Social Work

Research Proposals

A Workbook

Second Edition

Richard M. Grinnell, Jr.
Yvonne A. Unrau

Field Guide   Road Map   Workbook   Survival Guide

Dedicated to all social work students

Table of Contents

Preface for Instructors

OUR INEXPENSIVE, HIGHLY PRACTICAL BOOK is written in a straightforward manner for beginning social work students who are writing their first research proposals. Some students will be writing them as a part of their research methods courses, evaluation courses, administration courses, class projects, individual portfolios, capstone courses, internships, undergraduate and graduate theses, or even Ph.D. dissertations. We assume your students will have taken—or are now taking—a basic research methods course.

What Our Book Is About

WE HAVE ONLY PROVIDED our notion of what constitutes the rudimentary ingredients of a basic research proposal—section by section. We are fully aware, however, that some instructors will have different ideas about what needs to be added, subtracted, or modified in our basic ingredient list. We encourage creativeness, and urge you and your students alike to add, delete, and/or modify our book's content and organization to fit individual predilections. We encourage you to feel free to alter our suggested readings or add additional ones.

We assume your students' research proposals will be more quantitatively oriented than qualitatively oriented. Nevertheless, instructors and students alike can easily add qualitative content to appropriate sections in an effort to produce mixed-methods proposals—or what are currently referred to as mixed-model proposals.

We require students to read specific chapters in their research methods book *before* they even contemplate responding to the tips we provide within any of the 12 sections of the run-of-the-mill research proposal. We firmly believe that students need to understand basic research concepts before they can competently apply them within their proposals.

vi

It's pointless, for example, for students to start writing about how they plan to collect data without first understanding the advantages and disadvantages of the various data-collection methods. All of this content is addressed in their research methods texts. Thus, our book is designed to complement—not replace—your students' research methods book; that is, we want this book to be used in *conjunction with* any social work research methods text.

What's New in This Edition?

WITH THE NUMEROUS SUGGESTIONS offered by many of the instructors who adopted the previous edition, this one contains 107 new tips and a comprehensive glossary. We have also included a new section on assessing the ethical and cultural issues that need to be taken into account when writing research proposals (i.e., Section 8f).

Think of Our Book as a Bridge

AS YOU KNOW, STUDENTS STRUGGLE a bit when they try to apply the knowledge they gain from their classroom activities and required readings to writing research proposals. They have difficulty in applying what they learn—not an uncommon occurrence. For example, your students may have read a chapter from their research methods book on various sampling strategies, attended classes where these strategies were discussed, and perhaps even completed an individual or group assignment on some "sampling" topic.

They have acquired a lot of basic information. They now need some guidance on how to apply their newly gained expertise to writing their research proposals. They have a tendency to ask straightforward questions, such as What exactly am I supposed to write about for my sample when the maximum length of the Sampling section is only one to two paragraphs at best? What content do I have to include? What can I delete? How is it written? What are some of the things I should watch out for? Are there examples I can look at?

Our book addresses these legitimate questions in a step-by-step manner. Think of our book as a bridge, if you will—one that helps students to apply their basic research knowledge to writing research proposals. Let's now turn to see how this bridge works through homework assignments and proposal assignments.

Homework Assignments (Working Backward)

WE HAVE PROVIDED HOMEWORK ASSIGNMENTS at the end of each section of a research proposal. They require your students to read various sections of published research studies that have appeared as articles in social work journals. They are contained in boxes throughout this book. Some of the assignments use unpublished research proposals as well.

You can also have your students read different research studies than the ones we present if you want; that is, you can easily replace our selection with yours. Or you can let your students choose based on their own individual interests.

No matter which research study is selected, the homework assignments are designed to provide students with a bit of experience in applying the material they have learned from your class lectures, their individual and group assignments, their research methods book, and this book to actual social work research studies—ours, yours, or your students. It's up to you.

As we all know, a research proposal is developed *before* a research project actually begins—in theory, that is. It's written—or is at least thoroughly planned out in one's mind—*before* its implementation. With this in mind, we want students to write about what they think the research proposals *would have looked like* for published studies, given the content of their classroom materials, research methods book, and this book.

In essence, the homework assignments force students to work backward as they prepare make-believe sections of research proposals from published research studies. Think of it as reverse engineering. The homework assignments are not walks in the park, as illustrated in below:

The Process of Working Backward

Step 1: Read specific section of a published research study

Step 2: Read chapter(s) in their research methods book that is relevant to the section identified in Step 1

Step 3: Respond to tips in this book that are relevant to the section after completing Step 2

Step 4: Write a hypothetical section of a research proposal that could have been written for the published research study identified in Step 1

Proposal Assignments (Working Forward)

WE HAVE ALSO INCLUDED a proposal assignment at the end of each section. These help your students to develop their own individual (or group) research proposals. Each assignment simply requires them to write a section of their own research proposal in a systematic and highly integrated manner, as illustrated below:

The Process of Working Forward

Step 1: Read chapter(s) in their research methods book

Step 2: Respond to tips in this book after completing Step 1

Step 3: Write appropriate section of their research proposals after completing Step 2

Step 4 Implement research proposals after completing Step 3 (optional)

Practicality and Reality Prevail

UNNECESSARY INFORMATION OVERLOAD is avoided at all costs. Given our ever-changing student population, you as an instructor, could rightfully ask: What basic research proposal concepts can I realistically teach where my students will fully grasp, digest, and appreciate the rationale for creating research proposals, which in turn directly relate to successfully executing meaningful research studies? We believe the answer to this question, via tips, is contained within the pages that follow.

Templates Available (on following page)

YOU CAN REQUEST TEMPLATES for all homework assignments and proposal sections from the publisher (generalinfo@pairbondpublications.com). You can then distribute them to your students where they can fill them out and then submit them to you (and/or their fellow students) via hard paper copies, posts on D2L, or through e-mails—or not at all.

Templates for Homework Assignments:

Templates for Proposal Section:

Introduction for Students

WRITING A SOCIAL WORK RESEARCH PROPOSAL that you will be proud of takes a lot of time, so start early. Begin thinking about your research topic area well in advance of the final drop-dead date when you have to turn in your masterpiece to either your social work instructor or funding agency.

Make a habit of collecting and storing references while you are working on all sections of your proposal. Be prepared to write numerous drafts, and show them to your classmates and instructor as you go along. Make revisions based upon their feedback. Go over the language, style, and form of your proposal, after you have their feedback. Remember that your proposal will be revised many times, so plan accordingly. We have provided ample space within our book so you can write notes as your course goes along.

If you are writing your proposal under the supervision of a social work instructor, you should seek feedback throughout your writing process, especially while selecting your research problem area and formulating a specific research question (or hypothesis)—the toughest part of a proposal to master.

It's important to note that our book presents a basic generic framework and guidelines (via Tips) for preparing the standard research proposal. Your instructor may also want you to include (or exclude) additional content in your proposal. If this is the case, you need to obtain clarification from your instructor about what you are supposed to delete, add, or modify before you start writing your first word.

In addition, your instructor may want you to read different research studies than the ones we present in our book. Let's now go on to discuss the goals, objectives, and different types of research proposals you can write.

1

Goals of Research Proposals

SOCIAL WORK RESEARCH PROPOSALS have two primary goals:

1 To receive permission from your research instructor (or thesis/dissertation committee) to do a research study. This is probably the goal that you are working on if you're currently enrolled in a social work research methods course where your instructor requires you to author a research proposal as one of the course's requirements.

   Also, you need to remember that your instructor may or may not require you to actually implement the proposal you finally write—that is, will you be required to actually carry out what you propose after your proposal is finally completed? If so, be sure to write a proposal that is realistic for your time frame, finances, and skill level.

2 To request money from a funding agency to actually carry out your research proposal.

Objectives of Research Proposals

WITH THE ABOVE TWO GOALS OF RESEARCH PROPOSALS IN MIND, first-class proposals must quickly and easily respond to seven objectives. Whether you are trying to receive official permission to do a research study and/or are requesting funds to do it, you need to write a proposal that addresses seven highly integrated objectives:

1 You must ***convince other people*** of the value, significance, and usefulness of your proposed study. These folks could be your research instructor, your classmates, your fellow researchers, the agencies that fund research endeavors, the social work agencies where your study may take place, and your educational institution.

   In a nutshell, you must show them how your proposed research study will make a difference to someone besides yourself. What difference will your study make to your university, your fellow students, the profession of social work, the state, the nation, the world, the galaxy, the universe? In other words, "who cares?" You will answer this question under the following sections within your research proposal:

   - **Section 4:** Introduction
   - **Section 6:** Problem
   - **Section 10:** Significance

2 Once you have convinced other people that your problem area is important to study, you now need to ***demonstrate that you have a solid knowledge base*** in the problem area you propose to study. That is, you need to persuade key people that you know enough about your research topic to actually do a research study on it.

You will answer this question by brilliantly summarizing, comparing, and integrating all the relevant theory and existing research findings pertaining to your topic area within the following sections of your research proposal:

- **Section 5:** Literature Review
- **Section 6:** Problem
- **Section 7:** Research Question
- **Section 11:** References
- **Section 12:** Appendix M: Copies of Résumés of Key People

3 You must ***demonstrate that you have the research skills*** to actually carry out your proposed study. You may know a lot about your research topic, but do you have the skills to actually carry out the study? Simply put, you do this by writing a well-thought-out, practical, and feasible research proposal that clearly outlines how you plan to obtain and analyze the data your study will collect. These data will then answer your research question (or test your hypothesis).

Will your collected data be reliable and valid—and more importantly— will the data really be able to answer your research question (or test your hypothesis)? You will answer these questions under the following sections within your research proposal:

- **Section 8:** Method
  - **Section 8a:** Research Design
  - **Section 8b:** Sample
  - **Section 8c:** Instrumentation
  - **Section 8d:** Data Collection
  - **Section 8e:** Data Analysis
- **Section 9:** Limitations

4 Your proposal will ***serve as a financial and time-line contract***. Research projects sometimes involve contracts between several individuals or groups. Your research proposal should state clearly what each party is expected to bring to your research project, how you will use financial and human resources, and when your study will be completed. How much will your research study cost and how long will it take? You will answer these questions under the following section within your research proposal:

- **Section 12**: Appendixes
  — **Appendix A:** Letter(s) of permission
  — **Appendix B:** Cooperating agency description
  — **Appendix C:** Time line
  — **Appendix O:** Budget

5   The proposal also will *serve as a comprehensive planning tool.* Many research projects fail because they were not properly planned from the outset. When badly planned studies finally reach their conclusion, it is typically very stressful for the researchers. When a clear plan of action is in place from the beginning, the study is more likely to proceed smoothly to a successful conclusion than a vague, hazy, and fuzzy study that was planned at the last minute. All these concerns are addressed throughout your entire proposal.

6   The proposal will *serve as contract for engaging in ethical research practices.* Will you be doing research on humans? If so, what safeguards are you putting in place so you don't hurt them? You will answer these questions under the following sections within your research proposal:

- **Section 8b:** Sample
- **Section 8c:** Instrumentation
- **Section 8d:** Data Collection
- **Section 8f:** Ethical and Cultural Considerations
- **Section 12:** Appendixes
  — **Appendix E:** Consent Form
  — **Appendix F:** Assent Form
  — **Appendix G:** Institutional Review Board Approval

7   How does your proposed study *relate to the funding agency's interests?* This question is best answered in the cover letter you attach to your finished research proposal. You must highlight how your proposal is directly related and relevant to the agency's basic interests. This will not be an issue for you if you're not asking for funds to do your study.

Some funding agencies provide detailed instructions or guidelines concerning the preparation of research proposals (and, in some cases, forms on which they are to be typed); obviously, you must carefully read these guidelines *before* you begin to write your first sentence.

Types of Research Proposals

ON A GENERAL LEVEL, there are six types of research proposals:

1 **Social work students' classroom research proposals.** This type of proposal is probably the one that you are writing. It is used to demonstrate your knowledge of the complete social work research process, from selecting a research topic to study to disseminating the results from the study.

2 **Solicited proposals.** These proposals are submitted in response to specific solicitations issued by potential funding agencies. These solicitations, typically called Request for Proposals (RFP), are usually very specific in their requirements regarding what types of research problems areas they are willing to fund, in addition to providing the proposal's format, style, and level of detail.

3 **Unsolicited proposals.** These proposals are submitted to potential funding agencies that have not issued specific solicitations but are believed by the researchers to have interests in their research problem areas.

4 **Preproposals.** These are requested when potential funding sponsors wish to minimize applicants' efforts in preparing full-blown proposals. Preproposals are usually in the form of "letters of intent." After preproposals are reviewed, the funding agencies notify potential investigators if they should submit full proposals.

5 **Continuation or noncompeting proposals.** These types of proposals simply request continued funding of multiyear projects for which the sponsors have already provided funding for initial periods (normally one year). Continued financial support is usually contingent on satisfactory work progress and the availability of funds.

6 **Renewal or competing proposals.** These types of proposals request continued support for existing projects that are about to terminate. From the sponsors' viewpoint, these generally have the same status as unsolicited proposals.

Research Proposals Are Requests to Do Research Studies

AS YOU SHOULD KNOW BY NOW, before your research study gets underway, you are required to receive permission to do your study in the first place. And this permission is usually sought through a research proposal. Thus, a research proposal to do a research study is written *before* the research study even gets off the ground. On a very basic level there are 12 non-mutually exclusive sections within all research proposals. You will be expected to address all of these sections in yours.

After completing your research methods course (and using our book) you should have the skillset:

- to read a basic social work research study and then write a hypothetical research proposal the author could have written to receive permission to do the study. That is, you're going from reading a research study to writing a research proposal (see Figure A on page *viii*).
- to actually write a basic research proposal from beginning to end. That is, you're going from writing a research proposal to doing the research study based off of the proposal (see Figure B on page *ix*).

How to Use Our Tips

AS YOU WRITE EACH SECTION of your research proposal we encourage you to at least ponder the tips we believe you should think about when completing each of the 12 sections. Thus, we provide you with an opportunity to check whether or not you have addressed and contemplated—or at least thought about—our tips via simply checking one of four possible options below:

- NA (not applicable)
- TA (Thought about it but it's not necessary to include this content in my research proposal)
- Yes (Discussed it in my research proposal)
- No (Have not thought about it yet but will be in my research proposal if I find it relevant to include)

Let's now dig a bit deeper into the four possible responses that are available to you when you're addressing each tip.

NA

You will check "NA" for all tips that you believe are simply not applicable, or not relevant, to your particular research study. For example, Tip17 on page 13 wants you to check the title of your study to see if it contains an independent variable. If you plan on using a simple cross-sectional survey design, for example, then you would rate this tip as "NA" since this particular research design does not contain any independent variables. Simple as that!

TA

You will only check "TA" when you have thought about the tip—and have dealt with it—but believe it's not necessary to include a discussion of it within your proposal. For example, Tip 196 on page 100 states: Check to see that you have made a clear connection between the sampling method you are proposing to use (Section 8b) and your research design (Section 8a). Ideally, you would have already thought about the relationship between these two concepts but believe it's not really necessary to discuss it within the pages of your research proposal. So, in this case, you'll check it as "TA". Nevertheless, you need to have a rationale as to why you did not include a discussion of the tip in your proposal.

Yes

You would check "Yes" to a specific tip if you thought it was relevant enough to include a discussion of it in your research proposal. For example, if you plan on using appropriate ethically and culturally sensitive research participant consent forms (i.e., Tip 281 on page 152) in your study, then you'll simply check "Yes" and call it a day. Just be sure you include this content in the appropriate section of your research proposal and a copy of your consent form in an appendix.

No

You will only check "No" when you have not checked either "NA", "TA", or "Yes". Thus, when you check "No" you need to:

1 Describe how you plan to turn your "No" into a "NA", "TA", or "Yes".

2 State specifically where and how you plan on obtaining the necessary knowledge/skills to turn each "No" into a "NA", "TA", or "Yes". That is, in your ideal research proposal, all tips should not contain any "No's". So, in short, remember the phrase, "no No's".

PART I
Front Matter

Section 1: Title Page and Title

Section 2: Abstract

Section 3: Table of Contents

Sections 1–3 in a research proposal are usually written last—that is, after you have completed the other eight sections (Sections 4–12). However, they are presented first in our book so that you can jot down some initial ideas and revise these sections as your proposal develops over time. Note that the first three sections of a research proposal are typically called *Front Matter*.

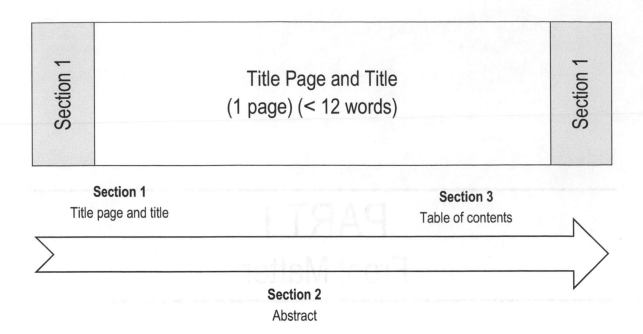

Front Matter of a Research Proposal

YOUR PROPOSAL'S TITLE will change many times as you write the remaining sections of your research proposal. Think of your title as "a working title." So be prepared to change your title as time goes on!

When writing your title, reexamine your research purposes, questions, or hypotheses to identify your main variables. These should be referred to in your title. The example below shows the purpose of a simple social work research proposal and a suggested corresponding title.

Example
Research purpose: The purpose of this research study will be to explore the relationship between administrative styles of social work supervisors and the effectiveness and efficiency of their supervisees.

Corresponding proposal title*:* This research study will determine if there is a relationship between the Administrative Styles of Social Work Supervisors and the Effectiveness and Efficiency of Their Supervisees

After you have successfully completed your research study you will need to disseminate your study's findings by submitting a manuscript for possible publication to a professional social work journal. The title of your research proposal

10

will be very similar to the title of the manuscript you finally submit for possible publication. For example:

Corresponding article title: This article presents the results of a research study that determined the relationship between the Administrative Styles of Social Work Supervisors and the Effectiveness and Efficiency of Their Supervisees

Writing a Title Page Section	QUICK TIPS
	Check to see if you have read pages 6–7 on how to use our tips.

#	Answers				Tips
1	NA	TA	Yes	No	Check to see if your research instructor (or funding agency you have in mind) has any specifications for your Title/Cover Page.
2	NA	TA	Yes	No	Check to be sure you included the names of key people who will be affiliated with your project. Usually the Title/Cover Page includes the people who will be involved in your proposed research study (e.g., Department Head, your research supervisor, your research instructor, Contracts Officer, Executive Director of the social work agency that your study will take place). Thus, if your proposed research study involves collaboration with other groups/organizations, it's a good idea to include their names on your Title/Cover Page.
3	NA	TA	Yes	No	Check to see if your Title Page looks professional and neat. However, do not waste time using fancy report covers, expensive binding, or other procedures that may send the wrong message to your potential funding agency. You are trying to impress them with how you really need funding, not the message that you do things rather expensively!

#	Answers				Tips
4	NA	TA	Yes	No	Check with your research instructor to see if he/she has any examples of title pages from other research proposals to show you.
Writing a Title Section				QUICK **TIPS**	
Check to see if you have read pages 6–7 on how to use our tips.					
#	**Answers**				**Tips**
5	NA	TA	Yes	No	Check to see if the title of your study is comprehensive enough to clearly indicate the nature of your proposed project. Your title should make sense standing all by itself.
6	NA	TA	Yes	No	Check to see if your title is logical, brief, and descriptive. It should not contain more than 20 words—the shorter the better.
7	NA	TA	Yes	No	Check to see if your title contains the important variables that you propose to study.
8	NA	TA	Yes	No	Check to see that your title is not a sentence and does not end with a period. If your title is getting too long, try removing some words. When all else fails, try using a two-part title with the parts separated by a colon (use only as a last resort!).
9	NA	TA	Yes	No	Check to see if you avoided the temptation to put the anticipated results of your study in the title.
10	NA	TA	Yes	No	Check to see if your title is concise and unambiguous. Resist trying to make it "cute".
11	NA	TA	Yes	No	Check to see if your title contains specific, familiar, and short words.
12	NA	TA	Yes	No	Check to see if your title is understandable and jargon-free.

13	NA	TA	Yes	No	Check to see if your title paints a quick overall picture of the key idea(s) that you propose to study.
14	NA	TA	Yes	No	Check to see if your title mentions the sample or population (research participants) you wish to study.
15	NA	TA	Yes	No	Check to see that your title contains the research setting where your study will be conducted (if appropriate of course).
16	NA	TA	Yes	No	Check to see that your title does not contain abbreviations.
17	NA	TA	Yes	No	Check to see that your title contains an independent variable (if appropriate of course).
18	NA	TA	Yes	No	Check to see that your title contains a dependent variable (if appropriate of course).
19	NA	TA	Yes	No	Check to see that your title contains the correct syntax (word order). The words you use in your title should clearly reflect the focus of your proposal. The most important words should come first, then the less important words. Try to remove words from your title that really are not necessary for understanding.
20	NA	TA	Yes	No	Check to see if your title is in *future tense*. Remember, you are proposing to do something (future tense), not reporting on what you found (present tense).
21	NA	TA	Yes	No	Check out titles of published research studies in the professional literature. See how they are written. Note that they are written in present tense since the authors' are describing what they *have found*, not what they *hope to find*.
22	NA	TA	Yes	No	Check with your research instructor to see if he/she has any examples of titles from other research proposals to show you.

Section 1
Writing a Title for Your Research Proposal

After reviewing all the previous tips, write a *tentative* title for your research proposal below.

- Use all the tips in this section to write your title (e.g., be sure it's not a sentence and doesn't end with a period).
- If possible, show your Title section to your classmates for their feedback.
- Revise your title based on your classmates' feedback.
- Submit your tentative title to your instructor for comments and feedback.

NOTE: As you know, you won't write the final version of your title until after you have completed Sections 4–12 of your research proposal. Thus, it's important for you to remember that at this point in the proposal-writing process your title should be considered a draft, which will transform into a masterpiece as your proposal develops over the semester.

Your Name(s):

Your Identification Number(s) (if any):

Type your *tentative* Title section here.
(Box will automatically expand as you type)

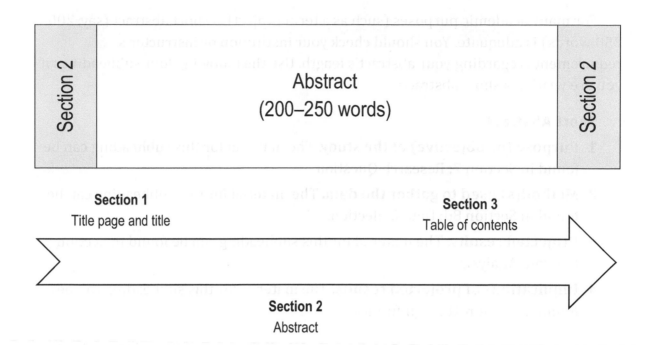

Front Matter of a Research Proposal

POTENTIAL FUNDERS USE ABSTRACTS to make initial decisions about whether they are interested in providing financial support for the proposals they receive. Reviewers, who usually read a high number of proposals, obtain their initial impressions by reading abstracts, thereby making abstracts a significant aspect of the review process.

An abstract is a summary that provides an overview of the proposal. When there are many competing proposals (such as for research funding), preparing a good abstract is exceedingly important because some reviewers may eliminate certain proposals based on their abstracts alone. For instance, if the funding agency is concentrating on pregnant adolescents and your abstract fails to mention this group, it may not get further consideration.

Generally, your abstract synthesizes the body of your proposal. While limiting the maximum number of words to between 200 and 250, you must clearly and concisely state your research question (or hypothesis), outline the means you'll use to answer that question (or test your hypothesis), and indicate your anticipated results and their significance to the social work profession. Just as we mentioned in the section about your title page (Section 1), your abstract will be refined over time and will be finally written after Sections 5–12 have been fully completed.

For many academic purposes (such as a term project), a short abstract (say, 200–250 words) is adequate. You should check your institution or instructor's requirements regarding your abstract's length. Use the following four subheadings if you are writing a short abstract:

Short Abstract

1 **Purpose (or objective) of the study.** The material for this subheading can be found in Section 7: Research Question.

2 **Method(s) used to gather the data.** The material for this subheading can be found in Section 8d: Data Collection.

3 **Projected results.** The material for this subheading can be found in Section 8e: Data Analysis.

4 **Implications of projected results.** The material for this subheading can be found in Section 10: Significance.

Longer abstracts simply need numerous subheadings to guide readers such as:

Long Abstract

1 **Problem area** (including importance). The material for this subheading can be found in Section 6: Problem.

2 **Research purpose** (or question or hypothesis). The material for this subheading can be found in Section 7: Research Question.

3 **Related literature** (brief overview of most salient aspects). The material for this subheading can be found in Section 5: Literature Review.

4 **Research participants** (including sampling plan). The material for this subheading can be found in Section 8b: Sample.

5 **Instrumentation** (types of instruments that will be used; names of instruments are usually not needed in the abstract). The material for this subheading can be found in Section 8c: Instrumentation.

6 **Methods of data collection.** The material for this subheading can be found in Section 8d: Data Collection.

7 **Method of data analysis** (descriptive and inferential, if any, or type of qualitative analysis). The material for this subheading can be found in Section 8e: Data Analysis.

8 **Potential implications.** The material for this subheading can be found in Section 10: Implications.

Writing an Abstract Section				QUICK TIPS
Check to see if you have read pages 6–7 on how to use our tips.				
#		**Answers**		**Tips**
23	NA	TA	Yes	No	Check to see that your abstract does not exceed 250 words.
24	NA	TA	Yes	No	Check to see if you clearly and concisely stated the **purpose** (or objective) of your study.
25	NA	TA	Yes	No	Check to see if you clearly and concisely stated the **method** of your study; that is, check to see if you clearly and concisely stated how you are going to answer your research question (or test your hypothesis).
26	NA	TA	Yes	No	Check to see if you clearly and concisely stated the anticipated **results** of your study.
27	NA	TA	Yes	No	Check to see if you clearly and concisely delineated the **significance** of your expected results; that is, how are your anticipated results going to be useful to social work practitioners, administrators, policy makers, or educators?
28	NA	TA	Yes	No	Check to see that you included "key words" at the bottom of your abstract.
29	NA	TA	Yes	No	Check to see that you clearly defined all abbreviations (except units of measurements), acronyms, and unique terms.
30	NA	TA	Yes	No	Check to see that your abstract reports accurate information that is in the body of the accompanying proposal.
31	NA	TA	Yes	No	Check to see if your abstract is extraordinarily clear to the common reader. Do not try to impress your friends with fancy words.

32	NA	TA	Yes	No	Check to see if you included enough relevant material to provide the ingredients that are needed for all four criteria that are usually required for abstracts that appear in professional social work journal articles: (1) purpose, (2) method, (3) results, and (4) implications.
33	NA	TA	Yes	No	Check to see if you wrote your abstract in the future tense.
34	NA	TA	Yes	No	Check to see if your abstract is clear, concise, specific, and to the point?
35	NA	TA	Yes	No	Check with your research instructor to see if he/she has any examples of proposal abstracts to show you.

After you have successfully completed your research study, you will need to disseminate your study's findings by submitting a manuscript for possible publication to a professional social work journal. The abstract of your research proposal should be very similar to the abstract of the manuscript you submit for possible publication.

Boxes 2.1 and 2.2 provide two examples of abstracts for articles that appeared in a professional social work journal. Note how the contents of the published abstracts are very similar to the ones for research proposals. The major difference between the two is that abstracts for research proposals are written in the future tense whereas abstracts for manuscripts that are submitted for possible publication are written in the present tense, as illustrated in Box 2.2. However, once in a while you will see published abstracts written in past tense, as demonstrated in Boxes 2.1 and 2.2.

BOX 2.1	Example of an Abstract from an Article That Appeared in a Professional Social Work Journal

Evaluating Culturally Responsive Group Work with Black Women[1]

Purpose: This study examined the efficacy of a culturally congruent group treatment model, entitled "Claiming Your Connections" (CYC) aimed at reducing depressive symptoms and perceived stress, and enhancing psychosocial competence (i.e., locus of control and active coping) among Black women. **Method:** A total of 58 Black women recruited from health and human service community-based organizations were randomly assigned to either the CYC intervention or a wait-list control group. Women in the CYC program attended weekly group intervention sessions over a 10-week period, and the wait-list control group did not receive any treatment for the same duration. **Results:** At pretreatment both groups indicated moderate levels of depressive symptoms, perceived stress, and psychosocial competence. After the intervention, the CYC group reported a significant reduction in depressive symptoms and perceived stress. There was no statistically significant change on these variables for the control group. **Implications:** Results suggest that the CYC group intervention program is effective with Black women who report having difficulty managing stressors of daily life.

---

[1]Jones, L.V., & Warner, L.A. (2011). Evaluating culturally responsive group work with Black women. *Research on Social Work Practice, 21*, 737–746.

BOX 2.2	Example of an Abstract from an Article That Appeared in a Professional Social Work Journal

Therapist Effects on Disparities Experienced by Minorities Receiving Services for Mental Illness[1]

Objectives: The authors examine if some of the reason clients from racial and ethnic minority groups experience outcome disparities is explained by their therapists. **Method:** Data from 98 clients (19% minority) and 14 therapists at two community mental health agencies where clients from racial and ethnic minority groups were experiencing outcome disparities were analyzed using hierarchical linear modeling with treatment outcomes at Level 1, client factors at Level 2, and therapists at Level 3. **Results:** There were substantial therapist effects that moderated the relationship between clients' race and treatment outcomes (outcome disparities). Therapists accounted for 28.7% of the variability in outcome disparities. **Conclusions:** Therapists are linked to outcome disparities and appear to play a substantial role in why disparities occur.

---

[1]Larrison, C.R., & Schoppelrey, S.L. (2011). Therapist effects on disparities experienced by minorities receiving services for mental illness. *Research on Social Work Practice, 21,* 727–736.

	Homework Assignment 2.1	

Writing *Short* Abstracts for Research Proposals

Box 2.1 presents an abstract from a social work journal article. Download and read the article. Now that you are familiar with the research study depicted in Box 2.1:

1 In the white space below, write a *short* hypothetical abstract you feel the authors *should have* written for the research proposal their study was based upon.

NOTE: You do not have a copy of the authors' research proposal. You only have a copy of the article that resulted from the implementation of their proposal.

- Use all the tips in this section to write your hypothetical proposal abstract (e.g., contains four subsections, written in future tense).

2 Submit your Abstract section to your instructor for comments and feedback.

Your Name(s):

Your Identification Number(s) (if any):

Assignment 2.1

Type your short Abstract section here.
(Box will automatically expand as you type)

	Homework Assignment 2.2	

Writing *Short* Abstracts for Research Proposals

Box 2.2 presents an abstract from a social work journal article. Download and read the article. Now that you are familiar with the research study depicted in Box 2.2:

1 In the white space below, write a *short* hypothetical abstract you feel the authors *should have* written for the research proposal their study was based upon.

   NOTE: You do not have a copy of the authors' research proposal. You only have a copy of the article that resulted from the implementation of their proposal.

   • Use all the tips in this section to write your hypothetical proposal abstract (e.g., contains four subsections, written in future tense).

2 Submit your Abstract section to your instructor for comments and feedback.

Your Name(s):

Your Identification Number(s) (if any):

Assignment 2.2

Type your short Abstract section here.

(Box will automatically expand as you type)

	Homework Assignment 2.3	

Writing *Long* Abstracts for Research Proposals

Box 2.1 presents an abstract from a social work journal article. Download and read the article. Now that you are familiar with the research study depicted in Box 2.1:

1 In the white space below, write a *long* hypothetical abstract you feel the authors *should have* written for the research proposal their study was based upon.

   NOTE: You do not have a copy of the authors' research proposal. You only have a copy of the article that resulted from the implementation of their proposal.

   • Use all the tips in this section to write your hypothetical proposal abstract (e.g., contains four subsections, written in future tense).

2 Submit your Abstract section to your instructor for comments and feedback.

Your Name(s):

Your Identification Number(s) (if any):

Assignment 2.3

Type your long Abstract section here.

(Box will automatically expand as you type)

	Homework Assignment 2.4	

Writing *Long* Abstracts for Research Proposals

Box 2.2 presents an abstract from a social work journal article. Download and read the article. Now that you are familiar with the research study depicted in Box 2.2:

1 In the white space below, write a *long* hypothetical abstract you feel the authors *should have* written for the research proposal their study was based upon.

   NOTE: You do not have a copy of the authors' research proposal. You only have a copy of the article that resulted from the implementation of their proposal.

   • Use all the tips in this section to write your hypothetical proposal abstract (e.g., contains four subsections, written in future tense).

2 Submit your Abstract section to your instructor for comments and feedback.

Your Name(s):

Your Identification Number(s) (if any):

Assignment 2.4

Type your long Abstract section here.

(Box will automatically expand as you type)

Section 2
Writing a Short Abstract for Your Research Proposal

Write a *short* abstract for your research proposal in the white space provided below.

- Use all the tips in this section to write your abstract (e.g., contains four subsections, written in future tense).
- If possible, show your abstract to your classmates for their feedback.
- Revise your abstract based on your classmates' feedback.
- Submit your abstract to your instructor for comments and feedback..

NOTE: As you know, you will actually write the *final version* of your abstract after you have completed Sections 4–12 of your research proposal. Thus, it is important for you to remember that at this point in the proposal-writing process your abstract should be considered a draft, which will transform into a masterpiece as your proposal develops over the semester.

Your Name(s):

Your Identification Number(s) (if any):

Title of Your Research Proposal:

Type your short Abstract section here.

(Box will automatically expand as you type)

Section 1
Title page and title

Section 3
Table of contents

Section 2
Abstract

Front Matter of a Research Proposal

A SHORT RESEARCH PROPOSAL with few parts does not need a table of contents. However, a longer and more detailed proposal may require not only a table of contents but a list of illustrations, figures, graphs, and tables as well.

Your Table of Contents section (along with your title and abstract) is finalized after you have completed Sections 4–12. Below is an example of the Table of Contents for a typical social work research proposal.

PART II
Identifying the Problem

Section 4: Introduction
Section 5: Literature Review
Section 6: Problem
Section 7: Research Question

This portion of your research proposal is all about introducing your readers to the general problem area you want to study and letting them know the specific research question you want to answer or hypothesis you want to test.

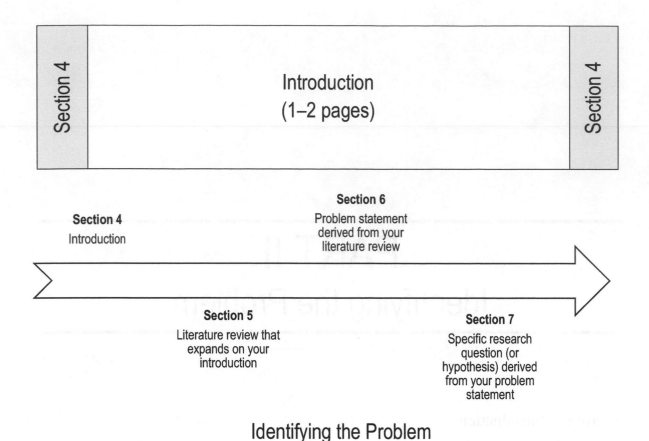

Identifying the Problem

THE INTRODUCTION SECTION of your research proposal is nothing more than an expansion of your abstract. It will contain three distinct subsections. Write your Introduction section in this specific order:

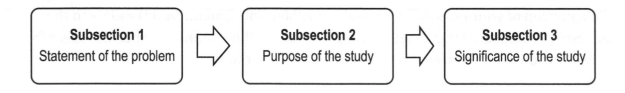

1 **Statement of the problem.** The first part of your Introduction section should begin with a succinct statement of what general problem area you are proposing to study. You need to briefly describe the major issues that your proposed research study will address and lay the broad foundation for the problem area that leads to your proposed study.

2 **Purpose of the study.** The second part provides a brief background of your problem area to enable an informed layperson to place your particular research problem in a context of common knowledge. In a nutshell, this subsection points out why your particular study is needed. This can be done in a number of ways. For example, you might be able to point out that various government agencies and/or prominent scholars have called for additional research in the problem area you wish to investigate further. You might also mention some statistics showing that the problem area affects many people you are proposing to investigate.

3 **Significance of the study.** The last subsection describes the practical and/or theoretical significance of your problem area and briefly refers to appropriate previously published studies and/or statistics. This part of your Introduction places your study within the larger context of the scholarly literature. It must clearly indicate what implications your study's findings will have for social work researchers, practitioners, administrators, educators, or policy makers.

If your study will involve working with a social work agency that also sees a need for your study, you need to include this information in this section and put a copy of the support letter written by the agency's Executive Director in an appendix (e.g., Appendix B in this book).

Your Introduction section needs to provide your readers with a broad overview of your proposal—a snapshot, if you will. This will show them the overall picture of what you are trying to do before they begin reading the specific details of exactly what you are going to do and how you are going to do it. All of these particulars are covered in detail in the remaining sections of your proposal.

Your Introduction section must form a strong impression in the minds of your readers. Thus, you must avoid giving your readers the opportunity to say things like:

- Not an original idea
- Rationale is weak
- Writing is vague
- Uncertain what is to be accomplished
- Problem area is not important
- Looks like the proposed study is unfocused, too large, or unrealistic

Writing an Introduction Section				QUICK TIPS
Check to see if you have read pages 6–7 on how to use our tips.				
#	**Answers**			**Tips**
36	NA	TA	Yes	No	Check to see that your Introduction section contains the three subsections in this order: (1) statement of the problem, (2) purpose of the study, and (3) significance of the study.
37	NA	TA	Yes	No	Check to see if you have "painted an overall descriptive picture" of your proposal in the minds of your readers.
38	NA	TA	Yes	No	Check to see that you have established a good argument for the importance of your problem area and why your study needs to be done.
39	NA	TA	Yes	No	Check to see that you have adequately described any underlying theories (if any) that you used to establish your problem area.
40	NA	TA	Yes	No	Check to see that you have provided a clear and concise overview of your proposed research methodology and data analysis plans.
41	NA	TA	Yes	No	Check to see if this section is written like an Executive Summary (the busy executive probably only has enough time to read your Introduction—not the entire proposal).
42	NA	TA	Yes	No	Check to see that the purpose of your proposed study clearly states your real intention. Does the purpose of your study break the problem area down into subsections for analysis?

43	NA	TA	Yes	No	Check to see if this section is specific and concise. Do not go into detail on aspects of your proposal that are further clarified at a later point in your proposal.
44	NA	TA	Yes	No	Check to see if you displayed your knowledge of the organization from which you are requesting funds (if any). Key concerns of a potential funding organization can be briefly identified in relation to your proposed project.
45	NA	TA	Yes	No	Check to see that your potential funding agency is committed to the same needs/problems that your proposal addresses. Clearly indicate how addressing the problems in your study helps your potential funding agency to fulfill its mission. Always keep the funding agency (or your research instructor) in your mind as a "cooperating partner" committed to the same concerns that you are. Recognizing them at the very beginning of your proposal can assist in strengthening their collaboration.
46	NA	TA	Yes	No	Check to see that you have avoided personal pronouns, subjective language, and awkward grammar.
47	NA	TA	Yes	No	Check to see that this section moves the reader, like a "funnel," from a general to a specific view of the problem area you propose to study.
48	NA	TA	Yes	No	Check to see that the problem area you propose to study is stated clearly, tersely, and objectively.
49	NA	TA	Yes	No	Check to see that your research problem is stated in the proper format (e.g., relationship between variables or difference between groups).

50	NA	TA	Yes	No	Check to see that the literature you refer to is really a true "synthesis," rather than a review, summary, or report. Also, check to see that it moves from topic to topic rather than from citation to citation.
51	NA	TA	Yes	No	Check to be sure that this section is no more than two to three typed, double-spaced pages in length.

The Introduction section that is written for a research proposal can easily be used for the Introduction section of the manuscript you finally submit for possible publication. Boxes 4.1 and 4.2 provide examples of Introduction sections for two articles that appeared in a professional social work journal. The Introduction sections in both published examples were very similar to the ones that were contained in their respective research proposals.

BOX 4.1	Example of an Introduction Section from an Article That Appeared in a Professional Journal

Readiness for College Engagement among Students Who Have Aged Out of Foster Care[1]

INTRODUCTION

There were over 423,000 children living in foster-care placements on any given day in the United States in 2009. Of these, over 32,000 exited the foster care system by "aging out" to independence (Child Welfare Information Gateway, 2011). Aging out is a legal event that occurs when the court formally discharges a young person from the state's custody based on the youth's chronological age. In most states, foster youth are discharged at 18 years of age; however, an increasing number of states are extending care to 21 years old as a result of the Fostering Connections to Success and Increasing Adoptions Act of 2008.

Previous research studies have indicated that most aged-out youth leaving foster care do so in unprepared and unplanned ways, and many either return to their families who were judged unfit by the court or begin living on their own (McMillen & Tucker, 1999). Upon aging-out of the system, these youth are abruptly initiated into adulthood and must rely heavily on their limited personal resources and income for their very survival (Iglehart, 1995).

Young people who have lived in foster care are less able to depend on family members for shelter, adult guidance, and financial support after high school than non-foster youth (Iglehart, 1995; Courtney, Dworsky, Lee, & Rapp, 2010). Educational attainment for foster youth lags far behind their non-foster-care peers, with just over half of foster youth completing high school (Wolanin, 2005; Sheehy et al., 2000).

Though estimates of high-school completion for foster youth vary across studies, the average of estimates suggests that approximately half of the youth between the ages of 18 and 24 who have aged out of foster care have high-school diplomas or general educational development (GED) diplomas in comparison to over 70 percent of non-foster youth (Wolanin, 2005). Other studies have found higher estimates of high-school achievement for foster youth, particularly when students attaining their GEDs are counted (Pecora et al., 2005).

This disparity has obvious implications for college entrance. Only 15 percent of foster youth are likely to enroll in college-preparatory classes during high school, whereas 32 percent of non-foster youth enroll in a high-school curriculum that helps to prepare them for college (Casey Family Programs, 2003).

Additionally, while college is a possible next step after high school, students growing up in foster care receive few encouraging messages from educators, social workers, and other adults regarding the pursuit of a college education (Davis, 2006). Only 20 percent of college-qualified foster youth attend college compared to 60 percent of their non-foster-care peers (Wolanin, 2005). Similarly, degree completion for foster youth, with estimates ranging from a low of 1 percent to a high of 10.8 percent, is substantially lower than the 24 percent degree-completion rate of non-foster youth (Pecora et al., 2006; Wolanin, 2005).

Research has generally suggested more negative outcomes for former foster youth compared to the general population, including disproportionate representation in the adult homeless population (Park, Metraux, & Culhane, 2005) as well as increased rates of unemployment and lack of health insurance (Reilly, 2003), mental illness (Courtney & Dworsky, 2006), and involvement in the criminal justice system (McMillen, Vaughn, & Shook, 2008).

In response to these dismal trajectories, federal legislation has provided monies to states to pay for services to help with the transition out of foster care into some form of independent living. For example, the Foster Care Independence Act of 1999 provides funding ($140 million) to state governments to improve and expand their current independent-living programs for foster youth who age out of the system.

The Promoting Safe and Stable Families Amendment of 2001 enhances the Foster Care Independence Act by providing additional funding ($60 million) for payments to state governments for post-secondary education and training. This funding pays for the Educational Training Voucher (ETV) program, which provides up to $5,000 per year up to age 23 for foster youth enrolled in post-secondary education as long as they enroll in the ETV program prior to 21 years of age.

The Fostering Connection to Success and Increasing Adoptions Act of 2008 permits states to claim federal reimbursement for foster-care maintenance payments made on behalf of foster youth to age 21. Foster youth living in states that take advantage of this policy and extend care can benefit by voluntarily remaining in the state's custody.

REFERENCES

Child Welfare Information Gateway. (2011). *Foster care statistics 2009.* Washington, DC: U.S. Department of Health and Human Services, Children's Bureau. Retrieved on June 7, 2011 from: http://www.childwelfare.gov/pubs/factsheets/foster.cfm

Courtney, M., Dworsky, A., Lee, J., & Raap, M. (2010). *Midwest evaluation of the adult functioning of former foster youth: Outcomes at ages 23 and 24.* Chicago: Chapin Hall Center for Children at the University of Chicago.

Iglehart, A.P. (1995). Readiness for independence: Comparison of foster care, kinship care, and non-foster care adolescents. *Children and Youth Services Review, 17,* 417–432.

McMillen, J.C. & Tucker, J. (1999). The status of older adolescents at exit from out-of-home care, *Child Welfare, 78,* 339–360.

McMillen, J.C., Vaughn, M.G., & Shook, J.J. (2008). Aging out of foster care and legal involvement: Toward a typology of risk. *Social Service Review, 82,* 419–446.

Park, J.M., Metraux, S., & Culhane, D.P. (2005). Childhood out-of-home placement and dynamics of public shelter utilization among young homeless adults. *Children and Youth Services Review, 27,* 533–546.

Pecora, P.J., Williams, J., Kessler, R.C., Hiripi, E., O'Brien, K., Emerson, J., Herrick, M.A., & Torres, D. (2006). Assessing the educational achievements of adults who were formerly placed in family foster care. *Child & Family Social Work, 11,* 220–231.

Reilly, T. (2003). Transition from care: Status and outcomes of youth who age out of foster care. Child Welfare, 82, 727–746.

Wolanin, T.R. (2005). *Higher education opportunities for foster youth: A primer for policymakers.* Washington, DC: Institute for Higher Education Policy.

---

[1]Unrau, Y.A., Font, S.A., & Rawls, G. (2012). Readiness for college engagement among students who have aged out of foster care. Children and Youth Services Review, 34, 76–83.

BOX 4.2	Example of an Introduction Section from an Article That Appeared in a Professional Journal

Exploring Out-of-Home Placement as a Moderator of Help Seeking Behavior among Adolescents Who Are High Risk[1]

Children placed in foster care are vulnerable to long-term physical and mental health problems owing to maltreatment and other trauma such as family separation. Many youth "age out" of foster care without high school diplomas or prospects of employment, leaving them unprepared for daily life as young adults.

Although adults with childhood foster care experience have been reported to fare less well on several social indicators such as educational achievement, community involvement, marital satisfaction, and occupational accomplishments, the reasons for their poor socialization may have as much to do with risks of poverty and family dysfunctions, as with risks associated with out-of-home placement (Buehler, Orme, Post, & Patterson, 2000). Research studies have not yet teased out which aspects of the foster care or group care experience, if any, are associated with long-term health and well-being.

Child welfare agencies play a significant role in the provision of mental health services while children live in out-of-home care (Kellam, Branch, Brown, & Russell, 1981). When children exit from foster care they often become ineligible for the various services that were once associated with their placements and must then seek help from other systems, such as schools, churches, medical clinics, families, and friends.

How well the foster care or group care experience prepares children—adolescents in particular—to seek professional help for their own needs is not yet fully known. Thus, the current study investigated whether a placement experience in either foster care or group care increased the likelihood of youth seeking professional help outside of the child welfare system for a variety of physical and mental health problems.

REFERENCES

Buehler, C., Orme, J.G., Post, J., & Patterson, D. A. (2000). The long term correlates of family foster care. *Children and Youth Services Review, 22,* 595–625.

Kellam, S., Branch, J., Brown, C., & Russell, G. (1981). Why teenagers come for treatment. *Journal of the American Academy of Child and Adolescent Psychiatry, 20,* 477–495.

―――――

[1] Unrau, Y.A., & Grinnell, R.M., Jr. (2005). Exploring out-of-home placement as a moderator of help-seeking behavior among adolescents who are high risk. Research on Social Work Practice, 6, 516–530.

	Homework Assignment 4.1	

Writing Introduction Sections for Research Proposals

Box 4.1 presents an Introduction section from a social work journal article. Download and read the article. Now that you are familiar with the research study depicted in Box 4.1:

1 In the white space below, write an Introduction section you feel the authors *should have* written for the research proposal their study was based upon.

   NOTE: You do not have a copy of the authors' research proposal. You only have a copy of the article that resulted from the implementation of their proposal.

   - Use all the tips in this section to write your hypothetical proposal's Introduction section (e.g., contains three distinct subsections).

2 Submit your revised Introduction section to your instructor for comments and feedback.

Your Name(s):
Your Identification Number(s) (if any):
Assignment 4.1

Type your Introduction section here.
(Box will automatically expand as you type)

	Homework Assignment 4.2	

Writing Introduction Sections for Research Proposals

Box 4.2 presents an Introduction section from a social work journal article. Download and read the article. Now that you are familiar with the research study depicted in Box 4.2:

1 In the white space below, write an Introduction section you feel the authors *should have* written for the research proposal their study was based upon.

   NOTE: You do not have a copy of the authors' research proposal. You only have a copy of the article that resulted from the implementation of their proposal.

   - Use all the tips in this section to write your hypothetical proposal's Introduction section (e.g., contains three distinct subsections).

2 Submit your revised Introduction section to your instructor for comments and feedback.

Your Name(s):
Your Identification Number(s) (if any):
Assignment 4.2

Type your Introduction section here.
(Box will automatically expand as you type)

Section 4
Writing an Introduction Section for Your Research Proposal

Write an Introduction section for your research proposal in the white space provided below.

- Use all the tips in this section to write your Introduction (e.g., contains three subsections).

- If possible, show your proposal's Introduction section to your classmates for their feedback.

- Revise your Introduction section based on your classmates' feedback.

- Submit your Title, Abstract, and Introduction sections to your instructor for comments and feedback.

NOTE: As you know, you will actually write the *final version* of your Introduction section after you have completed Sections 5–12 of your research proposal. Thus, it is important for you to remember at this point in the proposal-writing process that your Introduction section should be considered a draft, which will transform into a masterpiece as your proposal develops over the semester.

Your Name(s):
Your Identification Number(s) (if any):
Title of Your Research Proposal:
Abstract:

Type your Introduction section here.
(Box will automatically expand as you type)

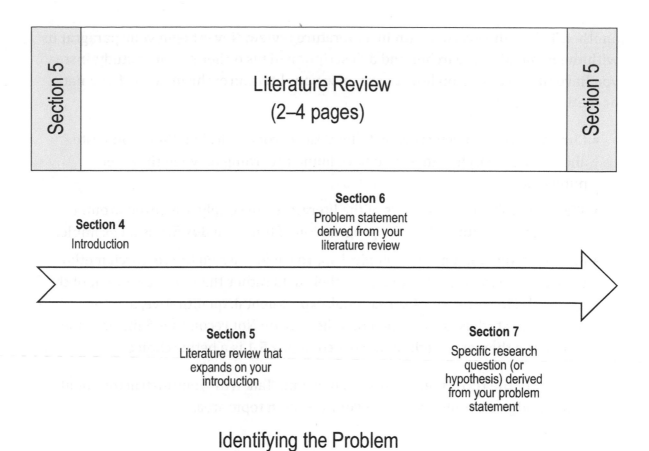

Identifying the Problem

IN GENERAL, YOUR LITERATURE REVIEW directly follows and expands on your Introduction section (Section 4), as previously described. Besides increasing your knowledge base on your problem area, writing a literature review provides you with an opportunity to demonstrate your skills in two areas:

1 **Information-seeking skills**: the ability to identify a set of useful articles and books by scanning the relevant literature efficiently, using manual and computerized methods.

2 **Critical appraisal skills**: the ability to identify and critique previously published research studies.

Whereas your Introduction section told your readers where your proposal is headed, by describing what you want to do, how you are going to do it, and why your work is significant, Section 5 validates your efforts and substantiates the need to study your problem area further. You will do this by citing other authoritative sources who are also knowledgeable about your problem area.

As you know, your literature review has to be professionally written; that is, it's Not simply a list of monotonous, mind-numbing descriptions of one study after another. This is the kiss of death in a literature review. Never begin your paragraphs with the name of a researcher and a description of his or her research study. Instead, you have three choices on how to organize your literature: chronological, thematic, or methodological.

- **Chronological.** If your review follows the chronological method, you write about the research studies you have found according to when they were published.

- **Thematic.** Thematic reviews of the literature are simply organized around a topic or issue, rather than the progression of time. See Box 5.1 as an example.

- **Methodological.** A methodological approach focuses on the research methods that the researchers used to gather their data rather than on the content of the material. Thus, survey, observational, experimental, quantitative, and/or qualitative studies are grouped together. We do Not recommend this method; rather, the thematic method illustrated in Box 5.1 is a better choice.

Pick one of the three methods—and only one. Talk with your instructor about which method you should use, given your research topic area.

Writing a Literature Review Section	QUICK TIPS
Check to see if you have read pages 6–7 on how to use our tips.	
Required	**Most important:** Check to see if you know how to write literature reviews and have read the appropriate chapter(s) in your research methods book before you complete Section 5.

#	Answers				Tips
52	NA	TA	Yes	No	Check to see if you know how to do electronic and manual literature searches.
53	NA	TA	Yes	No	Check to see if your literature review is written chronologically, thematically, or methodologically. Pick one theme and only one theme.

54	NA	TA	Yes	No	Check to see that you discussed the assumptions you are going to make before you begin your proposed research study.
55	NA	TA	Yes	No	Check to see that you have cited and discussed research studies that ran contrary to your perspective.
56	NA	TA	Yes	No	Check to see that you have shown how your proposed study relates to the larger, ongoing dialogue in the literature about your research area, filling in gaps and extending prior studies.
57	NA	TA	Yes	No	Check to see that you have critically analyzed the literature; that is, instead of just listing and summarizing study after study, did you assess them by discussing their strengths and weaknesses?
58	NA	TA	Yes	No	Check to see that you discussed the historical development of your research problem (or issue) over time.
59	NA	TA	Yes	No	Check to see that your literature review cited introductory texts, standard articles, chapters in books, grey material, online sources, and topical encyclopedias in an effort to sketch a solid orientation of the kinds of academic discussions in your problem area.
60	NA	TA	Yes	No	Check to see that you have been judicious in your choice of exemplars—the literature you select should be directly pertinent and relevant to your study.
61	NA	TA	Yes	No	Check to see that you have avoided statements that imply that little has been done in your problem area or that what has been done is too extensive to permit an easy summary. Statements of this sort are usually taken as indications that you are Not really familiar with the published literature.

62	NA	TA	Yes	No	Check to see that you cited previous projects and studies that are similar to what you are proposing.
63	NA	TA	Yes	No	Check to see that you discussed the research methods and data analyses that previous researchers have used when exploring your problem area.
64	NA	TA	Yes	No	Check to see that you have discussed all the key methodological issues that have arisen in your problem area: for example, problems in research designs (Section 8a), sampling (Section 8b), instrumentation (Section 8c), data collection methods (Section 8d), and data analyses (Section 8e). You don't want to make the same mistakes in your study.
65	NA	TA	Yes	No	Check to see that you have avoided the methodological and data analyses mistakes and/or errors that have been previously made by others.
66	NA	TA	Yes	No	Check to see that you have provided adequate conceptual and operational definitions of key terms (if appropriate).
67	NA	TA	Yes	No	Check to see that you have clearly outlined exactly what you are going to be investigating as the particular focus of your proposed research project. For example, is there a gap in the previous literature? In relation to current knowledge (as reflected in the literature), what exactly do you intend to do? What theoretical model relates to your research topic?
68	NA	TA	Yes	No	Check to see if you demonstrated how your project would extend the work that has been previously done.

69	NA	TA	Yes	No	Check to see that your literature review discussed the most recent research findings in your area of study.
70	NA	TA	Yes	No	Check to see if your literature review discussed the pressing problem that you want to address.
71	NA	TA	Yes	No	Check to see that your literature review listed new research questions that could be derived from previous research findings.
72	NA	TA	Yes	No	Check to see if you included a well-documented statement of the need/problem that is the basis for your project: that is, did you establish the need for your proposed research study?
73	NA	TA	Yes	No	Check to see that you clearly outlined the theoretical model (if any) that you are going to use in your research topic.
74	NA	TA	Yes	No	Check to see if you made your key points clearly and succinctly.
75	NA	TA	Yes	No	Check to see if you have selected and referenced only the more appropriate citations.
76	NA	TA	Yes	No	Check to see that you have been very careful in your use of language. It can be helpful to have a friend who is outside of your area of focus/expertise read your proposal to make sure that your language is readable and minimizes the use of jargon, trendy or "in" words, abbreviations, colloquial expressions, redundant phrases, and confusing language.
77	NA	TA	Yes	No	Check to see that your literature search was wide eNough to ensure that you have found all the relevant material. And has your search been narrow eNough to exclude irrelevant material? Is the number of sources you have provided appropriate for the scope of your research project?

78	NA	TA	Yes	No	Check to see if your overall literature review is brief, to the point, selective, and critical.
79	NA	TA	Yes	No	Check to see if the citations you used are in APA style.
80	NA	TA	Yes	No	Check to see that your readers will find your literature review relevant, appropriate, and useful.
81	NA	TA	Yes	No	Check to see that you have NOT made the following error in your literature review: Lacks organization and structure.
82	NA	TA	Yes	No	Check to see that you have NOT made the following error in your literature review: Lacks focus, unity, and coherence.
83	NA	TA	Yes	No	Check to see that you have NOT made the following error in your literature review: Is repetitive and verbose.
84	NA	TA	Yes	No	Check to see that you have NOT made the following error in your literature review: Fails to cite influential papers.
85	NA	TA	Yes	No	Check to see that you have NOT made the following error in your literature review: Fails to keep up with recent developments.
86	NA	TA	Yes	No	Check to see that you have NOT made the following error in your literature review: Fails to critically evaluate cited papers.
87	NA	TA	Yes	No	Check to see that you have NOT made the following error in your literature review: Cites irrelevant or trivial references.
88	NA	TA	Yes	No	Check to see that you have NOT made the following error in your literature review: Depends too much on secondary sources.

89	NA	TA	Yes	No	Check to see that your literature review did Not go over the double-spaced, three- to five-page limit. This page limit excludes the references that will go in your References section (Section 11).
90	NA	TA	Yes	No	Check to see that you distinguished between research, theory, and opinion.
91	NA	TA	Yes	No	Check to see that you provided enough information to convince others that your research study needed to be done.
92	NA	TA	Yes	No	Check to see that your cited literature justified your chosen research approach you plan to use (i.e., quantitative, qualitative, mixed-methods).
93	NA	TA	Yes	No	Check to see that you incorporated findings from original research studies into your literature review.
94	NA	TA	Yes	No	Check to see that your assumptions between and among variables actually make sense.
95	NA	TA	Yes	No	Check to see that your defined major concepts and operational definitions actually makes sense.
96	NA	TA	Yes	No	Check to see that you made reasonable assumptions of the relationship(s) between the independent and dependent variables (if any).
97	NA	TA	Yes	No	Check to see that you provided crystal clear conceptual definitions of key terms.
98	NA	TA	Yes	No	Check to see that you have indicated the basis for "factual" statements.
99	NA	TA	Yes	No	Check to see that your research question and hypothesis logically link with one another.
100	NA	TA	Yes	No	Check to see that your literature review is organized logically.
101	NA	TA	Yes	No	Check to see that you have provided a balanced review of differing viewpoints or findings.

102	NA	TA	Yes	No	Check to see that your literature review is Not one sided and/or ignores alternative evidence.
103	NA	TA	Yes	No	Check to see that your literature review is completely up to date.
104	NA	TA	Yes	No	Check to see that your literature review is actually convincing and doesn't bore your readers to death.
105	NA	TA	Yes	No	Check to see that your literature review is written critically (giving strengths and weaknesses of previous work).
106	NA	TA	Yes	No	Check to see that your literature review had reasonable parameters. (Why were certain bodies of literature included in the search and others excluded?)
107	NA	TA	Yes	No	Check to see that your literature sources came from reputable refereed journals.
108	NA	TA	Yes	No	Check to see that you have incorporated primary and secondary literature.
109	NA	TA	Yes	No	Check to see that you have incorporated recent developments in the literature.
110	NA	TA	Yes	No	Check to see that you have complete bibliographic data for each source you cite in your literature review.
111	NA	TA	Yes	No	Check to see that your literature review is sufficiently comprehensive when it comes to citations. (Use the "15–10" citation rule to assess its adequacy and comprehensiveness.)
112	NA	TA	Yes	No	Check to see that you discussed previous major research studies and their actual findings.
113	NA	TA	Yes	No	Check to see that you have cited previous research studies and have compared and contrasted their respective results.

114	NA	TA	Yes	No	Check to see that your literature review ends by delineating the "jumping-off place" for your proposed study. This will automatically lead to the next section of your proposal—the purpose of your study (Section 6).
115	NA	TA	Yes	No	Check with your research instructor to see if he/she has any examples of literature reviews from other research proposals to show you.

Box 5.1 provides an example of a literature review from an article that appeared in a professional social work journal. The content of a published literature review in an article is identical to one written for a research proposal. Simply remember that just about everything you write for the Literature Review section within your research proposal will be recycled in the manuscript you finally submit for possible publication.

BOX 5.1	Example of a Literature Review Section from an Article That Appeared in a Professional Publication

Readiness for College Engagement among Students Who Have Aged Out of Foster Care[1]

LITERATURE REVIEW

Foster Youths' Barriers to Higher Education

One barrier to entering higher education for foster youth is their difficulty in completing primary and secondary education. Teenagers in foster care are involved in special-education classes at comparatively higher rates during their secondary educational experiences than Non-foster-care teens (Courtney, Terao, & Bost, 2004; Pecora et al., 2006). Furthermore, they are more likely than their Non-foster-care counterparts to drop out of high school, repeat a grade, or be suspended or expelled (Courtney, Terao, & Bost, 2004; Blome, 1997). When compared to Non-foster youth, foster youth also have higher rates of changing schools that are related to their lower academic achievement and attainment (Blome, 1997; Pecora et al., 2006).

Foster youth also encounter general obstacles during their emerging years of young adulthood (i.e., 18–25 years of age). Youth aging out of foster care struggle more than other young adults across a number of important lifespan-developmental domains including: academics and education; finances and employment; housing; physical and mental health; social relationships and community connections; personal and cultural identity development; and life skills (Casey Family Programs, 2006).

Many foster youth enter young adulthood with significant educational deficits, and the lasting effects of these deficits are evident in their dismal educational attainment (Courtney & Dworsky, 2006). The problems encountered by foster youth in each of the domains can be barriers to education.

The struggles that foster youth have with practical or systemic barriers in other life domains make it difficult to access or stay in school after aging out of foster care. For example, it is estimated that only about one-third of youth aging out of foster care left the system with basic resources such as a driver's license, cash, or basic necessities such as dishes (Pecora et al., 2006). Most do Not have anyone to co-sign a loan or lease, which makes it difficult to secure safe housing.

Medicaid and funds for start-up goods are available in some states until age 21, but foster youth must be able to navigate the large and complicated state bureaucratic programs to receive these benefits. Courtney and colleagues (2010) found that the main barriers for higher-education access among foster youth were a lack of financial resources, the need to be in full-time employment, parenting responsibilities, and a lack of transportation. These practical and systemic obstacles provide some understanding as to why foster youth are less likely to access and succeed in college.

Nonetheless, several studies have reported that a significant number of foster youth want to pursue a college degree. Courtney and colleagues (2010), for example, reported that 79 percent of the foster youth in their study wanted to go to college. McMillen, Auslander, Elze, White, and Thompson (2003) reported similar findings whereby 70 percent of the foster youth they surveyed planned to attend college.

Foster Youth Attending College

A recent study that controlled for race and gender found that foster youth attending a four-year university were more likely to drop out of college compared to low-income first-generation students who had Not lived in foster care (Day, Dworsky, Fogarty, & Damashek, 2011). However, there is a paucity of research exploring the reasons foster youth are less likely to succeed in college. We found three studies that investigate how foster youth fare in college settings.

Merdinger, Hines, Osterling, and Wyatt (2005) surveyed an ethnically diverse sample of 216 college students who spent an average of seven to eight years, and three placements, in foster care. They found that only about one quarter of these students felt prepared to live independently upon exiting the foster-care system, and about the same percentage believed that the foster-care system had sufficiently prepared them for college.

The majority of the sample was succeeding academically, but reported challenges with finances, psychological distress, and access to health care. Social support from friends and family was identified as a factor that possibly contributed to the educational success of the sample.

Davis (2006) reviewed the many factors that inhibit the ability of foster youth to develop the strong academic foundation necessary to be successful in higher education. These factors included challenges encountered during primary and secondary education, multiple school changes, incidence of disruptive behaviors in the classroom, and higher incidence of learning delays.

Foster youth also had far less personal income than their peers but were awarded a sufficient level of financial aid so that it did Not impact their choice of institution. Davis Noted that although state and federal programs aim to provide financial support to former foster youth enrolled in postsecondary education, such support is inadequate when Not accompanied by structured social and academic support efforts.

Dworsky and Perez (2010) collected information from a Nonrandom sample of 98 college students who participated in a campus support program for former foster youth in Washington or California. The sample was racially diverse, primarily female, and had an average age of 20 years old. Nearly all participants placed value on academic guidance such as advice on choosing courses or declaring a major, and many also asserted the importance of mentoring and leadership opportunities.

Students overall reported that their campus support-program participation provided them with a sense of belonging in a way similar to that which one might feel in a family setting. Though students also found financial aid and housing assistance to be of great importance, Dworsky and Perez (2010) Noted that students were more likely to report gaining a sense of family through the program than they were to report receiving material assistance.

With the assistance of federal and state funding, foster youth are finding their way to higher-education institutions in increasing numbers (Fried, 2008). Colleges are starting to take Notice of these young adults as evidenced by the growing number of campus programs designed to provide financial, academic, and other supports to students who have aged out of the foster care system (Casey Family Programs, 2010a; Dworsky & Perez, 2010), yet little is known about foster youths' level of readiness to engage in college.

Even less is known about foster youths' personal, social, interpersonal, academic, and career-development needs during their transition into college and ways that child welfare and higher education professionals can offer assistance.

REFERENCES

Arnett, J.J. (2000). Emerging adulthood: A theory of development from the late teens through the twenties. *American Psychologist, 55*, 469–480.

Avery, R.J., & Freundlich, M. (2009). You're all grown up Now: Termination of foster care support at age 18. *Journal of Adolescence, 32*, 247–257.

Blome, W.W. (1997). What happens to foster kids: Educational experiences of a random sample of foster youth and a matched group of Non-foster youth. *Child and Adolescent Social Work Journal, 14*, 41–53.

Casey Family Programs (2006). *It's my life: Postsecondary education and training and financial aid excerpt.* Seattle, WA: Author. Retrieved on June 7, 2011 from: www.casey.org/Resources/Publications/IMLPostsecondaryEd.htm

Casey Family Programs (2009). *Providing effective financial aid assistance to students from foster care and unaccompanied homeless youth.* Seattle, WA. Retrieved on June 7, 2011 from: www.casey.org/Resources/Publications/ProvidingEffectiveFinancial Aid.htm.

Casey Family Programs (2010a). *Supporting success: Improving higher education outcomes for students from foster care* (Version 2.0). Seattle, WA: Author. Retrieved on June 7, 2011 from: http://www.casey.org/Resources/Publications/SupportingSuccess.ht m.

Casey Family Programs (2010b). *Improving higher education outcomes for young adults from foster care selected readings and resources.* Seattle, WA: Author.

Child Welfare Information Gateway. (2011). *Foster care statistics 2009.* Washington, DC: U.S. Department of Health and Human Services, Children's Bureau. Retrieved on June 7, 2011 from: http://www.childwelfare.gov/pubs/factsheets/foster.cfm

Cook, A., Blaustein, M., Spinazzola, & van der Kolk, B. (2003). *Complex trauma in children and adolescents.* White paper from the National Child Traumatic Stress Network. Retrieved on June 7, 2011 from: www.NCTSNet.org.

Courtney, M.E., & Dworksy, A. (2006). Early outcomes for young adults transitioning from out-of-home care in the USA. *Child and Family Social Work, 11*, 209–219.

Courtney, M.E., Dworsky, A., Lee, J., & Raap, M. (2010). *Midwest evaluation of the adult functioning of former foster youth: Outcomes at ages 23 and 24.* Chicago: Chapin Hall Center for Children at the University of Chicago.

Courtney, M.E., Terao, S., & Bost, N. (2004). *Midwest evaluation of the adult functioning of former foster youth: Conditions of the youth preparing to leave state care.* Chicago: Chapin Hall Center for Children at the University of Chicago.

Cueso, J. (2005). Decided, undecided, and in transition: Implications for academic advisement, career counseling, and student retention. In R.S. Feldman (Ed.), *Improving the first year of college: Research and practice* (pp. 27–48). Mahwah, NJ: Erlbaum.

Davis, R.J. (2006). *College access, financial aid and college success for undergraduates from foster care.* Washington, DC: National Association of Student Financial Aid Administrators.

Day, A. (2009). Coming full circle: From child victim to childcare professional. In W.K. Brown and J.R. Seita, *Growing up in the care of strangers.* Tallahassee, FL: William Gladden Foundation Press.

Day, A., Dworsky, A., Fogarty, K., & Damashek, A. (2011). An examination of post-secondary retention and graduation among foster care youth enrolled in a four-year university, *Children and Youth Services Review*, doi:10.1016/j.childyouth.2011.08.004.

Dworsky, A., & Courtney, M. (2009). Addressing the mental health service needs of foster youth during the transition to adulthood: How big is the problem and what can states do? *Journal of Adolescent Health, 44,* 1–2.

Dworsky, A., & Perez, A. (2010). Helping former foster youth graduate from college through campus support programs. *Children and Youth Services Review, 32,* 255–263.

Fried, T. (2008). Community colleges step up to support foster care students. *Community College Journal* (February/March), 38–39.

Geenan, S., & Powers, L.E. (2007). Tomorrow is aNother problem: The experiences of youth in foster care during their transition into adulthood. *Children and Youth Services Review, 29,* 1085–1101.

Hines, A.M., Merdinger, J., & Wyatt, P. (2005). Former foster youth attending college: Resilience and the transition to young adulthood. *American Journal of Orthopsychiatry, 75,* 381–394.

Iglehart, A.P. (1995). Readiness for independence: Comparison of foster care, kinship care, and Non-foster care adolescents. *Children and Youth Services Review, 17,* 417–432.

Jackson, S., & Martin, P.Y. (1998). Surviving the care system: Education and resilience. *Journal of Adolescence, 21,* 569–583.

Jehangir, R.R. (2010). *Higher education and first-generation students: Cultivating community, voice, and place for the new majority.* Basingstoke: Palgrave Macmillan.

Kools, S. (1997). Adolescent identity development in foster care. *Family Relations, 46,* 263–271.

Kools, S. (1999). Self-protection in adolescents in foster care. *Journal of Child and Adolescent Psychiatric Nursing, 12,* 139–152.

McMillen, J.C., Auslander, W., Elze, D., White, T., & Thompson, R. (2003). Educational experiences and aspirations of older youth in foster care. *Child Welfare, 82,* 475–495.

McMillen, J.C., & Raghavan, R. (2009). Pediatric to adult mental health service use of young people leaving the foster care system. *Journal of Adolescent Health, 44,* 7–13.

McMillen, J.C., & Tucker, J. (1999). The status of older adolescents at exit from out-of home care, *Child Welfare, 78,* 339–360.

McMillen, J.C., Vaughn, M.G., & Shook, J.J. (2008). Aging out of foster care and legal involvement: Toward a typology of risk. *Social Service Review, 82,* 419–446.

Merdinger, J.M., Hines, A.M., Osterling, K.L., & Wyatt, P. (2005). Pathways to college for former foster youth: Understanding factors that contribute to educational success. *Child Welfare, 84,* 867–896.

Park, J.M., Metraux, S., & Culhane, D.P. (2005). Childhood out-of-home placement and dynamics of public shelter utilization among young homeless adults. *Children and Youth Services Review, 27,* 533–546.

Pecora, P.J., Williams, J., Kessler, R.C., Hiripi, E., O'Brien, K., Emerson, J., Herrick, M.A., & Torres, D. (2006). Assessing the educational achievements of adults who were formerly placed in family foster care. *Child & Family Social Work, 11,* 220–231.

Reilly, T. (2003). Transition from care: Status and outcomes of youth who age out of foster care. *Child Welfare, 82,* 727–746.

Samuels, G.M., & Price, J.M. (2008). What doesn't kill you makes you stronger: Survivalist self-reliance and risk among young adults aging out of foster care. *Children and Youth Services Review, 30,* 1198–1210.

Seita, J.R. (2001). Growing up without family privilege. *Reclaiming Children and Youth, 10,* 130–132.

Sheehy, A., Oldham, E., Zanghi, M., Ansell, D., Correia, P., & Copeland, R. (2000). *Promising practices: Supporting the transition of youth served by the foster care system.* Baltimore: Annie E. Casey Foundation.

Stratil, M.L. (2001). *College Student Inventory Manual.* Iowa City, IA: Noel-Levitz, Inc.

Stratil, M.L. (2009). *College Student Inventory™: Form A.* Coralville, IA: Noel-Levitz, Inc.

Unrau, Y.A., & Grinnell, R.M., Jr. (2005). The impact of social work research courses on research self-efficacy for social work students. *Social Work Education, 24,* 639–651.

Unrau, Y.A., Seita, J.R., & Putney, K.S. (2008). Former foster youth remember multiple placement moves: A journey of loss and hope. *Children and Youth Services Review, 30,* 1256–1266.

van der Kolk, B.A. (2005). Developmental trauma disorder: Toward a rational diagNosis for children with complex trauma histories. *Psychiatric Annals, 35,* 401–408.

Wolanin, T.R. (2005*). Higher education opportunities for foster youth: A primer for policymakers.* Washington, DC: Institute for Higher Education Policy.

───────

[1]Unrau, Y.A., Font, S.A., & Rawls, G. (2012). Readiness for college engagement among students who have aged out of foster care. *Children and Youth Services Review, 34,* 76–83.

	Homework Assignment 5.1	
	Writing Literature Review Sections for Research Proposals	

Box 5.1 presents the Literature Review section from a social work journal article. Download and read the article. Now that you are familiar with the research study depicted in Box 5.1:

1 In the white space below, write the Literature Review section you feel the authors *should have* written for the research proposal that their study was based upon.

   NOTE: You do not have a copy of the authors' research proposal. You only have a copy of the article that resulted from the implementation of their proposal.

   - Use all the tips in this section to write your hypothetical proposal's Literature Review section (e.g., clear and succinct key points).

2 Submit your Literature Review section to your instructor for comments and feedback.

Your Name(s):

Your Identification Number(s) (if any):

Assignment 5.1

Type your revised Literature Review section here.

(Box will automatically expand as you type)

Section 5
Writing a Literature Review Section for Your Research Proposal

Write the Literature Review section for your research proposal in the white space provided below.

- Use all the tips in this section to write your literature review (e.g., clear and succinct key points).

- If possible, show your proposal's Literature Review section to your classmates for their feedback.

- Revise all four sections based on your classmates' feedback.

- Submit all four sections to your instructor for comment.

Your Name(s):

Your Identification Number(s) (if any):

Title of Your Research Proposal:

Abstract:

Introduction:

Type your Literature Review sections here.

(Box will automatically expand as you type)

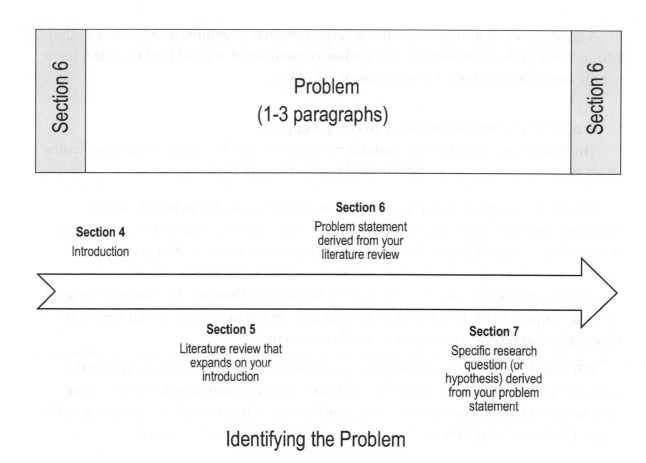

Identifying the Problem

SECTION 6 OF YOUR RESEARCH PROPOSAL is devoted to the problem area you wish to study, commonly referred to as a Problem Statement. It must be straightforwardly derived from your Literature Review section. Your research problem needs to be a one-sentence statement that provides a clear and concise description of a general "issue" that currently exists. And you want to study this issue further.

Your problem area must stand out. Your readers must easily recognize it as it provides the overall context for your proposed study and establishes the foundation for everything that will follow in your research proposal.

Furthermore, if the problem area you wish to study will involve the cooperation with a social work agency that sees a need for your study, your proposal should include a support letter from the agency's executive director. A copy of the letter is placed in an appendix (e.g., Appendix A in this book), but it should be referred to in this section.

A good Problem Statement generates the research question (or hypothesis) that you present in the next section. As previously mentioned, a good Problem Statement is only one sentence long. For example, it could be:

Problem Statement (without literary support)

The increasing use of micro-management techniques by social work supervisors is creating fear, anxiety, and a loss of productivity in their supervisees.

Yup, sure enough, this Problem Statement is one sentence in length. It now, however, needs to be accompanied by a few short sentences that elaborate on why the problem is a problem in the first place. These sentences need to present arguments—through the literature, of course—that make your problem area important enough for you to study further. More often than not, the sources for your literary support in Section 6 will have been mentioned previously when you were discussing the relevant literature in the last section.

While noting the rationale for your proposed project's boundaries and for the specified choice of your focus to the exclusion of others, you need to allude to the next section of your research proposal, the Research Question (Section 7), and to the research methodology you will use to answer your question (Section 8).

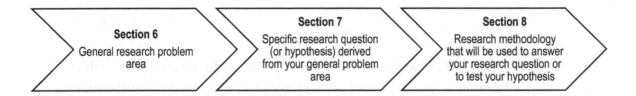

If appropriate, your Problem Statement should be presented within a context, and that context should be provided and briefly explained. That is, you should discuss the *conceptual or theoretical framework* in which your proposed study is embedded. Clearly and succinctly identify and explain the *theoretical framework* that underlies your proposed study and explain how you identified your "problem" as a problem. You should state your problem in terms intelligible to someone who is generally sophisticated but relatively uninformed in the problem area of your proposed study.

Box 6.1 provides an example of how a Problem Statement was formulated within a theoretical framework.

Writing a Problem Statement Section				QUICK TIPS
Check to see if you have read pages 6–7 on how to use our tips.				
Required				**Most important:** Check to see if you know how to write research problems and have read the appropriate chapter(s) in your research methods text before you complete Section 6!
#	**Answers**			**Tips**
116	NA	TA	Yes	No	Check to see that you have described the overall context of your proposed research study.
117	NA	TA	Yes	No	Check to see that your Problem Statement is either in a declarative form *or* in a question form. It can be either one. (This excludes the literature that supports the one-sentence statement, of course.)
118	NA	TA	Yes	No	Check to see that your Problem Statement is only one sentence in length. (This excludes the literature that supports it, of course.)
119	NA	TA	Yes	No	Check to see that your Problem Statement clearly indicates all the important variables your proposed study will address.
120	NA	TA	Yes	No	Check to see that your Problem Statement specifies a specific relationship between the variables you are studying. Note: In some research studies, a statement of variables will not be possible, such as those studies that involve qualitative research methods.
121	NA	TA	Yes	No	Check to see that you have provided a rationale for your Problem Statement.

122	NA	TA	Yes	No	Check to see that the problem area you propose to study is of current interest (or topical).
123	NA	TA	Yes	No	Check to see that your Problem Statement builds upon the past work of others.
124	NA	TA	Yes	No	Check to see that you have indicated how the population (research participants) you propose to use in your study is important, influential, or popular.
125	NA	TA	Yes	No	Check to see that you have indicated that the problem area you wish to study will in all likelihood continue into the future.
126	NA	TA	Yes	No	Check to see that your Problem Statement is not obscure, poorly formulated, or masked in an extended discussion.
127	NA	TA	Yes	No	Check to see that your Problem Statement is actually solvable given your time frame, resources, and commitment.
128	NA	TA	Yes	No	Check to see that you are *not* trying to answer too many research problems or test too many hypotheses in your proposed research project.
129	NA	TA	Yes	No	Check to see that your problem area really stands out.
130	NA	TA	Yes	No	Check to see that you have provided a discussion of the conceptual and/or theoretical framework in which your problem area is embedded.
131	NA	TA	Yes	No	Check to see that your Problem Statement contains only variables that are measurable. (More will be said about this in Section 8c on Instrumentation.)

132	NA	TA	Yes	No	Check to see that you have stated your problem in terms that are intelligible to someone who is generally sophisticated but relatively uninformed in the problem area of your proposed study.
133	NA	TA	Yes	No	Check to see that you have been judicious in your choice of exemplars—the literature you select must be directly pertinent and relevant to your problem area.
134	NA	TA	Yes	No	Check to see that your proposed study is replicable. The significance of your proposed project depends, in part, on its ability to be duplicated.
135	NA	TA	Yes	No	Check to see that you have identified the general analysis approach you propose to take. This more often than not is implicit in the statement.
136	NA	TA	Yes	No	Check to see that your Problem Statement did not go over the maximum three-paragraph limit. (This includes the supporting literature.)
137	NA	TA	Yes	No	Check with your research instructor to see if he/she has any examples of Problem Statements from other research proposals to show you.

BOX 6.1	Example of a Theoretical Framework and Problem Statement from an Article That Appeared in a Professional Journal

Exploring Out-Of-Home Placement as a Moderator of Help-Seeking Behavior among Adolescents Who Are High Risk[1]

COMPONENTS OF HELP-SEEKING BEHAVIORS

The first component of help-seeking behaviors is predisposing factors. The model suggests that service users possess a variety of predisposing factors that determine whether individuals seek out help for themselves. These include demographics (e.g., gender, race, age), social structure (e.g., education, occupation, social networks, culture), and health care beliefs (e.g., attitudes about health and health services).

The second component covers enabling factors, which are factors assumed to directly facilitate an individual's help-seeking behaviors. Availability and accessibility to services (e.g., health insurance and transportation), general know-how to gain use of services, and social relationships that assist with service use are included as enabling factors in Andersen's model.

The third component is known as the level of need factor, which is the severity of a problem suffered by the individual. It influences the likelihood of seeking help for oneself. Self-perceived need and professionally evaluated need are distinguished in the model

In sum, Andersen (1995) argued that all three factors—predisposing, enabling, and level of need—influence whether individuals set out to seek help for their problems. It should be noted that the current study does not test Andersen's model. Rather, his model is used as an organizing framework to examine the role that out-of home placement plays in the help-seeking behaviors among a group of adolescents who are high risk in relation to their physical and mental health problems.

Andersen's model provides a simple structure for describing complex relationships. Furthermore, others have applied it to foster care as a framework to critique health care utilization in the foster care system (Combs-Orme et al., 1991) and to investigate predictors of health service use by foster parents for children with psychiatric diagnoses (Zima, Bussing, Yang, & Belin, 2000).

There is a growing body of literature that investigates the factors predicting help-seeking behaviors between child and adolescent populations. This study's review of the literature was restricted to research studies that were conducted on North American samples that included youth between ages 13 and 19 years.

Previous research studies investigating help-seeking behaviors and service utilization were reviewed, **as the current study's aim is to understand which factors predict help-seeking behaviors in adolescent populations.**

REFERENCES

Andersen, R.M. (1995). Revisiting the behavioral model and access to medical care: Does it matter? *Journal of Health and Social Behavior, 36,* 1–10.

Combs-Orme, T., Chernoff, V., & Karger, R. (1991). Utilization of health care by foster children: Application of a theoretical model. *Children and Youth Services Review, 11,* 113–129.

Zima, B.T., Bussing, R., Yang, X., & Belin, T.R. (2000). Help-seeking steps and service use for children in foster care. *Journal of Behavioral Health Services & Research, 27,* 271–285.

_____

[1]Unrau, Y.A., & Grinnell, R.M., Jr. (2005). Exploring out-of-home placement as a moderator of help-seeking behavior among adolescents who are high risk. *Research on Social Work Practice, 15,* 516–530.

	Homework Assignment 6.1	

Writing Problem Sections for Research Proposals

Box 6.1 presents the Problem section from a social work journal article. Download and read the article. Now that you are familiar with the research study depicted in Box 6.1:

1 In the white space below, write the Problem section you feel the authors *should have* written for the research proposal their study was based upon.

NOTE: You do not have a copy of the authors' research proposal. You only have a copy of the article that resulted from the implementation of their proposal.

- Use all the tips in this section to write your hypothetical proposal's Problem section (e.g., builds upon past work of others).

2 Submit your Problem section to your instructor for comments and feedback.

Your Name(s):
Your Identification Number(s) (if any):
Assignment 6.1

Type your revised Problem section here.
(Box will automatically expand as you type)

Section 6
Writing a Problem Section for Your Research Proposal

Write a Problem section for your research proposal in the white space provided below.

- Use all the tips in this section to write your Problem section (e.g., builds on past work of others).
- If possible, show your Problem section to your classmates for their feedback.
- Revise your Problem section based on your classmates' feedback.
- Submit your Problem section to your instructor for comments and feedback.

Your Name(s):

Your Identification Number(s) (if any):

Title of Your Research Proposal:

Abstract:

Introduction:

Literature Review:

Type your Problem section here.

(Box will automatically expand as you type)

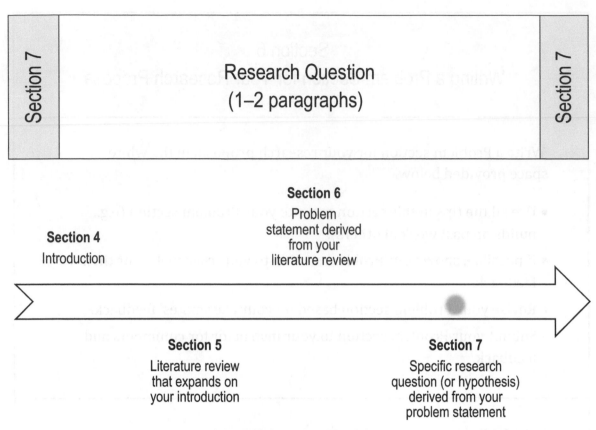

Identifying the Problem

SECTION 7 IS SHORT—very short. But just because it's short doesn't mean it's not important. It must follow logically from your Problem, which was logically derived from your Literature Review.

Section 7 simply provides the specific research question your study is going to answer, or the hypothesis you are going to test. If your research question (or hypothesis) is not extraordinarily clear to you, it won't be clear to those who read your proposal.

Many times, the Research Question (or hypothesis) section is a subsection of the Literature Review section, as illustrated below. In this instance, there would not be a separate Section 7 within the research proposal since it was incorporated into Section 5. And sometimes the Problem section is imbedded within the Literature Review section as well. So your outline could look like:

LITERATURE REVIEW (Section 5)   **or**   LITERATURE REVIEW (Section 5)

    Problem (Section 6)   Problem (Section 6)

    Research Question (Section 7)   Research Question (Section 7)

68

Whether your Research Question (or hypothesis) section is a subsection of the Problem section as previously illustrated or a subsection of the Literature Review, it has to be short and follow logically from your Problem section. Boxes 7.1 through 7.3 provide examples of how research questions can be written.

Writing a Research Question (or Hypothesis) Section				QUICK-TIPS
Check to see if you have read pages 6–7 on how to use our tips.				
Required				**Most important:** Check to see if you know how to write research questions and have read the appropriate chapter(s) in your research methods text before you complete Section 7!
#		**Answers**		**Tips**
138	NA	TA	Yes	No	Check to see that your research question to be answered (or your hypothesis to be tested) is logically linked to your Problem section; that is, this section must logically flow out of your Problem section.
139	NA	TA	Yes	No	Check to see that your research question starts with a sentence that begins "The purpose of this study is . . ." This will clarify your own mind as to your study's purpose, and it will directly and explicitly inform your readers about what exactly you propose to do.
140	NA	TA	Yes	No	Check to see that your research question to be answered (or your hypothesis to be tested) is an ethical one.
141	NA	TA	Yes	No	Check to see that you are prepared to interpret any possible outcomes with respect to your research question or hypothesis.

142	NA	TA	Yes	No	Check to see if you have visualized in your mind's eye the tables and other summary devices you will use that will eventually contain your study's results.
143	NA	TA	Yes	No	Check to see if you made a clear and careful distinction between your dependent and independent variables, and be certain they are clear to your readers. (Not all research studies contain independent and dependent variables.)
144	NA	TA	Yes	No	Check to see that your research question that can be adequately investigated.
145	NA	TA	Yes	No	Check to see that your research question can contribute to our profession's knowledge base.
146	NA	TA	Yes	No	Check to see that you research question has potentially strong implications for social work practice and/or policy, preferably both.
147	NA	TA	Yes	No	Check to see that your research question is based solidly within the profession of social work, including its intellectual history, its core values, the person-in-environment perspective, and its focus on vulnerable populations.
148	NA	TA	Yes	No	Check to see that your research question address clear gaps in the literature.
149	NA	TA	Yes	No	Check to see that your assumptions between and among variables make sense to you.
150	NA	TA	Yes	No	Check to see that your research question is researchable and feasible.
151	NA	TA	Yes	No	Check to see that your research question is ethically and culturally sensitive.
152	NA	TA	Yes	No	Check to see that your research question is thought provoking.
153	NA	TA	Yes	No	Check to see that your research question is directly related to your study's overall objectives.

154	NA	TA	Yes	No	Check to see that your research question is short and to the point.
155	NA	TA	Yes	No	Check to see that your research question is unambiguous and straightforward.
156	NA	TA	Yes	No	Check to see that your research question is formulated in a manner that will add to the available knowledge of social work practice.
157	NA	TA	Yes	No	Check to see that your research question is clearly stated, comprehensive, and used common vocabulary.
158	NA	TA	Yes	No	Check to be sure you were excruciatingly consistent in your use of terms. If appropriate, use the same pattern of wording (and word order) in all your research questions (or hypotheses).
159	NA	TA	Yes	No	Check to see if you have access to the data that are needed to answer your research question (or test your hypothesis).
160	NA	TA	Yes	No	Check to see that you did not go over the two-paragraph limit.
161	NA	TA	Yes	No	Check to see that you have all the necessary skills (or can develop them) to find an answer to your research question (or to test your hypothesis).
162	NA	TA	Yes	No	Check with your research instructor to see if he/she has any examples of research problems (or hypotheses) from other research proposals to show you.

BOX 7.1	Example of Research Questions from an Article That Appeared in a Professional Journal

Voucher Users and Revitalized Public-Housing Residents 6 Years after Displacement[1]

RESEARCH QUESTIONS

1 How did participants experience the application process of moving back to College Town?

2 How many residents moved back to College Town, and what reasons did they give for returning?

3 What reasons did residents give for not applying to move back to College Town?

4 How satisfied were residents who returned to College Town?

5 How did public-housing residents compare with voucher users on standardized measures of material hardship?

6 A total of 6 years after displacement, how did public-housing residents compare with voucher users for overall economic well-being?

_____

[1]Brooks, F., Lewinson, T., Aszman, J., & Wolk, J. (2012). Voucher users and revitalized public-housing residents 6 years after displacement. *Research on Social Work Practice, 22,* 10–19.

BOX 7.2	Example of Research Questions from an Article That Appeared in a Professional Journal

Evaluating Predictors of Program Attrition among Women Mandated into Batterer Intervention Treatment[1]

RESEARCH QUESTIONS

The current study addresses the following research questions:

1 What exactly are the differences in demographic and psychosocial variables between program completers versus program dropouts for women batterers, and what do these differences mean in terms of program planning and implementation?

2 Do referral source and level of supervision affect rates of program completion among women batterers, and if so, what are the implications for the criminal justice system?

_____

[1]Buttell, F., Powers, D., & Wong, A. (2012). Evaluating predictors of program attrition among women mandated into batterer intervention treatment. *Research on Social Work Practice, 22,* 20–28.

BOX 7.3	Example of Research Questions (Purpose) from an Article That Appeared in a Professional Journal

Readiness for College Engagement among Students Who Have Aged Out of Foster Care[1]

The purpose of this study, therefore, is twofold:

1 to identify and measure foster youths' readiness for college engagement, (i.e., academic motivation, social motivation, receptivity to student services, general coping).

2 to compare the readiness for college engagement among freshman foster youth prior to the start of college with the readiness for college engagement among freshman in general. In addition, this article describes the first-semester performance of freshman foster youth compared with other freshman enrolled in the same university.

---

[1]Unrau, Y.A., Font, S.A., & Rawls, G. (2012). Readiness for college engagement among students who have aged out of foster care. *Children and Youth Services Review, 34,* 76–83.

	Homework Assignment 7.1	

Writing Research Questions (or Hypotheses) Sections for Research Proposals

Boxes 7.1 to 7.3 present three Research Question sections from three different social work journal articles. Download and read one of the articles. Now that you are familiar with the research study depicted in the article you selected:

1 In the white space below, write a Research Question section you feel the authors *should have* written for the research proposal their study was based upon.

NOTE: You do not have a copy of the authors' research proposal. You only have a copy of the article that resulted from the implementation of their proposal.

- Use all the tips in this section to write your hypothetical proposal's Research Question section (e.g., is it ethical?).

2 Submit your Research Question section and a copy of the article to your instructor for comments and feedback.

Your Name(s):

Your Identification Number(s) (if any):

Assignment 7.1. Title of Selected Article:

Type your revised Research Question (or Hypothesis) section here.
(Box will automatically expand as you type)

Section 7
Writing a Research Question (or Hypothesis) Section for Your Research Proposal

Write a Research Question (or hypothesis) section for your research proposal in the white space provided below. Use all the tips in this section to write your Research Question (or hypothesis) section (e.g., is it ethical?).

- If possible, show your Research Question (or hypothesis) section to your classmates for their feedback.
- Revise your Research Question (or hypothesis) section based on your classmates' feedback.
- Submit your revised Research Question (or hypothesis) section to your instructor for comments and feedback.

Your Name(s):

Your Identification Number(s) (if any):

Title of Your Research Proposal:

Abstract:

Introduction:

Literature Review:

Problem:

Type your Research Question (or Hypothesis) section here.

(Box will automatically expand as you type)

PART III
Solving the Problem

Once you have specified the research question you want to solve (or the hypothesis you want to test) in Section 7, you now have to state how you are going to solve your research question (or test your hypothesis) in Section 8.

Method
(3–5 pages)

Section 8a: **Research Design:** What specific research design is going to be used?

Section 8b: **Sample:** How are the research participants going to be selected?

Section 8c: **Instrumentation:** How are the variables going to be measured?

Section 8d: **Data Collection:** How are the data going to be gathered?

Section 8e: **Data Analysis:** How are the data going to be analyzed?

Section 8f: **Ethical and Cultural Considerations:** How did you address all of the ethical and cultural issues that may need to be taken into account within the above sections?

In the last section you formulated a research question (or hypothesis) for your proposed study. You will now need to describe how you propose to answer your research question (or to test your hypothesis)—the main purpose of Section 8. The Method section contains six highly interrelated subsections listed above.

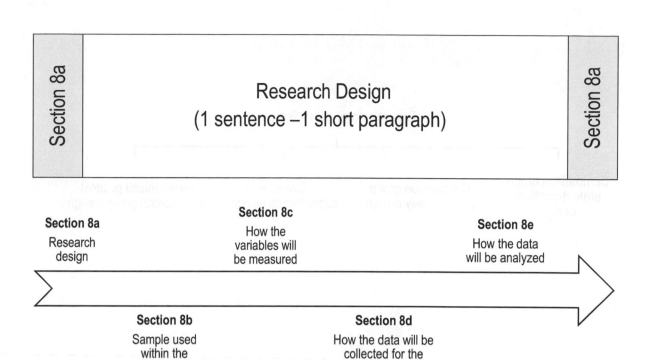

Solving the Problem

THERE ARE MANY WAYS to classify research designs. We are going to classify them into those that use only one group of research participants (known as one-group research designs) and those that use two or more groups of research participants (known as two-group designs) as illustrated:

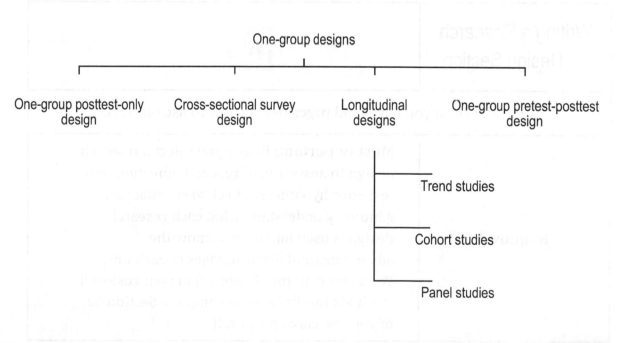

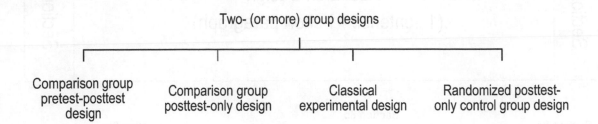

You need to justify the research design you propose to use that you believe will answer your research question (or to test your hypothesis). You then need to present a brief synopsis of your overall research design—quantitative, qualitative, or mixed (both quantitative *and* qualitative).

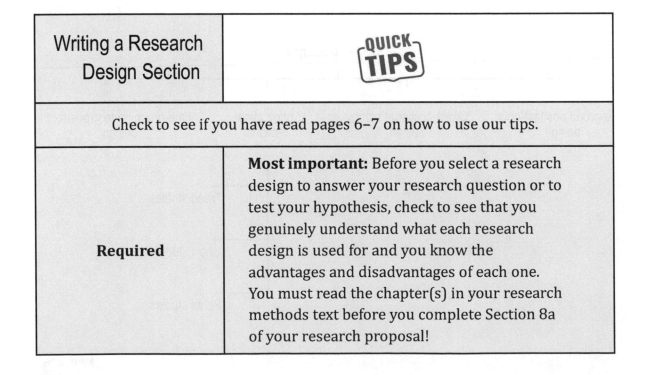

Writing a Research Design Section	QUICK TIPS
Check to see if you have read pages 6–7 on how to use our tips.	
Required	**Most important:** Before you select a research design to answer your research question or to test your hypothesis, check to see that you genuinely understand what each research design is used for and you know the advantages and disadvantages of each one. You must read the chapter(s) in your research methods text before you complete Section 8a of your research proposal!

#	Answers				Tips
163	NA	TA	Yes	No	Before you select a research design, check to see that you have considered the pros and cons of alternative designs, paying particular attention to how you are going to control extraneous variables that may produce bias and confounding results.
164	NA	TA	Yes	No	Check to see that you have made it extraordinary clear which specific research design you propose to use. State your selected design in words such as: This study will use a one-group posttest-only design.
165	NA	TA	Yes	No	Check to see that you have made a clear connection between the research question (or hypothesis) you formulated in Section 7 and the research design you are going to use to answer that question (or test your hypothesis), Section 8a.
166	NA	TA	Yes	No	Check to see that you have stated what your independent and dependent variables are (if you have any). You do not have to inform the readers at this point of how you are going to measure the variables—that's described in Section 8c on Instrumentation. Remember, your study does not have to have an independent or dependent variable.
167	NA	TA	Yes	No	Before you select a research design, check to see that you truly understand how the threats to internal and external validity factors affect each research design and especially the research design you have chosen to use in your proposed study.

168	NA	TA	Yes	No	Check to see that you have clearly stated how the research design you have finally selected for your proposed research study controls for one of the threats to internal validity: **history** (if applicable, of course). If your research design doesn't control for the effects of **history**, you need to point out that this is one of the limitations of your study that will be discussed further in Section 9—the section where you pay attention to how the internal validity threat of **history** directly affects the interpretation of your study's findings.
169	NA	TA	Yes	No	Check to see that you have clearly stated how the research design you have finally selected for your proposed research study controls for one of the threats to internal validity: **maturation** (if applicable, of course). If your research design doesn't control for the effects of **maturation**, you need to point out that this is one of the limitations of your study that will be discussed further in Section 9—the section where you pay attention to how the internal validity threat of **maturation** directly affects the interpretation of your study's findings.

170	NA	TA	Yes	No	Check to see that you have clearly stated how the research design you have finally selected for your proposed research study controls for one of the threats to internal validity: **testing (or initial measurement effects)** (if applicable, of course). If your research design doesn't control for the effects of **testing**, you need to point out that this is one of the limitations of your study that will be discussed further in Section 9—the section where you pay attention to how the internal validity threat of **testing** directly affects the interpretation of your study's findings.
171	NA	TA	Yes	No	Check to see that you have clearly stated how the research design you have finally selected for your proposed research study controls for one of the threats to internal validity: **instrumentation error** (if applicable, of course). If your research design doesn't control for the effects of **instrumentation error**, you need to point out that this is one of the limitations of your study that will be discussed further in Section 9—the section where you pay attention to how the internal validity threat of **instrumentation error** directly affects the interpretation of your study's findings.

172	NA	TA	Yes	No	Check to see that you have clearly stated how the research design you have finally selected for your proposed research study controls for one of the threats to internal validity: **statistical regression** (if applicable, of course). If your research design doesn't control for the effects of **statistical regression**, you need to point out that this is one of the limitations of your study that will be discussed further in Section 9—the section where you pay attention to how the internal validity threat of **statistical regression error** directly affects the interpretation of your study's findings.
173	NA	TA	Yes	No	Check to see that you have clearly stated how the research design you have finally selected for your proposed research study controls for one of the threats to internal validity: **differential selection of research participants** (if applicable, of course). If your research design doesn't control for the effects of **differential selection of research participants**, you need to point out that this is one of the limitations of your study that will be discussed further in Section 9—the section where you pay attention to how the internal validity threat of **differential selection of research participants** directly affects the interpretation of your study's findings.

174	NA	TA	Yes	No	Check to see that you have clearly stated how the research design you have finally selected for your proposed research study controls for one of the threats to internal validity: **mortality** (if applicable, of course). If your research design doesn't control for the effects **mortality**, you need to point out that this is one of the limitations of your study that will be discussed further in Section 9—the section where you pay attention to how the internal validity threat of **mortality** directly affects the interpretation of your study's findings.
175	NA	TA	Yes	No	Check to see that you have clearly stated how the research design you have finally selected for your proposed research study controls for one of the threats to internal validity: **reactive effects of research participants** (if applicable, of course). If your research design doesn't control for the effects of **reactive effects of research participants**, you need to point out that this is one of the limitations of your study that will be discussed further in Section 9—the section where you pay attention to how the internal validity threat of **reactive effects of research participants** directly affects the interpretation of your study's findings.

176	NA	TA	Yes	No	Check to see that you have clearly stated how the research design you have finally selected for your proposed research study controls for one of the threats to internal validity: **interaction effects** (if applicable, of course). If your research design doesn't control for **interaction effects**, you need to point out that this is one of the limitations of your study that will be discussed further in Section 9—the section where you pay attention to how the internal validity threat of **interaction effects** directly affects the interpretation of your study's findings.
177	NA	TA	Yes	No	Check to see that you have clearly stated how the research design you have finally selected for your proposed research study controls for one of the threats to internal validity: **diffusion of treatments** (if applicable, of course). If your research design doesn't control for **diffusion of treatments**, you need to point out that this is one of the limitations of your study that will be discussed further in Section 9—the section where you pay attention to how the internal validity threat of **diffusion of treatments** directly affects the interpretation of your study's findings.

178	NA	TA	Yes	No	Check to see that you have clearly stated how the research design you have finally selected for your proposed research study controls for one of the threats to internal validity: **compensatory equalization** (if applicable, of course).
					If your research design doesn't control for **compensatory equalization**, you need to point out that this is one of the limitations of your study that will be discussed further in Section 9—the section where you pay attention to how the internal validity threat of **compensatory equalization** directly affects the interpretation of your study's findings.
179	NA	TA	Yes	No	Check to see that you have clearly stated how the research design you have finally selected for your proposed research study controls for one of the threats to internal validity: **compensatory rivalry** (if applicable, of course).
					If your research design doesn't control for **compensatory rivalry**, you need to point out that this is one of the limitations of your study that will be discussed further in Section 9—the section where you pay attention to how the internal validity threat of **compensatory rivalry** directly affects the interpretation of your study's findings.

180	NA	TA	Yes	No	Check to see that you have clearly stated how the research design you have finally selected for your proposed research study controls for one of the threats to internal validity: **demoralization** (if applicable, of course). If your research design doesn't control for **demoralization**, you need to point out that this is one of the limitations of your study that will be discussed further in Section 9—the section where you pay attention to how the internal validity threat of **demoralization** directly affects the interpretation of your study's findings.
181	NA	TA	Yes	No	Check to see that you have clearly stated how the research design you have finally selected for your proposed research study controls for one of the threats to external validity: **pretest-treatment interaction** (if applicable, of course). If your research design doesn't control for **pretest-treatment interaction**, you need to point out that this is one of the limitations of your study that will be discussed further in Section 9—the section where you pay attention to how the external validity threat of **pretest-treatment interaction** directly affects the interpretation of your study's findings.

182	NA	TA	Yes	No	Check to see that you have clearly stated how the research design you have finally selected for your proposed research study controls for one of the threats to external validity: **selection-treatment interaction** (if applicable, of course). If your research design doesn't control for **selection-treatment interaction**, you need to point out that this is one of the limitations of your study that will be discussed further in Section 9—the section where you pay attention to how the external validity threat of **selection-treatment interaction** directly affects the interpretation of your study's findings.
183	NA	TA	Yes	No	Check to see that you have clearly stated how the research design you have finally selected for your proposed research study controls for one of the threats to external validity: **specificity of variables** (if applicable, of course). If your research design doesn't control for **specificity of variables**, you need to point out that this is one of the limitations of your study that will be discussed further in Section 9—the section where you pay attention to how the external validity threat of **specificity of variables** directly affects the interpretation of your study's findings.

184	N A	TA	Yes	No	Check to see that you have clearly stated how the research design you have finally selected for your proposed research study controls for one of the threats to external validity: **reactive effects** (if applicable, of course). If your research design doesn't control for **reactive effects**, you need to point out that this is one of the limitations of your study that will be discussed further in Section 9—the section where you pay attention to how the external validity threat of **reactive effects** directly affects the interpretation of your study's findings.
185	NA	TA	Yes	No	Check to see that you have clearly stated how the research design you have finally selected for your proposed research study controls for one of the threats to external validity: **multiple-treatment interference** (if applicable, of course). If your research design doesn't control for **multiple-treatment interference**, you need to point out that this is one of the limitations of your study that will be discussed further in Section 9—the section where you pay attention to how the external validity threat of **multiple-treatment interference** directly affects the interpretation of your study's findings.

186	NA	TA	Yes	No	Check to see that you have clearly stated how the research design you have finally selected for your proposed research study controls for one of the threats to external validity: **researcher bias** (if applicable, of course). If your research design doesn't control for **researcher bias**, you need to point out that this is one of the limitations of your study that will be discussed further in Section 9—the section where you pay attention to how the external validity threat of **researcher bias** directly affects the interpretation of your study's findings.
187	NA	TA	Yes	No	Check to see that you have provided all the necessary information about the research design so it could be reproduced or replicated.
188	NA	TA	Yes	No	Check to see that you have demonstrated why your chosen research design (and data-collection method, 8d) are well suited to your research question.
189	NA	TA	Yes	No	Check to see that you have clearly described the independent variable(s) and dependent variable(s), if any.
190	NA	TA	Yes	No	Check to see that you have ensured study's research design, methods, and procedures are sufficiently transparent, balanced, and objective.
191	NA	TA	Yes	No	Check to see that you have stated how long it will take to complete your entire study.
192	NA	TA	Yes	No	Check to see that you have made explicit any assumptions that your research design rests upon.
193	NA	TA	Yes	No	Check to see that you have the skills to carry out the research design you have selected.

BOX 8a.1	Example of a Research Design Section from an Article That Appeared in a Professional Journal

Evaluation of a Program to Educate Disadvantaged Parents to Enhance Child Learning[1]

A one-group pretest–posttest ($O_1 X O_2$) design was employed to test the hypotheses that gains would be made in child learning as well as in parental social support and self-efficacy and that child behavior problems and parenting stress would be reduced upon completion of the program.

---

[1]Leung, C., Tsang, S., & Dean, S. (2010). Evaluation of a program to educate disadvantaged parents to enhance child learning. *Research on Social Work Practice, 20,* 591–599.

BOX 8a.2	Example of a Research Design Section (and Sample Section) from an Article That Appeared in a Professional Journal

Readiness for College Engagement among Students Who Have Aged Out of Foster Care[1]

METHOD

The convenience sample for this exploratory cross-sectional survey was 81 former foster youth who graduated from high school and were admitted as freshman in the 2009 ($n = 35$) and 2010 ($n = 46$) fall semesters. Participants were identified by their enrollment in the Seita Scholars Program.

---

[1]Unrau, Y.A., Font, S.A., & Rawls, G. (2012). Readiness for college engagement among students who have aged out of foster care. *Children and Youth Services Review, 34*, 76–83.

BOX 8a.3	Example of a Research Design Section from a Research Proposal

**Chatham-Kent Children's Services (CKCS) Help-Seeking
Project for Adolescents in Out-of-Home Placement:
A Research Proposal[1]**

RESEARCH DESIGN

An experimental classical two-group pretest-posttest design will be
utilized in this study with two follow-up points. All participants will be
randomly assigned to either the experimental or the control condition
of the study. Random assignment will continue until 60 youth have
been assigned to each group ($N = 120$).

The figure below illustrates the basic layout of the research design.
More specifically, it shows that the experimental group will receive the
three-part intervention (described earlier) while the control group will
not. It also shows that data will be collected from youth in both groups
at four time points (i.e., study onset, 5 weeks, 10 weeks, 20 weeks), and
the amount of remuneration (i.e., $10, $15, $20, $30) that each youth
will receive for participating at each data collection point.

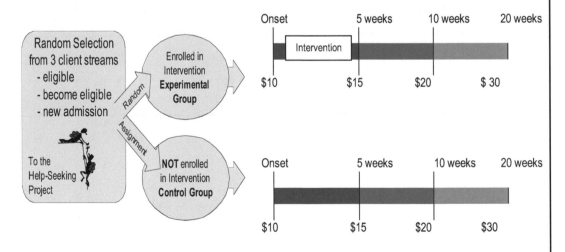

[1]Unrau, Y., & Grinnell, R.M., Jr. (2005). *Chatham-Kent Children's
Services (CKCS) Help-Seeking Project for Adolescents in Out-of-
Home Placement: A Research Proposal. S*ubmitted to Provincial
Centre of Excellence for Child and Youth Mental Health at CHEO.
Ottawa, Ontario, Canada K1H 8L1.

	Homework Assignment 8a.1	

Writing Research Design Sections for Research Proposals

Boxes 8a.1 and 8a.2 present two Research Design sections from two different social work journal articles. Download and read one of the articles. Now that you are familiar with the research study depicted in the article you selected:

1 In the white space below, write a Research Design section you feel the authors *should have* written for their research proposal.

- Use all the tips in this section to write your Research Design section (e.g., is the research design clearly stated?).

2 Submit your Research Design section along with your selected article to your instructor for comments and feedback.

Your Name(s):
Your Identification Number(s) (if any):
Assignment 8a.1. Title of Selected Article:

Type your revised Research Design section here.
(Box will automatically expand as you type)

	Homework Assignment 8a.2	
	Writing Research Design Sections for Research Proposals	

Box 8a.3 presents a Research Design section from a research proposal.

1 In the white space below, write a Research Design section you feel the authors *should have* written for the research proposal.

  - Use all the tips in this section to write your Research Design section.

2 Submit your Research Design section to your instructor for comments and feedback.

Your Name(s):

Your Identification Number(s) (if any):

Assignment 8a.2

Type your revised Research Design section here.

(Box will automatically expand as you type)

Section 8a
Writing a Research Design Section for Your Research Proposal

Write a Research Design section for your research proposal in the white space provided below.

- Use all the tips in this section to write your Research Design section (e.g., is it clear what research design is being used?).
- If possible, show your Research Design section to your classmates for their feedback.
- Revise your Research Design section based on your classmates' feedback.
- Submit your revised Research Design section to your instructor for comments and feedback.

Your Name(s):

Your Identification Number(s) (if any):

Title of Your Research Proposal

Abstract:

Introduction:

Literature Review:

Problem:

Research Question:

Type your Research Design section here.

(Box will automatically expand as you type)

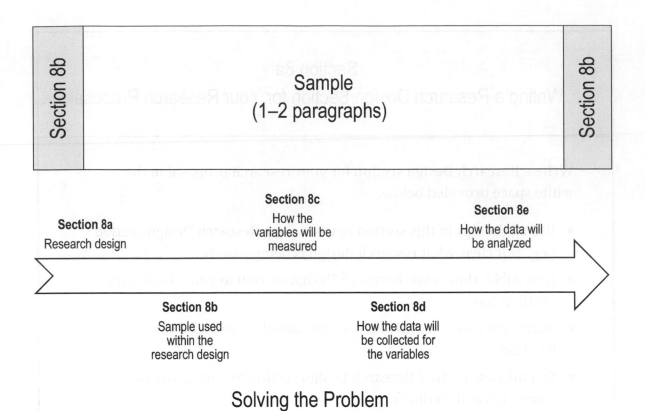

Solving the Problem

NOW THAT YOU HAVE SELECTED the research design you propose to use in your study (Section 8a), you need to select a sampling strategy that you will use to select your research participants. These research participants will be the folks who supply you with the data you will need to answer your research question (or test your hypothesis). Obviously, not all research studies use humans in their samples. For example, they can use case files or existing databases.

As you know from your research methods book, samples that are used within research studies can be categorized into two general types: (1) probability and (2) nonprobability.

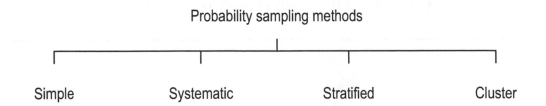

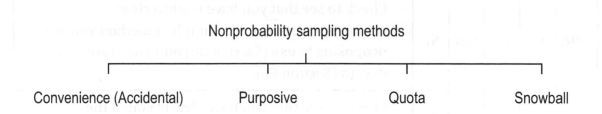

Nonprobability sampling methods

Convenience (Accidental)   Purposive   Quota   Snowball

Writing a Sample Section	QUICK TIPS
Check to see if you have read pages 6–7 on how to use our tips.	
Required	**Very important:** Check to see that you genuinely understand the advantages and disadvantages of using probability and nonprobability sampling strategies. This means that you must read the sampling chapter in your textbook before you start to complete this section of your research proposal.

#	Answers				Tips
194	NA	TA	Yes	No	Check to see that you have made it clear what specific sampling frame you are going to use to draw your sample from. State the sampling frame in words such as "The sampling frame for this study will include all high school students enrolled in XYZ High School in the academic year 2013."
195	NA	TA	Yes	No	Check to see that you have made it clear what specific sampling strategy you are proposing to use. State the sampling method in words such as "This study will use a snowball sampling procedure."

196	NA	TA	Yes	No	Check to see that you have made a clear connection between the sampling method you are proposing to use (Section 8b) and your research design (Section 8a).
197	NA	TA	Yes	No	Check to see that you have clearly stated the projected size (*N*) of your proposed sample.
198	NA	TA	Yes	No	Check to see that the overall size of your proposed sample is adequate to answer your research question (or to test your hypothesis).
199	NA	TA	Yes	No	Check to see that you have explained how you have determined the size and type of the sample you are going to be using, including the relative importance of Type I error (false positive) and Type II error (false negative).
200	NA	TA	Yes	No	Check to see that it is realistically feasible for you to obtain the necessary number of research participants for your proposed study.
201	NA	TA	Yes	No	Check to see that you have the support of your potential research participants to move ahead with your research study.
202	NA	TA	Yes	No	Check to see that you have included specific relevant information on the population (your potential research participants) that you intend to focus on.
203	NA	TA	Yes	No	Check to see that your proposed sample will be representative of the population from which you will be drawing it. That is, you need to ask the question, "How representative will my sample be?"
204	NA	TA	Yes	No	Check to see that you have made arrangements to write informed consent (and/or assent) letters to potential research participants. Copies of these documents are placed in your appendixes (e.g., Appendixes E and F in this book).

205	NA	TA	Yes	No	Check to see that you have provided the specific instructions that your human research participants will receive in reference to how they will provide the data requested of them. Place a copy of the instructions in the appendixes (e.g., Appendixes H and/or I in this book).
206	NA	TA	Yes	No	Check to see that you have provided a clear description of the sampling method that you propose to use to recruit research participants for your study. That is, what sampling method(s) will you use in selecting your sample (e.g., random, stratified random, cluster, stage, purposive, quota, snowball, accidental [or convenience]?
207	NA	TA	Yes	No	Check to see that you have described the inclusion and exclusion criteria that you propose to use to select your sampling frame.
208	NA	TA	Yes	No	Check to see that you have specified the time frame for sample selection.
209	NA	TA	Yes	No	Check to see that you have specified your estimated study's final sample size.
210	NA	TA	Yes	No	Check to see if you discussed any salient characteristics (e.g., demographic, clinical, diagnostic) of your proposed study's sample in clear detail to permit comparisons of your particular sample with those used in prior (and future) research studies.
211	NA	TA	Yes	No	Check to see if your study's proposed sample is going to be representative of the larger population from which it's drawn.
212	NA	TA	Yes	No	Check to see if you discussed any unique features of your proposed sample.
213	NA	TA	Yes	No	Check to see that you have made explicit any assumptions that your sampling strategy rests upon.

| 214 | NA | TA | Yes | No | Check to see that you have the skills to carry out your selected sampling strategy. If not, obtain the skills before you start your sampling procedures. |
| 215 | NA | TA | Yes | No | Check with your research instructor to see if he/she has any examples of Sample sections from other research proposals to show you. |

BOX 8b.1	Example of a Sample Section from a Research Proposal

Chatham-Kent Children's Services (CKCS) Help-Seeking Project for Adolescents in Out-of-Home Placement: A Research Proposal[1]

RESEARCH SETTING AND SAMPLE

The study will take place at Chatham-Kent Children's Services (CKCS), which has since 1996 operated as an amalgamated agency offering child protection, children's mental health, and child development/prevention services to children and families living in the Chatham-Kent Municipality.

The agency, which is funded by the Ministry of Children and Youth Services, the Municipality of Chatham-Kent, the United Way, and others, was recently recommended for accreditation with Ontario Association of Children's Aid Societies and Children's Mental Health Ontario.

The agency's mission statement is: "Working with our community to strengthen families and promote the well being and safety of children and youth," and the values of the agency clearly communicate that children are the priority of service delivery.

Random Selection from the Population

Eligibility criteria for study participation include: (1) 12 to 17 years old and living in out-of-home placement with CKCS during the period of the study, (2) discharge from care is not expected to occur within 20 weeks, (3) youth do not have severe cognitive delays or IQ scores less than 80, and (4) youth do not have severe medical needs or physical disabilities that would prevent them from participating in a group session with peers or having a 30-minute telephone conversation. Participants for the study will be selected from three streams of clientele at CKCS.

1 **Eligible:** At the start point of the study, CKCS will have approximately 140 adolescents meeting the above eligibility criteria in care. About one-half of these adolescents are placed in foster homes, one-third in group homes, and one-fifth have room-and-board living arrangements.

2 **Become Eligible:** Over a 21-month period of time CKCS estimates that approximately 26 children already in care at the start of the study will become eligible for participation as they pass their 12th birthdays.

3 **New Admissions:** Over a 21-month period of time CKCS estimates that another 30 new admissions (meeting the eligibility criteria above) will enter CKCS out-of-home placements.

Study participants will be selected from the three streams of clientele just mentioned: (1) 64 study participants will be randomly selected from a list of eligible youth that are in CKCS care at the start of the study, (2) approximately 26 youth who have their 12th birthdays during the course of the study will be added to the sample as they become eligible for participation along with another 30 eligible youth entering out-of-home placement with CKCS during the study period. It is important to note that study participants ($N = 120$) will be randomly assigned to experimental or control groups with $N = 60$ per group.

Approach to Recruitment

Youth will be invited to participate in the study using informed consent procedures, which have received the approval of both the Research Ethics and Review Committee at CKCS and the Human Subject Institutional Review Board at Western Michigan University.

In sum, the project manager will be trained by the researchers to follow protocols for seeking informed consent from selected participants. These procedures include: informing youth about the details of the study—including incentives, explaining that participation is voluntary, and making it clear that there is no penalty for not participating.

---

[1]Unrau, Y., & Grinnell, R.M., Jr. (2005). *Chatham-Kent Children's Services (CKCS) Help-Seeking Project for Adolescents in Out-of-Home Placement: A Research Proposal.* Submitted to Provincial Centre of Excellence for Child and Youth Mental Health at CHEO. Ottawa, Ontario, Canada K1H 8L1.

BOX 8b.2	Example of a Sample Section from an Article That Appeared in a Professional Journal

Feasibility of Using Virtual Reality to Assess Nicotine Cue Reactivity during Treatment[1]

SAMPLING PROCEDURE

Participants ($n = 46$) were recruited through advertisements in a local paper in the Atlanta metropolitan area and were involved in a treatment study. The following were the inclusion criteria for study participation: (a) cigarette smokers with current Diagnostic and Statistical Manual, Fourth Edition, Text Revision (DSM-IV-TR; American Psychiatric Association, 2000) diagnosis of nicotine dependence, who were daily smokers for the past 2 years; and (b) good physical health and willing to wear a nicotine patch.

The following were exclusion criteria: (a) current DSM-IV-TR (American Psychiatric Association, 2000) psychiatric diagnosis of chronic, severe mental illness (e.g., schizophrenia, bipolar disorder, depression with psychosis, and schizoaffective disorder), or substance abuse other than nicotine dependence; (b) treated with any smoking cessation, (c) history of serious medical conditions (e.g., heart condition); (d) fear of closed spaces or visual problems that may impair ability to view VR materials.

REFERENCE

American Psychiatric Association (2000). *Diagnostic and statistical manual of mental disorders* (4th ed., Text Revision). Washington, DC: Author.

———————

[1]Kaganoff, E., Bordnick, P.S., & Carter, B.L. (2012). Feasibility of using virtual reality to assess nicotine cue reactivity during treatment. *Research on Social Work Practice, 22*, 159–165.

BOX 8b.3	Example of a Sample Section from an Article That Appeared in a Professional Journal

Motivations, Values, and Conflict Resolution: Students' Integration of Personal and Professional Identities[1]

Participants consisted of students currently enrolled in a MSW program at a private, Midwestern university. An e-mail describing the study was sent to all MSW students, and interested students were asked to contact the researcher directly. A nonrandom, purposive, maximum variation-sampling frame was used. Maximum-variation sampling involves selecting participants who vary widely along dimensions of interest (Patton, 2001). Dimensions of interest were religious affiliation, age, gender, sexual orientation, race, and family socioeconomic status. Interested students who did not identify with majority-group characteristics (Caucasian, heterosexual, and female) were automatically selected for participation.

Interested students who did identify with these majority-group demographics were further evaluated according to age and religious affiliation and enrolled based on the overall contribution to the maximum variation of the sample. Purposive recruitment attempts were made to students known to self-identify as male, non-Caucasian, and/or nonheterosexual.

In line with Glaser and Strauss' (1967) idea of theoretical sampling, active recruitment of advanced students was initiated when a pattern encompassing differences among foundation students, advanced standing students, and concentration students began to emerge. Based on additional recruitment efforts, seven more participants were enrolled, yielding a total sample of 20 interviewees.

REFERENCES

Glaser, B.G., & Strauss, A.L. (1967). *The discovery of grounded theory: Strategies for qualitative research.* Hawthorne, NY: Aldine de Gruyter.

Patton, M. Q. (2001). *Qualitative research and evaluation methods* (3rd ed.). Thousand Oaks, CA: Sage.

[1]Osteene, P.J. (2011). Motivations, values, and conflict resolution: students' integration of personal and professional identities. *Journal Social Work Education, 47,* 423–44

BOX 8b.4	Example of a Sample Section from an Article That Appeared in a Professional Journal

Measuring Parenting Practices among Parents of Elementary School–Age Youth[1]

SAMPLING PROCEDURE

The study used data from a point in time, self-reported survey of parents ($n = 1,153$) with children under <11 years of age who were randomly selected from a population of parents residing in a southeastern state in 2007. Respondents resided in one of the eight counties in urban, suburban, and rural areas of the state. The counties were selected through a stratified process based on population density and region. Within each county, parents were randomly selected from the American Student List database of eligible parents.

[1]Randolph, K.A., & Radey, M. (2011). Measuring parenting practices among parents of elementary school–age youth. *Research on Social Work Practice, 21,* 88–97.

	Homework Assignment 8b.1	

Writing Sample Sections for Research Proposals

Box 8b.1 presents a Sample section from a research proposal.

1 In the white space below, write a Sample section you feel the authors *should have* written for their research proposal. Your main objective is to edit, revise, rearrange, and/or modify the authors' Sample section in an effort to make it clearer, more concise, and easier to read and follow.

  • Use all the tips in this section to rewrite your Sample section (e.g., the specific sampling strategy is clearly stated).

2 Submit your revised Sample section to your instructor, pointing out all the revisions you made and why you made them.

Your Name(s):

Your Identification Number(s) (if any):

Assignment 8b.1

Type your revised Sample section here.

(Box will automatically expand as you type)

	Homework Assignment 8b.2	

Writing Sample Sections for Research Proposals

Boxes 8b.2 to 8b.4 present three Sample sections from three different social work journal articles. Download and read one of the articles. Now that you are familiar with the research study depicted in the article you selected:

1   In the white space below, write a Sample section you feel the authors *should have* written for the research proposal that their study was based upon.

NOTE: You do not have a copy of the authors' research proposal. You only have a copy of the article that resulted from the implementation of their proposal.

   • Use all the tips in this section to write your hypothetical proposal's Sample section (e.g., is the research design clearly stated?).

2   Submit your Sample section along with the journal article to your instructor for comments and feedback.

Your Name(s):
Your Identification Number(s) (if any):
Assignment 8b.2. Title of Selected Article:

Type your revised Sample section here.
(Box will automatically expand as you type)

Section 8b
Writing a Sample Section for Your Research Proposal

Write a Sample section for your research proposal in the white space provided below. The box will expand as you type.

- Use all the tips in this section to write your Sample section (e.g., is it clear what sampling strategy is being used?).
- If possible, show your Sample section to your classmates for their feedback.
- Revise your Sample section based on your classmates' feedback.
- Submit your Sample section to your instructor for comments and feedback.

Your Name(s):

Your Identification Number(s) (if any):

Title of Your Research Proposal:

Abstract:

Introduction:

Literature Review:

Problem:

Research Question:

Research Design:

Type your Sample section here.

(Box will automatically expand as you type)

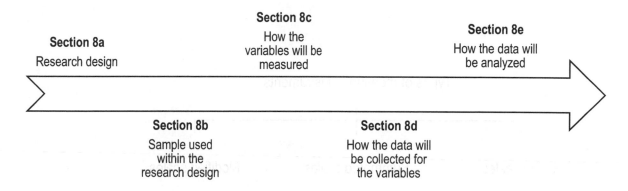

Section 8a
Research design

Section 8c
How the variables will be measured

Section 8e
How the data will be analyzed

Section 8b
Sample used within the research design

Section 8d
How the data will be collected for the variables

Solving the Problem

EVERY VARIABLE CONTAINED WITHIN SECTION 7 has to be measured. Now comes the moment of truth: How are you going to measure them? That is the purpose of Section 8c.

As you know from your research methods text, there are many ways you can measure variables, commonly referred to as *instrumentation* in research lingo. In reality, you will always measure your variables by standardized and/or unstandardized measuring instrument(s) of some kind or another.

As a last resort, you can even make up your own measuring instrument such as a mailed survey or interview schedule. As you know from your research methods text, you should always use an existing standardized measuring instrument whenever possible, feasible, and practical.

The Instrumentation section of your proposal basically provides a visual copy of each measuring instrument that you propose to use for every variable contained in your research question (or hypothesis). If you are going to use a measuring instrument that has been previously used in a study similar to yours, you will need to identify it by name, put a copy in your appendixes, and discuss its reliability and validity. If your measuring instrument is homegrown—that is, you are creating it

111

yourself—you will need to outline the procedures you will take to develop and test its reliability and validity.

Copies of all your measuring instruments (whether standardized or homegrown) must be included in your appendixes—one appendix for each instrument (e.g., Appendix D in this book).

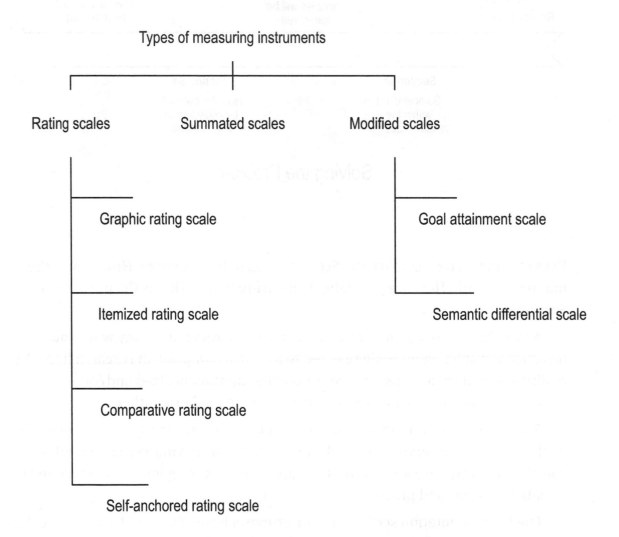

Writing an Instrumentation Section	QUICK TIPS
Check to see if you have read pages 6–7 on how to use our tips.	

Required	**Very Important:** Check to see that you genuinely understand the advantages and disadvantages of the various ways to measure variables. This means that you must read the chapters on measurement and measuring instruments in your textbook!

#	Answers				Tips
216	NA	TA	Yes	No	Check to see that you have made it clear which specific measuring instrument you are proposing to use for each variable in your study. State each measuring instrument in words such as "This study will use the *Problem Solving Inventory* to measure the problem-solving skills of the clients."
217	NA	TA	Yes	No	Check to see that you have made a clear connection between the measuring instrument you are proposing to use (Section 8c), your research design (Section 8a), and most importantly, your variables contained within your Research Question (Section 7). After all, your measuring instruments will measure the variables contained within your research question (or hypothesis).

218	NA	TA	Yes	No	Check to see that you have selected a standardized measurement instrument (if at all possible) to measure each of your variables. If you have selected a standardized measuring instrument, then be sure you have answers to basic questions about how the instrument used **research participants (sample)** in its construction. **(Tips 219–223):**
219	NA	TA	Yes	No	Check to see if the samples are representative of pertinent populations.
220	NA	TA	Yes	No	Check to see if the sample sizes are sufficiently large
221	NA	TA	Yes	No	Check to see if the samples are homogeneous.
222	NA	TA	Yes	No	Check to see if the subsamples are pertinent to your research participants' demographics.
223	NA	TA	Yes	No	Check to see if the data obtained from the samples are up to date.
224	NA	TA	Yes	No	Check to see that you have selected a standardized measurement instrument (if at all possible) to measure each of your variables. If you have selected a standardized measuring instrument, then be sure you have answers to basic questions about the instrument's **validity (Tips 225–231):**
225	NA	TA	Yes	No	Check to see that the instrument's content domain is clearly and specifically defined.
226	NA	TA	Yes	No	Check to see if there was a logical procedure for including the items, or questions on the instrument.
227	NA	TA	Yes	No	Check to see if the criterion measure is relevant to the instrument.

228	NA	TA	Yes	No	Check to see if the criterion measure is reliable and valid.
229	NA	TA	Yes	No	Check to see if the theoretical construct is clearly and correctly stated.
230	NA	TA	Yes	No	Check to see if the instrument's scores converge with other relevant measures.
231	NA	TA	Yes	No	Check to see if the instrument's scores discriminate from irrelevant variables.
232	NA	TA	Yes	No	Check to see that you have selected a standardized measurement instrument (if at all possible) to measure each of your variables. If you have selected a standardized measuring instrument, then be sure you have answers to basic questions about the instrument's **reliability (Tips 233–235):**
233	NA	TA	Yes	No	Check to see if there is sufficient evidence of the instrument's internal consistency.
234	NA	TA	Yes	No	Check to see if there is equivalence between various forms of the instrument.
235	NA	TA	Yes	No	Check to see if there is stability of the instrument over a relevant time interval.
236	NA	TA	Yes	No	Check to see that you have selected a standardized measurement instrument (if at all possible) to measure each of your variables. If you have selected a standardized measuring instrument, then be sure you have answers to basic questions about the instrument's **practicality (Tips 237–244):**
237	NA	TA	Yes	No	Check to see if the instrument is an appropriate length.
238	NA	TA	Yes	No	Check to see if the instrument is socially acceptable to your research participants.

239	NA	TA	Yes	No	Check to see if the instrument is feasible to complete.
240	NA	TA	Yes	No	Check to see if the instrument is relatively direct.
241	NA	TA	Yes	No	Check to see if the instrument have utility.
242	NA	TA	Yes	No	Check to see if the instrument is relatively nonreactive.
243	NA	TA	Yes	No	Check to see if the instrument is sensitive to measuring change.
244	NA	TA	Yes	No	Check to see if the instrument is feasible to score.
245	NA	TA	Yes	No	Check to see that you have provided a short description for each measuring instrument in your proposal.
246	NA	TA	Yes	No	Check to see that your potential research participants have commented upon your proposed measuring instrument and how it's administered. That is, pilot test your measurements on some of your potential research participants to ascertain what they liked and did not like about your measurements and procedures.
247	NA	TA	Yes	No	Check to see that you have included a copy of each measuring instrument in an individual appendix at the end of your proposal.
248	NA	TA	Yes	No	Check to see that you have provided an explicit description of how to score the measuring instrument (see Appendix D as an example).
249	NA	TA	Yes	No	Check to see that you have made explicit any assumptions that your measuring instruments rest upon.

250	NA	TA	Yes	No	Check to see that you have the skills to actually administer the measuring instruments to your proposed research participants.
251	NA	TA	Yes	No	Check with your research instructor to see if he/she has any examples of instrumentation sections from other research proposals to show you.

BOX 8c.1	Example of an Instrumentation Section from a Research Proposal

**Chatham-Kent Children's Services (CKCS) Help-Seeking Project for Adolescents in Out-of-Home Placement:
A Research Proposal[1]**

INSTRUMENTATION

Data for the study will be collected through five self-report instruments that will be completed by youth in care, in addition to a case file review. Each instrument is summarized below.

1 The *Brief Child and Family Phone Interview (BCFPI)* is a computer-assisted, 30-minute, clinical telephone interview. It is a key assessment instrument used by CKCS and other Ontario agencies that provide mental health services to children. The *BCFPI—Adolescent Version* provides risk assessment information about child functioning, as well as externalizing (i.e., impulsivity, cooperativeness, conduct) and internalizing (i.e., separation from parents, anxiety, mood) behaviors. The *BCFPI-Adolescent Version* is supported by reports of adequate reliability and validity (Cunningham, Pettingill, & Boyle, 2004). This instrument will measure youth demographic variables as well as youth mental health problems (a need factor in Andersen's Behavioral Health Model). A copy of this instrument can be found in Appendix L.

2 The *Client Engagement in Child Protective Services (CECPS)* (Yatchmenoff, 2005) is composed of 19 items that are rated on a 5-point scale (5 = strongly agree to 1 = strongly disagree), with higher scores indicating higher engagement. Items assess four dimensions of client engagement in nonvoluntary child welfare services, which include receptivity, buy-in, working relationships, and mistrust. The *CECPS* is supported by sound reliability and construct validity (Yatchmenoff, 2005), and we have permission from the instrument's developer to modify the instrument for use with adolescents in our project. This instrument will measure youths' beliefs about the help available through Chatham-Kent Children's Service (CKCS), a predisposing factor in Andersen's Behavioral Health Model. A copy of this measuring instrument can be found in Appendix M.

3 The brief version of *Barriers to Adolescents Seeking Help (BASH)* (Kuhl, Jarkon-Horlick, & Morrissey, 1997; Wilson , Deane, Ciarrochi, & Rickwood, 2005) is composed of 11 items that target belief-based barriers to seeking help for psychological problems from mental health professionals. Each item is rated on a 6-point scale (1 = strongly disagree to 6 = strongly agree), and higher scores indicate more barriers. The instrument reports good internal consistency ($r = .84$) (Wilson, Deane, & Ciarrochi, 2005) and has been used in several research studies investigating help-seeking behavior of adolescents. This instrument will measure youths' barriers to help seeking (a predisposing factor). A copy of this measuring instrument can be found in Appendix N.

4 The *Barriers to Engagement in Treatment Screen (BETS)* (Wilson, Fogarty, & Deane, 2002) is composed of 11 items that measure specific barriers related to youths' engagement with their caseworkers. Each item is rated on a 4-point scale (0 = Agree to 3 = disagree), and higher scores indicate more barriers. The *BETS* has been used primarily as a screening tool, which is intended to facilitate discussion between youth and the service provider at the outset of treatment. Psychometrics for the *BETS* are currently being tested but show promising results (C.J. Wilson, personal communication, November, 2005). This instrument will measure the youths' engagement with CKCS workers (a predisposing factor). A copy of this measuring instrument can be found in Appendix O.

5 The *General Help Seeking Questionnaire (GHSQ)* was developed by a group of Australian researchers (Deane, Wilson, & Ciarrochi, 2001; Wilson, Deane, Ciarrochi, & Rickwood, 2005) and is composed of 10 specific help sources. For each source, youth rate the likelihood of seeking help for suicidal thoughts and personal-emotional problems on a 7-point scale (1 = extremely unlikely to 7 = extremely likely). Higher scores indicate greater intention to seek help. The GHSQ is designed to allow modifications of the list of specific help sources so that language used will reflect job titles that are consistent with CKCS. Help-seeking intention is examined as a mean score per problem-type, and is well suited to measuring change in help-seeking intentions. The GHSQ is reported to have satisfactory reliability and validity (Wilson, Deane, Ciarrochi, & Rickwood, 2005), and good 3-week test-retest reliability for suicidal ($r = .88$) and personal-emotional ($r = .86$) problems

(Wilson, Deane, & Ciarrochi, 2005). It has also been shown to relate to actual help-seeking in the past month, and to predict future help-seeking behaviors (Deane, Ciarrochi, Wilson, et al., 2001; Wilson, Deane, Ciarrochi, & Rickwood, 2005). This instrument will measure youths' intentions to seek help as well as actual requests for help (date of request and type of problem), which is the outcome or dependent variable of the study. A copy of this measuring instrument can be found in Appendix P.

6 *Case File Review:* Data collected from case files will be facilitated by use of a standard checklist recording form that will be specifically created for this study in order to promote consistency of data recording. Information gathered from case file information will include: demographic variables, placement characteristics, and additional documentation related to youths' requests for help from CKCS workers. A copy of this measuring instrument can be found in Appendix Q.

REFERENCES

Cunningham, C.E., Pettingill, P., & Boyle, M.H. (2004). *The Brief Child and Family Phone Interview Version 3: Interviewer's Manual.* Hamilton: BCFPI Works.

Deane, F.P., Wilson, C.J. & Ciarrochi, J. (2001). Suicidal ideation and help negation: Not just hopelessness or prior help. *Journal of Clinical Psychology, 57,* 901–914.

Deane, F.P., Wilson, C.J., Ciarrochi, J. & Rickwood, D. (2002). *Mental Health Help-Seeking in Young People.* Report to the National Health and Medical Research Council of Australia, Canberra, Australia, Grant YS060. Wollongong, NSW: University of Wollongong, Illawarra Institute for Mental Health.

Kuhl, J., Jarkon-Horlick, L., & Morrissel, R. F. (1997). Measuring barriers to help-seeking in adolescents. *Journal of Youth and Adolescence, 26,* 637–650.

Wilson, C.J., Deane, F.P., & Ciarrochi, J. (2005). Can hopelessness and adolescents' beliefs and attitudes about seeking help account for help negation? *Journal of Clinical Psychology, 61,* 1525–1539.

Wilson, C.J., Deane, F.P., Ciarrochi, J., & Rickwood, D. (2005). Measuring help-seeking intentions: Properties of the General Help-Seeking Questionnaire. *Canadian Journal of Counseling, 39,* 15–28.

Wilson, C.J., Deane, F.P., & Fogarty, K. (2004). *GPs in schools: Building bridges to general practice* (2nd ed.). Participant training manual for "Youth Friendly" General Practitioners in strategies for classroom presentation and outreach. Illawarra Division of General Practice, Wollongong, Australia. Funded by the Commonwealth Department of Health and Aging.

Wilson, C.J., Fogarty, K., & Deane, F.P. (2002). *The essential youth friendly GP kit.* An evidence-based information and resource pack to increase GP competencies when dealing with young people. Illawarra Institute for Mental Health, University of Wollongong, Wollongong, Australia.

Yatchmenoff, D.K. (2005). Measuring client engagement from the client's perspective in nonvoluntary child protective services. *Research on Social Work Practice, 15,* 84–96.

---

[1]Unrau, Y., & Grinnell, R.M., Jr. (2005). *Chatham-Kent Children's Services (CKCS) Help-Seeking Project for Adolescents in Out-of-Home Placement: A Research Proposal.* Submitted to Provincial Centre of Excellence for Child and Youth Mental Health at CHEO. Ottawa, Ontario, Canada K1H 8L1.

BOX 8c.2	Example of an Instrumentation Section from an Article That Appeared in a Professional Journal

Evaluation of a Program to Educate Disadvantaged Parents to Enhance Child Learning[1]

MEASURES

The parent participants were requested to complete the following questionnaires before and after the HOPE program and midway through the program (Week 15):

1 The *Eyberg Child Behavior Inventory* (ECBI; Eyberg & Ross, 1978): a 36-item multidimensional measure of parental perception of disruptive behavior in children, which incorporates two scores, namely, the intensity and problem scores, the Chinese version of which was validated by Leung, Chan, Pang, and Cheng (2003).

2 The *Parenting Stress Index* (PSI; Lam, 1999): a 36-item questionnaire on issues related to parenting stress. Apart from the total score, three subscale scores can also be calculated, namely, Parental Distress (PD), Parent-Child Dysfunctional Interaction (PCDI), and Difficult Child (DC). The Chinese version of the scale was validated by Lam (1999).

3 The *General Self-Efficacy Scale* (Schwarzer, 1993): a 10-item scale measured on a 4-point Likert-type scale ranging from 1 (not at all true) to 4 (exactly true). A validated Chinese version is available (Zhang & Schwarzer, 1995).

4 The *Duke-UNC Functional Social Support Questionnaire* (Broadhead, Gehlbach, de Gruy, & Kaplan, 1988): an 8-item questionnaire on perceived social support in various areas. The questionnaire has been translated into Chinese using back translation, and it has been used with Chinese immigrants in Hong Kong with satisfactory reliability (.94; Leung et al., 2007).

REFERENCES

Broadhead, W.E., Gehlbach, S.H., de Gruy, F.V., & Kaplan, B.H. (1988). The Duke-UNC functional social support questionnaire: Measurement of social support in family medicine patients. *Medical Care, 26*, 709–723.

Eyberg, S.M., & Ross, A.W. (1978). Assessment of child behavior problems: The validation of a new inventory. *Journal of Clinical Psychology, 16,* 113–116.

Lam, D. (1999). Parenting stress and anger: The Hong Kong experience. *Child and Family Social Work, 4,* 337–346.

Leung, C.M., Chan, S.C.M., Pang, R.C.Y., & Cheng, W.K.C. (2003). *Validation of the Chinese version of the Eyberg Child Behavior Inventory for use in Hong Kong.* Unpublished manuscript, Education Bureau, Hong Kong.

Leung, C., Leung, S. S. L., & Chan, R. (2007). The adaptation of mainland Chinese immigrant parents of preschool children in Hong Kong. *E-Journal of Applied Psychology, 3,* 43–57. Retrieved from ttp://ojs.lib.swin.edu.au/index.php/ejap/article/view/79/106.

Schwarzer, R. (1993). *Measurement of perceived self-efficacy: Psychometric scales for cross-cultural research.* Berlin, Germany: Zentrale Universitats Druckerei der FU Berlin.

Zhang, J.X., & Schwarzer, R. (1995). Measuring optimistic self-beliefs: A Chinese adaptation of the General Self-Efficacy Scale. *Psychologia, 38,* 174–181.

---

[1]Leung, C., Tsang, S., & Dean, S. (2011). Evaluation of a program to educate disadvantaged parents to enhance child learning. *Research on Social Work Practice, 20,* 591–599.

	Homework Assignment 8c.1	
	Writing Instrumentation Sections for Research Proposals	

Box 8c.1 presents the Instrumentation section from a research proposal.

1 In the white space below, write an Instrumentation section you feel the authors *should have* written for the research proposal. Your main objective is to edit, revise, rearrange, and/or modify the authors' Instrumentation section in an effort to make it clearer, more concise, and easier to read and follow.

- Use all the tips in this section to rewrite your Instrumentation section (e.g., is each instrument referred to in the appendix?).

2 Submit your revised Instrumentation section to your instructor, pointing out all the revisions you made and why you made them.

Your Name(s):
Your Identification Number(s) (if any):
Assignment 8c.1

Type your revised Instrumentation section here.
(Box will automatically expand as you type)

| | Homework Assignment
8c.2 | |

Writing Instrumentation Sections for Research Proposals

Box 8c.2 presents the Instrumentation section (Measures) from a social work journal article. Download and read the article. Now that you are familiar with the research study depicted in the article:

1 In the white space below, write an Instrumentation section you feel the authors *should have* written for the research proposal that their study was based upon.

   NOTE: You do not have a copy of the authors' research proposal. You only have a copy of the article that resulted from the implementation of their proposal.

   • Use all the tips in this section to write your hypothetical proposal's Instrumentation section (e.g., is the research design clearly stated?).

2 Submit your Instrumentation section to your instructor for comments and feedback..

Your Name(s):
Your Identification Number(s) (if any):
Assignment 8c.2

Type your revised Instrumentation (Measures) section here.
(Box will automatically expand as you type)

Section 8c
Writing an Instrumentation Section for Your Research Proposal

Write an Instrumentation section for your research proposal in the white space provided below. The box will expand as you type.

- Use all the tips in this section to write your Instrumentation section (e.g., is it clear how each variable is measured?).
- If possible, show your Instrumentation section to your classmates for their feedback.
- Revise your Instrumentation section based on your classmates' feedback.
- Submit your Instrumentation section to your instructor for comments and feedback.

Your Name(s):

Your Identification Number(s) (if any):

Title of Your Research Proposal:

Abstract:

Introduction:

Literature Review:

Problem:

Research Question:

Research Design:

Sample:

Type your Instrumentation section here.

(Box will automatically expand as you type)

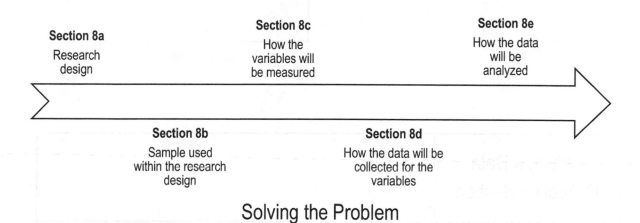

Data Collection
(1–2 paragraphs for each data collection method)

Section 8a

Research design

Section 8c

How the variables will be measured

Section 8e

How the data will be analyzed

Section 8b

Sample used within the research design

Section 8d

How the data will be collected for the variables

Solving the Problem

AS YOU NOW FROM YOUR RESEARCH METHODS TEXT, you can collect new data and/or existing data to answer your research question (or test your hypothesis).

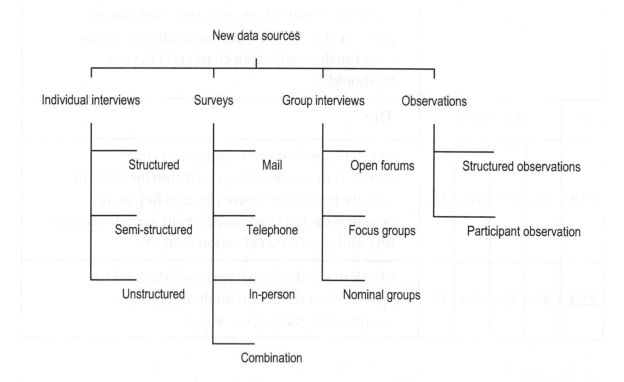

New data sources

| Individual interviews | Surveys | Group interviews | Observations |

Structured — Mail — Open forums — Structured observations

Semi-structured — Telephone — Focus groups — Participant observation

Unstructured — In-person — Nominal groups

Combination

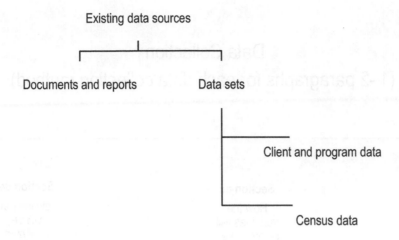

Writing a Data Collection Section				
Check to see if you have read pages 6–7 on how to use our tips.				
Required				**Very important:** Check to see that you genuinely understand the advantages and disadvantages of using the various data collection methods as previously outlined. This means that you must read the data collection chapter(s) in your textbook!
#	**Answers**			**Tips**
252	NA	TA	Yes	No	Check to see that you have made a clear connection between the measuring instrument you are proposing to use (Section 8c), your research design (Section 8a), your sample (Section 8b), and your data collection method.
253	NA	TA	Yes	No	Check to see that you have made clear which specific data collection method(s) you are proposing to use in your study.

254	NA	TA	Yes	No	Check to see that you have made a clear data-collection plan, as illustrated in Table 8d.1. Do not submit your proposal without such a plan.
255	NA	TA	Yes	No	Check to see that you have covered all the necessary logistical considerations to collect data in the most efficient manner possible.
256	NA	TA	Yes	No	Check to see that you have indicated how you will deal with those folks who do not respond, are unavailable, or refuse to respond to your questionnaire.
257	NA	TA	Yes	No	Check to see that you have made explicit any assumptions that your data collection method(s) rest upon.
258	NA	TA	Yes	No	Check to see that you have made it crystal clear *when* your data will bc collected.
259	NA	TA	Yes	No	Check to see that you have made it crystal clear *where* your data will be collected.
260	NA	TA	Yes	No	Check to see that you have made it crystal clear *how* your data will be collected.
261	NA	TA	Yes	No	Check to see that you have made it crystal clear who actually will provided the data? That is, who is the data source?
262	NA	TA	Yes	No	Check to see that you have stated that your data-collection method will be pretested before it's finally implemented to your full sample or population.
263	NA	TA	Yes	No	Check to see that you have stated how long it will take for the data-collectors to collect the data.
264	NA	TA	Yes	No	Check to see that you have described your study's data-collection process in enough detail so it can be readily replicated by other researchers.

265	NA	TA	Yes	No	Check to see that you have described your data collector's relationship with your research participants.
266	NA	TA	Yes	No	Check to see that you have the skills to actually collect the data via your selected data collection method(s) for your proposed research study.
267	NA	TA	Yes	No	Check with your research instructor to see if he/she has any examples of Data Collection sections from other research proposals to show you.

Table 8d.1
Example of a Data-Collection Plan for Two Variables

a	b	c	d	e	f	g
Indicator	*How indicator is measured*	*Who provides the data*	*How data are gathered*	*When data are gathered*	*Where data are gathered*	*Who collects the data*
Increase the self-esteem of pregnant adolescents after they have their babies	*Rosenberg Self-Esteem Scale* (Appendix Q)	Client	1. Self-administered 2. Self-administered 3. Self-administered	1. Intake 2. Exit interview 3. 3 months after intervention	1. Waiting room 2. Social worker's office 3. Client's home	1. Receptionist 2. Social Worker 3. Case-aid
Increase the social support systems of pregnant adolescents after they have their babies	*Scale of Perceived Social Support* (Appendix R)	Client	1. Self-administered 2. Self-administered in group setting 3. Self-administered in a group setting	1. Intake 2. Last day of intervention 3. 1 month after intervention	1. Waiting room 2. In last group session 3. Group interview in coffee shop	1. Receptionist 2. Group leader 3. Research assistant

a = This column is where you list specifically what indicator(s) you are going to use to measure each of your variables. Theoretically, you can have multiple indicators to measure the same variable.

b = This column is where you list specifically how you are going to measure each indicator in column *a*. For example, the indicators for self-esteem and social support can be measured by many different means. In our example, we chose one standardized measuring instrument for each variable: the *Rosenberg Self-Esteem Scale* for our self-esteem variable and the *Scale of Perceived Social Support* for our social support variable.

c = This column is where you list specifically who is going to provide the data, via the use of your selected measuring instrument (*b*). In a nutshell, this person, called a data source, is the one who is going to provide the data for the measuring instrument. Once again, a measuring instrument can be completed by a variety of different data sources.

d = This column is where you list specifically how the measuring instrument is going to be administered. Not only can you use a variety of measuring instruments to measure an indicator (*b*), but you also have a variety of options for how to administer them. For example, you can read the items or questions on the measuring instrument to your clients, or you can have your clients fill out the instrument themselves. You can also have clients complete them individually with no one around or in group settings such as parks, waiting rooms, and coffee shops.

e = This column is where you state the exact time frame in which the measuring instrument is going to be completed. Once again, there are many options available. For example, clients could complete measuring instruments at home on Friday nights before bedtime or at the beginning of your interview.

f = This column, which is highly related to the previous column (*e*), is where you list the specific location where the measuring instrument will be completed. For example, you can have your clients complete the *Rosenberg Self-Esteem Scale* in your program's waiting room, at home, or in your office.

g = This column is where you list specifically who is going to collect the data via the measuring instrument when it is completed. After the data source (*c*) has provided the data for the measuring instrument (*b*), who's going to collect the completed instrument for analysis? And, more importantly, who is going to collate all the data into a databank for further analyses?

BOX 8d.1	Example of a Quantitative Data Collection Section (and an Instrumentation Section) from a Research Proposal

Students' Persistence in the University of Nebraska at Lincoln: A Mixed Methods Study[1]

PHASE I: QUANTITATIVE DATA COLLECTION AND INSTRUMENTATION

The first, quantitative phase of the study will focus on identifying internal and external factors contributing to and/or impeding students' persistence in the ELHE-DE program. The cross-sectional survey design, which implies the data will be collected at one point in time (McMillan, 2000), will be used.

The primary technique for collecting the quantitative data will be a self-developed questionnaire, containing items of different formats: multiple choice, asking either for one option or all that apply, dichotomous answers like "Yes" and "No," self-assessment items, measured on the 7-point Likert-type, and open-ended questions. A panel of professors teaching in the ELHE-DE program was used to secure the content validity of the survey instrument. The questionnaire consists of 24 questions, which are organized into six sections or scales.

1 The first section of the survey asks questions related to the ELHE-DE program and participants' experiences in it. It includes the selection questions related to the status of subjects in the program and within each of the four groups, factors contributing to the decision to proceed or withdraw, UNL support services, and participants' experiences in the program. The latter are measured on a 7-point Likert-type scale from "Strongly Disagree" to "Strongly Agree" and will provide data regarding how the program-, faculty-, and institutional-related factors impact ELHE-DE students' persistence.

2 The second section will measure participants' comfort level with the online learning environment and will provide additional data about the impact of institutional-related factors. A 7-point rating scale from "Very Uncomfortable" to "Very Comfortable" is used.

3 The third section is focused on participants' experiences with their academic advisors and will provide data regarding the role of an advisor in pursuing the doctoral degree in CMAL. A 7-point rating scale from "Extremely Negative" to "Extremely Positive" is used.

4 The fourth section asks for self-evaluation of how motivated the students are to pursue doctoral degree via distributed means. The scale from 1 to 7, from "Strongly Disagree" to "Strongly Agree," is used.

5 The fifth section is focused on how selected external factors have influenced participants' progress in the program. This scale will provide data to answer the fifth research question. These experiences are measured on a 7-point Likert-type scale from "Strongly Disagree" to "Strongly Agree." Demographic questions constitute the sixth, final section of the questionnaire. They will provide information regarding participants' age, gender, employment, and Nebraska residency status, degrees earned, and family structure. Some questions in the survey have an open-ended "Other (specify)" option to provide one correct answer for every subject in the study. A choice of "Not Applicable" (NA) is included, when necessary.

6 The last question on the survey is open-ended and will ask for additional information about students' experiences in the ELHE-DE program.

The survey questionnaire will be web-based and accessed through the URL, which will be sent to all current and former ELHE-DE students identified by the Department of Educational Administration. One of the advantages of web-based surveys is that participants' responses will automatically be stored in a database and can be easily transformed into numeric data in Excel or SPSS formats. Last known working e-mail addresses are available for all the potential participants in the study.

An informed consent form will be posted on the web as an opening page of the survey. Participants will click on the button below, saying, "I agree to complete this survey," thus expressing their compliance to participate in the study and complete the survey. The survey instrument will be pilot tested on the 5% randomly selected participants representing the former and current students in the ELHE-DE program. The goal of the pilot study is to validate the instrument and to test its reliability. All names from the eligible ELHE-DE participants identified in the database will be entered into the SPSS computer analysis system.

A random proportionate by group sample of 15 participants will be selected. These participants will be excluded from the subsequent major study. The results of the pilot survey will help establish stability and internal consistency reliability, face, and content validity of the questionnaire. Based on the pilot test results, the survey items will be revised if needed.

A week before the survey is available on the web, participants will receive a notification from the department about the importance of their input for the study. This will help escape a low response rate, which is typical for web-based surveys. To decrease the response rate error and solicit a relatively high response rate of the survey, a three-phase follow-up sequence will be used (Dillman, 2000).

To those subjects who will have not responded by the set date (1) five days after distributing the survey URL, an e-mail reminder will be sent out; (2) ten days later, the second e-mail reminder will be sent; (3) two weeks later, the third e-mail reminder will be sent stating the importance of the participant's input for the study.

REFERENCES

Dillman, D.A. (2000). *Mail and Internet surveys: The tailored design method* (2nd ed.). New York: John Wiley.

McMillan, J.H. (2000). *Educational research: Fundamentals for the consumer* (3rd ed.). New York: Addison Wesley Longman.

———————

[1]Ivankova, N.V. (2002). *Students' persistence in the University of Nebraska at Lincoln: A mixed methods study.* Doctoral dissertation proposal submitted for partial fulfillment of the requirements for the degree of Doctor of Philosophy. Graduate College at the University of Nebraska at Lincoln.

BOX 8d.2	Example of a Qualitative Data Collection Section from a Research Proposal

Students' Persistence in the University of Nebraska at Lincoln: A Mixed Methods Study[1]

PHASE II: QUALITATIVE DATA COLLECTION

The second, qualitative phase in the study will focus on explaining the results of the statistical tests, obtained in the first, quantitative phase. The multiple case studies design (Stake, 1995) will be used for collecting and analyzing the qualitative data. A case study is a type of ethnographic design (Creswell, 2002; LeCompte & Schensul, 1999) and is an exploration of a "bounded system" or a case over time, through detailed, in-depth data collection involving multiple sources of information and rich in context (Merriam, 1988; Creswell & Maitta, 2002).

In this study, the instrumental multiple cases (Stake, 1995) will serve the purpose of "illuminating a particular issue" (Creswell, 2002, p. 485), such as persistence in the ELHE-DE program, and they will be described and compared to provide insight into an issue. The primary technique will be conducting in-depth semi-structured telephone interviews with four students, one from each group (Beginning, Matriculated, Graduated, and Withdrawn/Inactive). Individual interviews with the significant others of these selected participants might also be conducted. Triangulation of different data sources is important in case study analysis (Creswell, 1998). Academic transcripts will be used to validate the information obtained during the interviews.

The participants will be asked for consent to access their transcripts, while the information regarding the courses and grades will be received through the researcher's advisor. I will also ask participants to provide elicitation materials or physical artifacts that might have a relationship to their persistence or non-persistence in the ELHE-DE program. Selected online classes taken by the participants and archived on a Lotus Notes or Blackboard server will also be examined for supporting information.

The Interview Protocol will include 10 to 15 open-ended questions, and will be pilot tested. The content of the protocol questions will be grounded in the results of the statistical tests of the relationships between the participants' group membership and the predictor factors as related to students' persistence in the program, and will elaborate on them.

The questions will focus on the issue of persistence in the ELHE-DE program and about the details of the cases selected on maximal variation principle. The protocol will be pilot tested on three students selected from the same target population, but then excluded from the full study.

Debriefing with the participants will be conducted to obtain information on the clarity of the interview questions and their relevance to the study aim. The participants will receive the interview questions prior to the scheduled calling time, and will be informed the interview will be tape-recorded and transcribed verbatim. Respondents will have an opportunity to review and, if necessary, correct the contents of the interview after it has been transcribed.

REFERENCES

Creswell, J.W. (1998). *Qualitative inquiry and research design: Choosing among five traditions.* Thousand Oaks, CA: Sage.

Creswell, J.W. (2002). *Educational research: Planning, conducting, and evaluating quantitative and qualitative approaches to research.* Upper Saddle River, NJ: Merrill/Pearson Education.

Creswell, J.W., & Maitta, R. (2002). Qualitative research. In N. Salkind (Ed.), *Handbook of research design and social measurement* (pp. 143–184). Thousand Oaks, CA: Sage.

LeCompte, M.D., & Schensul, J.J. (1999). *Designing and conducting ethnographic research. Ethnographer's Toolkit, 1.* Walnut Creek, CA: AltaMira.

Merriam, S.B. (1998). *Qualitative research and case study applications in education: Revised and expanded from case study research in education.* San Francisco, CA: Jossey-Bass.

Stake, R. E. (1995). *The art of case study research.* Thousand Oaks, CA: Sage.

[1]Ivankova, N.V. (2002). *Students' persistence in the University of Nebraska at Lincoln: A mixed methods study.* Doctoral dissertation proposal submitted for partial fulfillment of the requirements for the degree of Doctor of Philosophy. Graduate College at the University of Nebraska at Lincoln.

	Homework Assignment 8d	

Writing Data Collection Sections for Research Proposals

Boxes 8d.1 and 8d.2 present a Data Collection section from a research proposal. Box 8d.1 contains the quantitative data that are to be collected (Phase I), and Box 8d.2 describes how the qualitative data will be collected (Phase II).

1 In the white space below, write the two Data Collection sections (Phases I and II) you feel the author *should have* written for her research proposal. Your main objective is to edit, revise, rearrange, and/or modify the author's Data Collection section in an effort to make it clearer, more concise, and easier to read and follow.

- Use all the tips in this section to rewrite your two Data Collection sections (e.g., how are nonresponses to be dealt with?).

2 Submit your revised Data Collection sections to your instructor, pointing out all the revisions you made and why you made them.

Your Name(s):
Your Identification Number(s) (if any):
Assignment 8d

Type your revised Data Collection section here.
(Box will automatically expand as you type)

Section 8d
Writing a Data Collection Section for Your Research Proposal

Write a Data Collection section for your research proposal in the white space provided below.

- Use all the tips in this section to write your Data Collection section (e.g., did you construct a Data Collection table like Table 8d.1?).
- If possible, show your Data Collection section to your classmates for their feedback.
- Revise your Data Collection section based on your classmates' feedback.
- Submit your Data Collection section to your instructor for comments and feedback.

Your Name(s):

Your Identification Number(s) (if any):

Title of Your Research Proposal:

Abstract:

Introduction:

Literature Review:

Problem:

Research Question:

Research Design:

Sample:

Instrumentation:

Type your Data Collection section here.

(Box will automatically expand as you type)

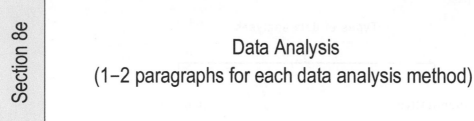

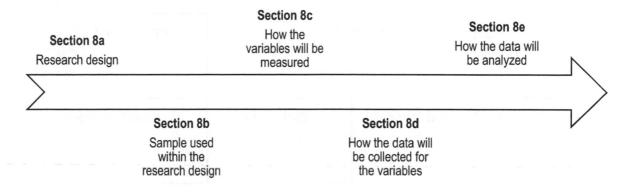

Solving the Problem

AS YOU KNOW FROM YOUR RESEARCH METHODS TEXT there are two general types of data analyses—quantitative and qualitative. In short, you can collect data for your study's variables in the form of numbers and/or words. Numbers are analyzed via quantitative methods and words by qualitative ones.

One of the most neglected areas of the average social work research proposal is that dealing with the collection of data and the resulting analysis and interpretation of them. Nevertheless, a major part of your proposed project will be spent analyzing and interpreting the data you have collected.

The type of data analysis you will use depends on whether you have collected quantitative and/or qualitative data. It is important to realize, however, that although that the data collection section and data analysis section are discussed separately in a research proposal, the sections are always written simultaneously.

You should not make decisions about your data collection method (Section 8d) without also *simultaneously* deciding which data analysis method (Section 8e) you will use to analyze the data you have collected. In a nutshell, data collection and analysis go hand in hand.

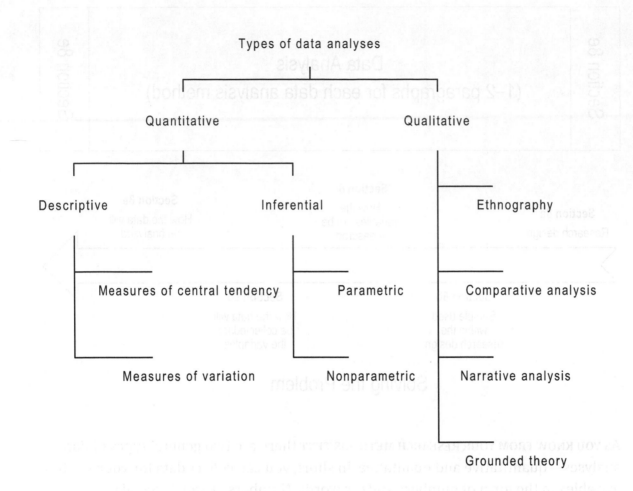

Writing a Data Analysis Section				QUICK TIPS
Check to see if you have read pages 6–7 on how to use our tips.				
Required				**Very important:** Check to see that you know how to do simple quantitative and qualitative data analyses. This means that you must read the two or more chapters in your textbook that describe how to do these two types of data analyses!
#	**Answers**			**Tips**
268	NA	TA	Yes	No	Check to see that you have made a clear connection between the measuring instrument(s) you are proposing to use (Section 8c), your research design (Section 8a), your data source(s) (Section 8d), your sample (Section 8d), and your data analysis plan.
269	NA	TA	Yes	No	Check to see that you have made clear which specific data analysis method(s) you are proposing to use in your study.
270	NA	TA	Yes	No	Check to see that you have indicated what attempts you will make to investigate possible sources of bias and their influence on your study's results.
271	NA	TA	Yes	No	Check to see that you have covered how you will handle any missing data. That is, how will you handle the effects of research participants who do not complete all the data-gathering instruments or only complete portions of them?
272	NA	TA	Yes	No	Check to see that you have stated in straightforward language how you will be handing your data analysis.

273	NA	TA	Yes	No	Check to see that you have made a clear data analysis plan, as illustrated in Table 8.e1. Your research proposal must contain a data-analysis table such as Table 8.e1.
274	NA	TA	Yes	No	Check to see that you have provided a well-thought-out rationale for your decision to use the data analysis you have selected.
275	NA	TA	Yes	No	Check to see that you have indicated the specific statistical software packages you plan to use when you analyze your data (e.g., AM Software from American Institutes for Research, Bascula from Statistics Netherlands, CENVAR from U.S. Bureau of the Census, CLUSTERS from University of Essex, Epi Info from Centers for Disease Control, Generalized Estimation System (GES) from Statistics Canada, IVEware from University of Michigan, PCCARP from Iowa State University, R survey package from the R Project, SAS/STAT from SAS Institute, SPSS from SPSS Inc., Stata from Stata Corporation, SUDAAN from Research Triangle Institute, VPLX from U.S. Bureau of the Census, WesVar from Westat, Inc.).
276	NA	TA	Yes	No	Check to see that you have used the appropriate statistic with each one of your hypotheses (if any).
277	NA	TA	Yes	No	Check to see that you have provided sample charts, graphs, or tables that will show how your data will be organized and reported in your final paper. It's always a great idea to create fake tables (with appropriate titles and headings) as templates you can use when you enter the data into them.
278	NA	TA	Yes	No	Check to see that you have made explicit any assumptions that your data analyses method(s) rest upon.

279	NA	TA	Yes	No	Check to see that you have the skills to actually analyze the data for your study.
280	NA	TA	Yes	No	Check with your research instructor to see if he/she has any examples of Data Analyses sections from other research proposals to show you.

Table 8e.1

Example of a Data-Analysis Plan for One Variable Measured before and after Treatment

a	b	c	d	e
Name of variable	Name of measuring instrument	Measurement level	When data are going to be collected	How data are going to be analyzed
Self-Esteem	*Index of Self-Esteem* (Appendix D)	Ordinal (treated as interval)	Time 1: Intake interview Time 2: Exit interview	• Descriptive statistics • One group *t*-test between Time 1 and Time 2 scores

BOX 8e.1	Example of a Data Analysis Section from a Research Proposal

**Chatham-Kent Children's Services (CKCS) Help-Seeking
Project for Adolescents in Out-of-Home Placement:
A Research Proposal[1]**

DATA ANALYSIS PLAN

The first step in the analysis will be to generate descriptive statistics
for all variables included in the study. Subsequently, we will examine
preliminary relationships between each of the independent and total
scores of the dependent variables using appropriate bivariate tests.
Our primary interest is determining whether the experimental
intervention has a positive impact on two particular dependent
variables—(1) youths' requests for help from a CKCS worker (mental
health or child protection) and (2) youths' intentions to seek help from
others.

Since we expect to find statistically significant relationships
between other independent variables and the dependent variables, we
will proceed with multivariate analysis. Specifically, Poisson or zero-
inflated regression will be used to test for differences between the
experimental and control groups for count variables (e.g., number of
times help requested), while event-history analysis (Cox regression)
will be used to investigate differences in time-to-first request for help
(Hypothesis #1). Analysis of covariance will be used to investigate
differences between groups in terms of youths' intentions to seek help
from others (Hypothesis #2).

---

[1]Unrau, Y., & Grinnell, R.M., Jr. (2005). *Chatham-Kent Children's Services
(CKCS) Help-Seeking Project for Adolescents in Out-of-Home
Placement: A Research Proposal.* Submitted to Provincial Centre of
Excellence for Child and Youth Mental Health at CHEO. Ottawa,
Ontario, Canada K1H 8L1.

BOX 8e.2	Example of a Data Analysis Section from an Article That Appeared in a Professional Journal

Vida Alegre:
Preliminary Findings of a Depression Intervention
for Immigrant Latino Mothers[1]

ANALYSIS

Due to the small sample size, nonparametric techniques were used. Among nonparametric techniques, we conducted a Wilcoxon signed-rank test to assess the magnitude of the change in the CES-D test scores at different points in time. Similar to the paired samples *t* test, the signed-rank test examines whether we can reject the null hypothesis that no significant difference exists between the pretest and posttest scores and the pretest and follow-up scores. However, unlike other nonparametric statistics, the Wilcoxon test also assesses the magnitude of any difference that might occur. The *Statistical Package for the Social Sciences* (SPSS) was used to produce the Wilcoxon test, which calculated the number of positive and negative differences, the *Z* score, and the associated probability level. The outcome thus allows an analysis of the direction and magnitude of change.

---

[1]Piedra, L.M., & Byoun, S. (2012). Vida alegre: Preliminary findings of a depression intervention for immigrant Latino mothers. *Research on Social Work Practice, 22*, 138–150.

<table>
<tr><td></td><td style="text-align:center">**Homework Assignment 8e.1**</td><td></td></tr>
</table>

Writing Data Analysis Sections for Research Proposals

Box 8e.1 presents a Data Analysis section from a research proposal.

1 In the white space below, write a Data Analysis section you feel the authors *should have* written for the research proposal. The box will expand as you type. Your main objective is to edit, revise, rearrange, and/or modify the authors' Data Analysis section in an effort to make it clearer, more concise, and easier to read and follow.

 • Use all the tips in this section to rewrite your Data Analysis section (e.g., is each instrument referred to in the appendix?).

2 Submit your revised Data Analysis section to your instructor, pointing out all the revisions you made and why you made them.

Your Name(s):
Your Identification Number(s) (if any):
Assignment 8e.1

Type your revised Data Analysis section here.
(Box will automatically expand as you type)

Homework Assignment
8e.2

Writing Data Analysis Sections for Research Proposals

Box 8e.2 presents the Data Analysis section from a social work journal article. Download and read the article. Now that you are familiar with the research study depicted in the article:

1 In the white space below, write a Data Analysis section you feel the authors *should have* written for the research proposal that their study was based upon.

   NOTE: You do not have a copy of the authors' research proposal. You only have a copy of the article that resulted from the implementation of their proposal.

   - Use all the tips in this section to write your hypothetical proposal's Data Analysis section (e.g., is the research design clearly stated?).

2 Submit your revised Data Analysis section to your instructor for comments and feedback.

Your Name(s):
Your Identification Number(s) (if any):
Assignment 8e.2

Type your revised Data Analysis section here.
(Box will automatically expand as you type)

Section 8e
Writing a Data Analysis Section for Your Research Proposal

Write a Data Analysis section for your research proposal in the white space provided below.

- Use all the tips in this section to write your Data Analysis section (e.g., Is Table 8e.1 fully completed and done correctly?)
- If possible, show your Data Analysis section to your fellow classmates for their feedback.
- Revise your Data Analysis section based on your classmates' feedback.
- Submit your Data Analysis section to your instructor for comments and feedback.

Your Name(s):

Your Identification Number(s) (if any):

Title of Your Research Proposal:

Abstract:

Introduction:

Literature Review:

Problem:

Research Question:

Research Design:

Sample:

Instrumentation:

Data Collection:

Type your Data Analysis section here.
(Box will automatically expand as you type)

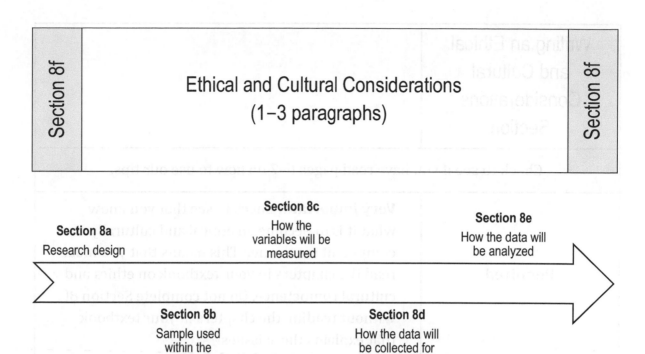

Section 8f

Ethical and Cultural Considerations
(1–3 paragraphs)

Section 8a
Research design

Section 8b
Sample used within the research design

Section 8c
How the variables will be measured

Section 8d
How the data will be collected for the variables

Section 8e
How the data will be analyzed

Addressing Ethical and Cultural Considerations for Sections 8a–8e

AS YOU KNOW FROM YOUR RESEARCH METHODS TEXT you need to address all ethical and cultural issues that will crop up when doing your research proposal.

Writing an Ethical and Cultural Considerations Section					
Check to see if you have read pages 6–7 on how to use our tips.					
Required					**Very important:** Check to see that you know what it is to become an ethical and culturally competent researcher. This means that you must read the chapters in your textbook on ethics and cultural competence. Do not complete Section 8f without reading the chapters in your textbook that explains these issues!
#	**Answers**				**Tips**
281	NA	TA	Yes	No	Check to see that you propose to use appropriate ethically and culturally sensitive *consent* forms.
282	NA	TA	Yes	No	Check to see that you propose to use appropriate ethically and culturally sensitive *assent* forms.
283	NA	TA	Yes	No	Check to see that you have addressed all the *ethical considerations* that can spring up in reference to your proposed data collection strategy.
284	NA	TA	Yes	No	Check to see that you have addressed all the *cultural considerations* that can spring up in reference to your proposed data collection strategy.
285	NA	TA	Yes	No	Check to see that you plan to submit your proposal to appropriate IRBs for official approval to do your study.
286	NA	TA	Yes	No	Check to see that you have minimized the risk of harm to your research participants.

287	NA	TA	Yes	No	Check to see that you have provided *anonymity* to your research participants (if appropriate, of course)
288	NA	TA	Yes	No	Check to see that you have provided *confidentiality* to your research participants (if appropriate, of course)
289	NA	TA	Yes	No	Check to see that you have avoided deceptive practices.
290	NA	TA	Yes	No	Check to see that you have provided your research participants with information on their rights to withdraw from your study for any reason whatsoever.
291	NA	TA	Yes	No	Check to see that you have addressed the contextuality of your study—that is, do you have an understanding of the sociocultural, political, and historical context of where your research participants live?
292	NA	TA	Yes	No	Check to see that you have addressed your study's relevance—that is, does your study's research question (or hypothesis) address meaningful issues faced by your research participants, and Does it serve the interests of improving their lives?
293	NA	TA	Yes	No	Check to see that your communication style is appropriate—that is, you have an understanding of the preferred communication styles of your research participants and their communities and the subtleties and variations inherent in the language used?
294	NA	TA	Yes	No	Check to see that you have displayed an awareness of identity and power differences—that is, are aware of researcher–participant power differences, the establishment of credibility, and the development of more horizontal relationships?

295	NA	TA	Yes	No	Check to see that you have used appropriate disclosures—that is, do you avoid the use of secrecy and build trust with your research participants?
296	NA	TA	Yes	No	Check to see that you are fully aware of reciprocation—that is, does your research study meet the mutual goals and objectives for you, the researcher, and your research participants?
297	NA	TA	Yes	No	Check to see that you used an empowerment approach to the research process—that is, does your research process contribute to empowering your research participants?
298	NA	TA	Yes	No	Check to see that you are aware of the concept of time—that is, do you use a flexible approach within the research process in terms of quantity and quality of time spent with your research participants?
299	NA	TA	Yes	No	Check to see that you will be respectful to people with other perspectives throughout the study.

	Homework Assignment 8f	

Select a Journal Article of Your Choice

1 In the white space below, write an Ethical and Cultural Considerations section you feel the authors *should have* written for the research proposal that their study was based upon.

   - Use all the tips in this section to write your Ethical and Cultural Considerations section (e.g., Tip 299: Will you be respectful to people with other perspectives throughout your study?)

2 Submit your Ethical and Cultural Considerations section (along with a copy of your selected article) to your instructor for comments and feedback.

Your Name(s):

Your Identification Number(s) (if any):

Assignment 8f

Type your Ethical and Cultural Considerations section here.
(Box will automatically expand as you type)

Section 8f
Writing an Ethical and Cultural Considerations
Section for Your Research Proposal

Write an Ethical and Cultural Considerations section for your research proposal in the white space provided below.

- Use all the tips in this section to write your Ethical and Cultural Considerations section.

- If possible, show your Ethical and Cultural Considerations section to your fellow classmates for their feedback.

- Revise your Ethical and Cultural Considerations section based on your classmates' feedback.

- Submit your revised Ethical and Cultural Considerations section to your instructor for comments and feedback.

Your Name(s):

Your Identification Number(s) (if any):

Title of Your Research Proposal:

Abstract:

Introduction:

Literature Review:

Problem:

Research Question:

Research Design:

Sample:

Instrumentation:

Data Collection:

Data Analysis:

Type your Ethical and Cultural Considerations section here.

(Box will automatically expand as you type)

PART IV
Evaluating the Proposed Solution

Section 9: Limitations
Section 10: Significance

It's now time to evaluate the first eight sections of your research proposal, to delineate your study's limitations and significance.

All research proposals (and, of course, the findings that are ultimately derived from them) have limitations. This includes your proposed study as well. Section 9 gives you the opportunity to inform your readers that you know what your study's limitations are.

It's also the time to discuss the overall practical and/or theoretical merits of your study. As you know, you briefly suggested the study's significance in two previous sections: Abstract and Introduction. Section 10 is where you expand on your study's overall significance to the social work profession.

157

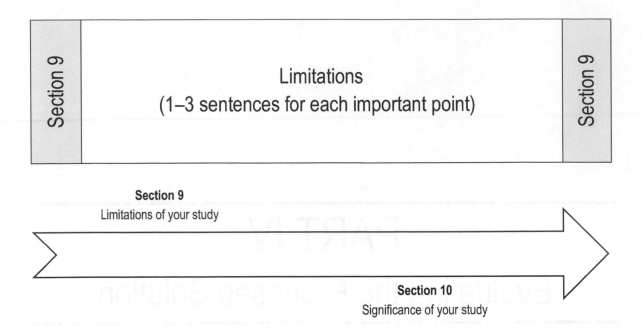

Evaluating the Proposed Solution

A *LIMITATION* **IS A WEAKNESS OF YOUR PROPOSED STUDY,** and all research studies have them—and that includes yours! Think, for a moment, about your overall research design, your sample, the measuring instruments you are going to use, and your data collection and analysis plans.

Think about all the threats to internal and external validity that may have been impossible for you to avoid or even minimize. You need to explain to the readers that you know what your study's limitations are. Simple examples of limitations might include the following:

1 Due to the small availability, nonrandom sample that I want to use, my results will not be generalizable beyond the specific population from which I'm going to draw my sample.

2 Because some of my randomly selected research participants may not respond to my questionnaire, my results may not accurately reflect the opinions of all members within my sampling frame.

3 Due to the 3-year duration of my study, a significant number of my research participants who were available at the beginning of my study may not be available (or may be unwilling to participate) in the final stage of my study.

Scrupulously stating all the limitations of your study will help your readers understand some of the fundamental problems you will probably encounter when

158

you actually perform your study. Nevertheless, you must design and conduct your proposed study in a manner that precludes having so many limitations that the results derived from it are unusable and impractical.

As you know from your research methods book, research designs that control for (or account for) the various threats to internal and external validity will ensure that your study's results are not only internally valid and reliable but externally generalizable as well. This in turn will keep your study's limitations to a reasonable number.

What's a delimitation? A *delimitation* addresses how your proposed study has to be narrow in scope in an effort to make it practical to implement; that is, your study, by necessity, has to be bounded to some degree—all research studies have delimitations.

Section 9 is also the place to explain the things that you are not going to do and why you have chosen not to do them: the literature you will *not* review (and why), the population you are *not* studying (and why), and the methodological procedures you will *not* use (and why). Your delimitations should be limited to the things that your readers might reasonably expect you to do but that you—for clearly explained reasons—have decided not to do.

Technically, limitations (factors you cannot control) are distinct from delimitations (factors you control). Examples of delimitations might include the following:

1 To ensure the manageability of my data collection plan, my measuring instruments will only use closed-ended response items and will not include open-ended items.
2 Because I will be collecting data through intensive 2-hour client interviews, my sampling frame will contain only those clients who reside in Cook County.

On an overly simplified level, Section 9 of your research proposal is a crude evaluation of how well your Method section was thought out:

8a the appropriateness of the research design you selected that will answer your research question (or test your hypothesis)

8b the rationale as to how, why, where, and when you selected your sample

8c the appropriateness of the kind of measurements you plan to use to measure your variables

8d the appropriateness of the sample (data source) you plan to use, and what data collecting methods you chose to use to gather data from your sample

8e the appropriateness of your proposed data analysis techniques

Writing a Limitations Section				QUICK TIPS
Check to see if you have read pages 6–7 on how to use our tips.				
#	**Answers**			**Tips**
300	NA	TA	Yes	No	**Research Design.** Check to see that you addressed each of the tips in Section 8a.
301	NA	TA	Yes	No	**Sample.** Check to see that you addressed each of the tips in Section 8b.
302	NA	TA	Yes	No	**Instrumentation.** Check to see that you addressed each of the tips in Section 8c.
303	NA	TA	Yes	No	**Data Collection.** Check to see that you addressed each of the tips in Section 8d.
304	NA	TA	Yes	No	**Data Analysis.** Check to see that you addressed each of the tips in Section 8e.
305	NA	TA	Yes	No	**Ethical and Cultural Considerations.** Check to see that you addressed each of the tips in Section 8f.
306	NA	TA	Yes	No	Check with your research instructor to see if he/she has any examples of Limitations sections from other research proposals to show you.

BOX 9.1	Example of a Limitations Section from an Article That Appeared in a Professional Journal

Vida Alegre:
Preliminary Findings of a Depression Intervention
for Immigrant Latino Mothers[1]

STUDY LIMITATIONS AND DIRECTIONS FOR FUTURE RESEARCH

Although this study demonstrated feasibility—participants exposed to the intervention experienced a sustained reduction in depressive symptoms—limitations presented themselves.

First, the high dropout rate led to a small sample size that limited our ability to control other variables that might contribute to lower levels of depression, such as taking psychotropic medication or seeking out other forms of therapy. In addition, the high drop-out rate suggest that future studies with this population must include a better tracking system for participants, as a subgroup of women would have moved and/or changed her number before the intervention ends.

Second, because the study aimed to establish feasibility, this study does not include a comparison group; therefore, threats to internal validity cannot be dismissed. Therefore, a study with a larger sample and a randomized experimental design is needed to further test the strength of the intervention.

A third limitation rests on the use of bilingual students; the replication of this intervention is limited to communities that can draw upon institutions of higher education within close proximity. For those communities without such institution, training models need to be developed that equip members of the Hispanic community to work as paraprofessionals or peer counselors.

Fourth, despite overcoming a number of obstacles that affect service access—the lack of bilingual providers, the availability of child care, and the lack of culturally tailored services for immigrants—Vida Alegre was unable to overcome the problem of transportation. Although the lack of transportation may negatively bias the effect of the intervention, in a real world sense, transportation remains a formidable obstacle across services sectors.

[1]Piedra, L.M., & Byoun, S. (2012). Vida Alegre: Preliminary findings of a depression intervention for immigrant Latino mothers. *Research on Social Work Practice, 22*, 138–150.

BOX 9.2	Example of a Limitations Section from an Article That Appeared in a Professional Journal

Readiness for College Engagement among Students Who Have Aged Out of Foster Care[1]

LIMITATIONS

The research design for this exploratory study was a one-group cross sectional survey and is thus subject to the usual limitations of such a design. A noteworthy limitation is selection bias with respect to our sample of former foster youth. As discussed earlier, most foster youth do not make it to college. Our sample earned high school GPAs and ACT scores that were necessary to gain admittance to a four-year college. This notable achievement alone suggests the 81 students from foster care in our sample may have perceived themselves as better prepared for college than other foster youth whose academic qualifications limited them to community colleges or other post-secondary educational programs.

Moreover, students in our sample had enrolled in a comprehensive college support program that provided support in the areas of education, finances, housing, health, socialization, identity development, and life skills. However, since they did not begin this program until after completing the CSI, program enrollment could not have affected the students' perceptions, but it is possible that students' expectations of the program may have played a role in their ratings.

Another limitation is that the study measured self-perceptions of readiness for college prior to starting the college experience; therefore, the findings of the study are best understood as a measure of the students' intentions and not their actions: How they *think* they will feel and behave regarding their college coursework based on their high-school experiences and any limited exposure to college life.

---

[1]Unrau, Y.A., Font, S.A., & Rawls, G. (2012). Readiness for college engagement among students who have aged out of foster care. *Children and Youth Services Review, 34,* 76–83.

Homework Assignment 9a

Writing Limitations Sections for Research Proposals

Boxes 9.1 and 9.2 present two Limitations sections from two different social work journal articles. Download and read one of the articles. Now that you are familiar with the research study depicted in the article you selected:

1 In the white space below, write a Limitations section you feel the authors *should have* written for the research proposal that their study was based upon.

   NOTE: You do not have a copy of the authors' research proposal. You only have a copy of the article that resulted from the implementation of their proposal.

   • Use all the tips in this section to write your hypothetical proposal's Limitations section.

2 Submit your Limitations section to your instructor for comments and feedback.

Your Name(s):
Your Identification Number(s) (if any):
Assignment 9. Title of Selected Article:

Type your revised Limitation section here.
(Box will automatically expand as you type)

	Homework Assignment 9b	
Select a Journal Article of Your Choice		

1 In the white space below, write a Limitations section you feel the authors *should have* written for the research proposal that their study was based upon.

- Use all the tips in this section to write your Limitations section

2 Submit your Limitations section (along with a copy of your selected article) to your instructor for comments and feedback.

Your Name(s):

Your Identification Number(s) (if any):

Assignment 8f

Type your Limitations section here.

(Box will automatically expand as you type)

Section 9
Writing a Limitations Section for Your Research Proposal

Write a Limitations section for your research proposal in the white space provided below.

- Use all the tips in this section to write your Limitations section.
- If possible, show your Limitations section to your classmates for their feedback.
- Revise your Limitations section based on your classmates' feedback.
- Submit your Limitations section to your instructor for comments and feedback.

Your Name(s):

Your Identification Number(s) (if any):

Title of Your Research Proposal:

Abstract:

Introduction:

Literature Review:

Problem:

Research Question:

Research Design:

Sample:

Instrumentation:

Data Collection:

Data Analysis:

Ethical and Cultural Considerations:

Type your Limitations section here.
(Box will automatically expand as you type)

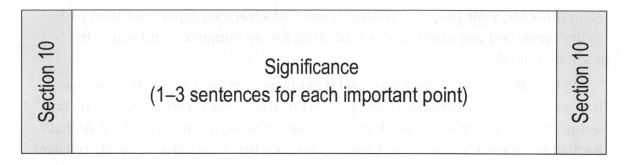

Significance
(1–3 sentences for each important point)

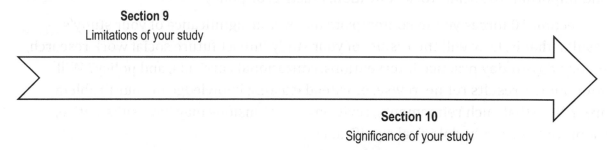

Section 9
Limitations of your study

Section 10
Significance of your study

Evaluating the Proposed Solution

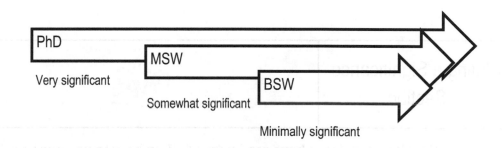

PhD

MSW

Very significant

BSW

Somewhat significant

Minimally significant

Significance of Research Proposals by Social Work Degree

SECTION 10 IS AN EXTREMELY DIFFICULT SECTION TO WRITE—especially if you are an undergraduate who may not have a lot of social work practice experience under your belt. Where you are in school determines how significant your study should be to the advancement of civilization and the universe.

If your research proposal is being completed as a requirement for an undergraduate course, for example, then the overall practical day-to-day significance of your proposed study does not have to be truly astonishing and an effort to save humanity.

167

In this case, your proposal writing is more of a learning experience than a life-saving event, and you may wish to hold off on saving humanity until you're in graduate school.

On the other hand, if your proposal is being written for a graduate-level course, then your instructor would obviously expect it to be more directly relevant to day-to-day contemporary social work practice than an undergraduate venture. And at the doctoral level, it goes without saying that your proposal must be totally relevant and important to social work education, practice, or policy.

Section 10 forces you to contemplate the overall significance of your study's results; that is, how will the results of your study impact future social work research, theory, day-to-day practice interventions, educational curricula, and policy? Will your study's results refine, revise, or extend existing knowledge in your problem area? Note that such refinements, revisions, or extensions may have substantive, theoretical, or methodological significance.

As you know, your Abstract and Introduction sections contained subsections when it comes to the "significance" of your study. In a nutshell, Section 10 is just an extensive elaboration of those two subsections.

Writing a Significance Section				QUICK-**TIPS**
Check to see if you have read pages 6–7 on how to use our tips.				
#	**Answers**			**Tips**
307	NA	TA	Yes	No	Check to see that you have discussed what the results of your study will mean to the theoretical framework that framed your study.
308	NA	TA	Yes	No	Check to see that you have provided various suggestions that subsequent research studies may focus upon given the projected findings of your study.

309	NA	TA	Yes	No	Check to see that you have provided concrete suggestions how the results of your study could affect social work educators, practitioner, and policy makers (if appropriate).
310	NA	TA	Yes	No	Check to see that you have provided concrete suggestions on how the results of your study could affect social work programs and agencies (if appropriate).
311	NA	TA	Yes	No	Check to see that you have made suggestions as what is to be improved or changed as a result of your proposed research study.
312	NA	TA	Yes	No	Check with your research instructor to see if he/she has any examples of significance sections from other research proposals to show you.

BOX 10.1	Example of a Significance for Future Research Section from an Article That Appeared in a Professional Journal

Readiness for College Engagement among Students Who Have Aged Out of Foster Care[1]

RESEARCH IMPLICATIONS

This study adds to the literature by highlighting foster youths' readiness to engage in college and comparing their readiness to the general population of freshman FTIAC students. With the proliferation of campus-based programs supporting students from foster care on two- and four-year college campuses, researchers will have more opportunities to study this vulnerable and under-served population.

It is important that future research include variables to measure the foster-care experience itself, since foster youth can vary on many factors such as age of entry into the foster care system, number and type of foster care placements they have received, and level of support from the foster family after their cases are closed. The variation in childhood histories and foster care experiences likely influence the degree of academic motivation, social motivation, receptivity to services, and coping among former foster-care youth in the young adult years.

Foster-care research strongly suggests that the aspirations of foster youth do not match up to their behaviors or actions; that is, intentions do not automatically translate into actions. And, since this study measured perception and not action, further studies of a longitudinal nature are needed to determine if students from foster care are more or less likely to actually utilize campus-based services and support compared to their non-foster-care student peers.

Including a wider range of psychological variables and their effects on the coping strategies of students from foster care would also increase understanding of how best to assist these students when obstacles that interfere with academic progress arise.

---

[1]Unrau, Y.A., Font, S.A., & Rawls, G. (2012). Readiness for college engagement among students who have aged out of foster care. *Children and Youth Services Review, 34*, 76–83.

BOX 10.2	Example of a Significance for Social Work Practice Section from an Article That Appeared in a Professional Journal

Readiness for College Engagement among Students Who Have Aged Out of Foster Care[1]

PRACTICE IMPLICATIONS

The findings of this study shed light on how child welfare and education professionals can address the needs of students from foster care. Past research studies have strongly made the case that students from foster care have a high risk of dropping out of college. Lack of family privilege, the premature launch into independence, financial difficulties, housing instability, and lack of access to health care are among the significant barriers that students from foster care must tackle above and beyond the normal stresses of college life.

Educating child welfare and college professionals about the unique educational obstacles faced by students from foster care as well as their higher-than-average levels of academic and social motivation and openness to academic and counseling services can give these professionals a better perspective on how to engage this unique student group. Early engagement with foster youth in college is critical since foster youth may possess greater confidence than competence to engage in the college environment.

The Appendix provides a selective list of policy and practice resources prepared by Casey Family Programs that can inform professionals about the needs of, and the supports and programs for, students from foster care who are often a hidden and fragmented population on college campuses. Professionals working in ways to support college students from foster care must be skillful in engaging students and eliciting relevant information to perform the job of assisting students in need. Casey Family Programs has developed recommendations for financial-aid staff about sensitive approaches to communication with students from foster care and unaccompanied homeless youth.

For example, they suggest that students from foster care find it helpful when college staff professionals conduct conversations that include asking personal questions in environments where they cannot be overheard; take time to explain questions and make sure students understand the answers before ending the interaction; walk students through next steps (e.g., completion of a form, escort to next department and introduce them to someone before leaving); and follow up with students via e-mail, text, or phone to ensure they completed all steps.

_____

[1]Unrau, Y.A., Font, S.A., & Rawls, G. (2012). Readiness for college engagement among students who have aged out of foster care. *Children and Youth Services Review, 34,* 76–83.

	Homework Assignment 10	
	Writing Significance Sections for Research Proposals	

Boxes 10.1 and 10.2 present one Significance section from a social work journal article. The authors divided the section into two parts: (Research Implications and Practice Implications). Download and read the article. Now that you are familiar with the research study depicted in the article:

1 In the white space below, write one Significance section with two subsections (one for *research* and the other for *practice*) you feel the authors *should have* written for the research proposal that their research study was based off of.

- Use all the tips in this section to write your Significance section (e.g., is each instrument referred to in the appendix?).

2 Submit your Significance section to your instructor for comments and feedback.

Your Name(s):
Your Identification Number(s) (if any):
Assignment 10

Type your revised Significance section here.
(Box will automatically expand as you type)

Section 10
Writing a Significance Section for Your Research Proposal

Write a Significance section for your research proposal in the white space provided below.

- Use all the tips in this section to write your Significance section.
- If possible, show your Significance section to your classmates for their feedback.
- Revise your Significance section based on your classmates' feedback.
- Submit your Significance section to your instructor for comments and feedback.

Your Name(s):

Your Identification Number(s) (if any):

Title of Your Research Proposal:

Abstract:

Introduction:

Literature Review:

Problem and Research Question:

Research Design:

Sample:

Instrumentation:

Data Collection:

Data Analysis:

Ethical and Cultural Considerations:

Limitations:

Type your Significance section here.
(Box will automatically expand as you type)

PART V
Back Matter

Section 11: References

Section 12: Appendixes

The back matter of a research proposal includes two sections: Section 11 contains the references you cited throughout your proposal, and Section 12 comprises all your appendixes. Unfortunately, most naïve proposal writers neglect the back matter of their proposals. This is a serious mistake because the people who review research proposals for potential funding pay particular attention to how these two sections are completed—especially Section 12, which contains your appendixes.

175

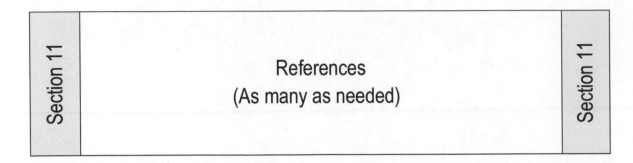

Section 11

References
(As many as needed)

Section 11

Section 11
References cited within the proposal

Section 12
Appendixes that support the proposal

Back Matter

SECTION 11 IS ONLY A LIST OF YOUR REFERENCES. We assume you know how to format your references in APA style. You can use this book as a guide to how they are formatted if your memory needs a bit of refreshing.

Writing a References Section	QUICK TIPS
\multicolumn{2}{}{Check to see if you have read pages 6–7 on how to use our tips.}
Required	**Very Important:** Check to see that you really understand how to reference material for your papers. If not, obtain one of the many inexpensive books that can be found on Amazon.com that deal with the subject.

#	Answers				Tips
313	NA	TA	Yes	No	Check to see that each and every reference in this section is 100% complete and accurate.
314	NA	TA	Yes	No	Check to see that all of your references are formatted to APA specifications.
315	NA	TA	Yes	No	Check to see that your references are alphabetized correctly.
316	NA	TA	Yes	No	Check to see that each reference is contained in the body of your proposal.
317	NA	TA	Yes	No	Check to see that only the references cited in your proposal are included in your reference list.
318	NA	TA	Yes	No	Check with your research instructor to see if he/she has any examples of References sections from other research proposals to show you.

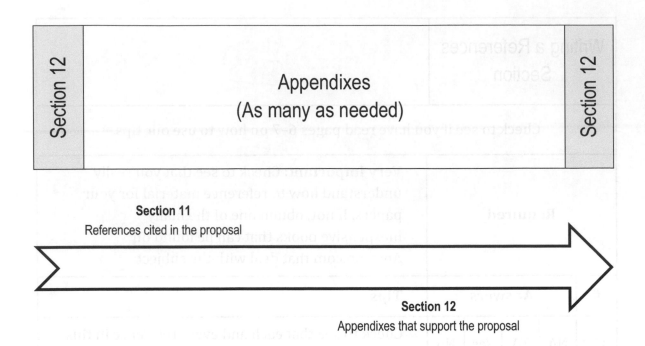

Section 12

Appendixes
(As many as needed)

Section 12

Section 11
References cited in the proposal

Section 12
Appendixes that support the proposal

Back Matter

APPENDIXES ARE ABSOLUTELY ESSENTIAL to include in your research proposal. They can easily make or break your proposal. They should be devoted to those aspects of your project that are of secondary interest to your readers. In short, appendixes are used for the material that can't be included in the body of the paper due to space limitations.

First, assume that many of your readers will only have a short amount of time to read your proposal, will only read its main body, and will skip the appendixes. Second, assume that some of your readers *will* want additional information that is not found in the body of your proposal—that is the purpose of the appendixes.

It is more than likely that you won't use all the appendixes we have included in this section. These appendixes are required no matter what kind of study you propose: C, D, G, J, K, L, M, N, and O. However, if you are not proposing to do your study within a social work agency, you will not need Appendixes A and B. Likewise, if you are not going to use human research participants in your study, you won't include Appendixes E, F, H, and I.

Appendix A Copies of official letters of permission to conduct your research study in a social work agency or program (if needed)

Appendix B Cooperating agency description (if needed)

Appendix C Time lines

Appendix D Measuring instruments (an individual appendix for each instrument)

Appendix E Copy of informed consent form (if needed)

Appendix F Copy of informed assent form (if needed)

Appendix G Copy of institutional review board (IRB) approval from your university/college (check with your instructor to see if an IRB is required)

Appendix H Verbatim instructions given to your research participants (if needed)

Appendix I Interview protocols (if needed)

Appendix J Data collection plan

Appendix K Data analysis plan

Appendix L Personnel (if needed)

Appendix M Copies of resumes of key people

Appendix N Dissemination plan

Appendix O Budget

Appendix A
(Permission to do your study, if applicable)

APPENDIX A IS THE PLACE TO INCLUDE LETTERS from an agency's Executive Director who has provided permission for you to implement your proposal within the agency. Your study would more than likely use some of the agency's resources and clientele. It is very important that the person who signs the letter of permission actually knows what your study is all about. There should be no surprises when you show up at the door.

In a nutshell, make sure the agency's Executive Director has thoroughly read your research proposal and understands exactly *what* you are going to do, *why* you are going to do it, *who* are you going to do it to, *how* you are going to do it, *when* you are going to do it, *where* are you going to do it, and more importantly, *how* are you obtaining informed consent and/or assent for your research participants—who just happen to be the clientele of the agency.

Appendix A is not needed if you don't require any letters of support to do your study. Please note that Appendix A is not the place for the Institutional Review Board (IRB) approval letters; those are contained in Appendix G. You will need a support letter from an agency's Executive Director to include in your proposal that you submit to your university/college's IRB.

Box A is an actual example of how an agency's Executive Director wrote a letter of support and at the same time provided permission for researchers to do a research study within his agency and use the agency's clientele as research participants.

Funding agencies would like to know that others (besides yourself) feel strongly enough about your proposed project that they are willing to write a letter of support. The more support letters the better. Do not write a support letter for the agency's Executive Director to sign. Have the Executive Director write it.

The support letter must be substantive in nature and addressed to the funding agency and not to "To Whom It May Concern." This dreaded phrase makes it appear that you are applying to many different potential funding agencies and the Executive Director is using the same letter for each. In reality this may be the case, however, so

180

make sure the Executive Director personalizes each letter to the specific potential funding agency.

BOX A	Example of a Support Letter for a Research Study to Take Place within a Social Work Agency

Chatham-Kent Children's Services (CKCS) Help-Seeking Project for Adolescents in Out-of-Home Placement: A Research Proposal[1]

Dear Ms. Funder:

We are pleased to provide you with the attached research proposal as a response to your "Request for Proposals."

We are a large, integrated, multiservice agency that serves the protection, mental health, and developmental needs of the children and youth in our community. In addition, we have the mandate to deliver prevention and community services for children and their families.

We are glad to once again have the collaboration of Drs. Grinnell and Unrau from the School of Social Work at Western Michigan University in Kalamazoo, Michigan. I personally have had the opportunity to previously collaborate with both Drs. Grinnell and Unrau on a wide range of child welfare–related topics. You will note from our attached vitas that we have collaborated on child sexual abuse, in-home support, and related program evaluation issues.

Over the years, and as a team, I believe we have developed relevant and useable practice findings. The research topic is not only timely but we should be able to put the results to good use to improve the lives of youth in our care and better prepare them for independence.

If you have any questions whatsoever please don't hesitate to contact me.

Mike Stephens, MSW
Chief Executive Officer

Appendix B
(Cooperating agency description, if applicable)

IF YOU WILL BE WORKING WITH A SOCIAL WORK AGENCY, it is a good idea to provide a detailed description of what it does in Appendix B. All you need to do is provide the six pieces of information below on one sheet of paper:

1 Name of the agency

2 Complete address of the agency

3 General telephone number of the agency

4 Brief description of the major services the agency provides

5 Specific persons within the agency that you will be working with along with each one's telephone number and/or extension

6 Description of what the role of each person will be in reference to your research study; that is, what will each person specifically be responsible for?

If you will be working with more than one agency, you will need to prepare a single-page description for each one that follows the same format. Remember, one page for each agency.

Appendix B is also a good place to put a copy of a letter written by the agency's Executive Director (or similar person) that specifies how the agency plans on using the results of your study (if appropriate, of course).

Box B is an example of how an agency plans to implement the results of a research study into its day-to-day practices if the proposal is funded and how the results of the study will benefit the social service delivery system within the agency.

182

BOX B	Example of a Support Letter That Addresses How the Agency Will Use the Results from a Research Study

Chatham-Kent Children's Services (CKCS) Help-Seeking Project for Adolescents in Out-of-Home Placement: A Research Proposal[1]

Dear Ms. Funder,

Please find enclosed 10 copies of our "Phase 2" grant proposal that we wish to submit to your organization for funding: "Chatham-Kent Children's Services Help-Seeking Project for Adolescents in Out-of-Home Placement." Our proposal is a direct result of the $10,000 Grants in Aid funds we received from your organization last year.

We're really excited about our project. In fact, if our intervention is shown to be successful, we will implement it in our day-to-day practice activities via reorganizing our service delivery structure. Since we initially received your "Phase 1" funding, we, along with the two researchers from WMU, have been thinking through various in-house strategies toward sustaining the intervention without extra funding from outside sources.

If you have any questions, please do not hesitate to contact me at your earliest convenience.

I look forward to hearing from you, and thank you for your time.

Sincerely,

Mike Stephens, MSW
Chief Executive Officer

----

[1]Unrau, Y., & Grinnell, R.M., Jr. (2005). *Chatham-Kent Children's Services (CKCS) Help-Seeking Project for Adolescents in Out-of-Home Placement: A Research Proposal.* Submitted to Provincial Centre of Excellence for Child and Youth Mental Health at CHEO. Ottawa, Ontario, Canada K1H 8L1.

Appendix C
(Time lines)

As you know, Appendixes A and B are optional because they will not be relevant if your study is not going to use a social work agency. Appendix C, however, is not optional—it's required as it outlines your proposed work schedule, outlining the various activities you will be doing with specific time lines for each activity.

It is important that you present accurate, realistic time lines that allocate an adequate amount of time for all the different activities you will perform in your proposed project. Don't forget to include time for revising, revising, revising, editing, editing, editing, and producing the final product.

More often than not, most social work students seriously underestimate the amount of time it will take them to conduct the research and write the final research reports (manuscripts) that are based on their research proposals. Thus, you need to make a best guesstimate time line that outlines the amount of time it will take for each of your activities—from your literature review to the final submission of your manuscript for possible publication.

The example here is a crude sample time line submitted by one student. Keep in mind that time lines can vary dramatically, depending on the circumstances of the research endeavor. In this case, the student is preparing a preliminary literature review for the proposal and will need to complete it by the time the study is actually over. Other students may compile the complete literature review while preparing their proposals. Also, this student was employed full-time and could devote only evenings and weekends to carrying out the research study (Patten, 2010).

1   Complete literature review from my research proposal. (1 month)

2   Have completed literature review assessed by my instructor. (2 weeks)

3   Obtain mailing lists of research participants from the Department of Social Services. (2 weeks)

4   Prepare survey cover letter and first draft of questionnaire. (1 week)

5 Have cover letter and questionnaire reviewed by my instructor. (1 week)

6 Pilot test cover letter and questionnaire. (3 weeks)

7 Revise cover letter and questionnaire based on feedback from pilot test. (2 weeks)

8 Have revised cover letter and questionnaire reviewed by my instructor. (2 weeks)

9 Obtain approval from my university's institutional review board. (3 weeks)

10 Write the Method section of the final research report. (2 weeks)

11 Have the Method section reviewed by my instructor. (2 weeks)

12 Mail letter and questionnaire to sample, and wait for responses. (3 weeks)

13 Mail follow-up questionnaire and wait for responses. (2 weeks)

14 Tabulate responses. Conduct descriptive and inferential analyses. (3 weeks)

15 Write the Findings section of the final research report. (2 weeks)

16 Have the Findings sections reviewed by my instructor. (2 weeks)

17 Assemble the first draft of the complete report. Have it reviewed by my instructor and at the University Writing Center for mechanical flaws in grammar, punctuation, etc. (2 weeks)

18 Submit the complete first draft (revised in light of previous step) to my instructor for initial review. (2 weeks)

19 Rewrite and revise in light of the previous step, and resubmit for feedback. (2 weeks)

20 Make final changes based on previous step; format the final report and submit it to a social work journal for possible publication. (4 weeks)

REFERENCE

Patten, M.L. (2010). *Understanding research methods: An overview of the essentials* (7th ed.). Glendale, CA: Pryczak.

Appendix D
(Measuring instruments)

ATTACHING STANDARDIZED MEASURING INSTRUMENTS

Appendix D starts the appendixes that contain good, clear copies of your standardized measuring instruments *along with* their appropriate scoring instructions. There must be a separate appendix for each measuring instrument (and the instructions on how to complete them) that you plan to use. Or, to put it another way, one instrument for each variable you plan to measure—simple as that.

Thus, if you have five variables, you will have an appropriate measuring instrument for each, and five separate appendixes: D_1, D_2, D_3, D_4, and D_5.

Figure D_1 contains an example of a standardized measuring instrument that measures self-esteem, and Figure D_2 contains basic information about the instrument.

If a measuring instrument is copyrighted, you need to state that you will obtain official written permission from the copyright holder to reproduce the instrument for your study *before* you actually begin to implement your study.

As you know, you will be referring to each measuring instrument (and thus each individual appendix) in your Research Design section (8a), Sampling section (8b), Instrumentation section (8c), Data Collection section (8d), and Data Analysis section (8e).

ATTACHING YOUR OWN HOMEGROWN INSTRUMENTS

If you are creating your own instrument(s), include a draft copy of the actual measuring instrument you plan to use, such as a survey, questionnaire, or interview schedule. This will let your reviewers know that you're serious about your proposed project. Put "DRAFT" at the top of each homegrown measuring instrument, and make them look as much like the final product as possible.

186

If you will be using interviews as your data collection method, include a draft copy of the specific questions that you plan to use. Remember, the questions you ask and the answers you receive must be directly relevant to your research question (or hypothesis).

Under no circumstances should you dump copies of all of your measuring instruments into one appendix in a sloppy manner. It will not impress your reviewers the least bit.

Figure D_1 illustrates how a measuring instrument needs to be displayed, and Figure D_2 (Continued) demonstrates the material that should accompany the instrument.

Name:_____ Today's Date:_____

This questionnaire is designed to measure how you see yourself. It is not a test, so there are no right or wrong answers. Please answer each item as carefully and as accurately as you can by placing a number beside each one as follows:

1 = None of the time
2 = Very rarely
3 = A little of the time
4 = Some of the time
5 = A good part of the time
6 = Most of the time
7 = All of the time

1. __ I feel that people would not like me if they really knew me well.
2. __ I feel that others get along much better than I do.
3. __ I feel that I am a beautiful person.
4. __ When I am with others I feel they are glad I am with them.
5. __ I feel that people really like to talk with me.
6. __ I feel that I am a very competent person.
7. __ I think I make a good impression on others.
8. __ I feel that I need more self-confidence.
9. __ When I am with strangers I am very nervous.
10. __ I think that I am a dull person.
11. __ I feel ugly.
12. __ I feel that others have more fun than I do.
13. __ I feel that I bore people.
14. __ I think my friends find me interesting.
15. __ I think I have a good sense of humor.
16. __ I feel very self-conscious when I am with strangers.
17. __ I feel that if I could be more like other people I would have it made.
18. __ I feel that people have a good time when they are with me.
19. __ I feel like a wallflower when I go out.
20. __ I feel I get pushed around more than others.
21. __ I think I am a rather nice person.
22. __ I feel that people really like me very much.
23. __ I feel that I am a likeable person.
24. __ I am afraid I will appear foolish to others.
25. __ My friends think very highly of me.

Figure D$_1$
Hudson's *Index of Self-Esteem*

AUTHOR: Walter W. Hudson

PURPOSE: To measure problems with self-esteem.

DESCRIPTION: The *ISE* is a 25-item scale designed to measure the degree, severity, or magnitude of a problem the client has with self-esteem. Self-esteem is considered as the evaluative component of self-concept. The *ISE* is written in very simple language, is easily administered, and easily scored. Because problems with self-esteem are often central to social and psychological difficulties, this instrument has a wide range of utility for a number of clinical problems.

The *ISE* has a cutting score of 30 (+ or − 5), with scores above 30 indicating the respondent has a clinically significant problem and scores below 30 indicating the individual has no such problem. Another advantage of the *ISE* is that it is one of nine scales of the *Clinical Measurement Package* (Hudson, 1982), all of which are administered and scored the same way.

NORMS: This scale was derived from tests of 1,745 respondents, including single and married individuals, clinical and nonclinical populations, college students, and nonstudents. Respondents included Caucasians, Japanese, and Chinese Americans, and a smaller number of members of other ethnic groups. Not recommended for use with children under the age of 12.

SCORING: For a detailed description on how to score the *ISE,* see: www.walmyr.com.

RELIABILITY: The *ISE* has a mean alpha of .93, indicating excellent internal consistency, and an excellent (low) S.E.M. of 3.70. The *ISE* also has excellent stability with a two-hour test-retest correlation of .92.

VALIDITY: The *ISE* has good know-groups validity, significantly distinguishing between clients judged by clinicians to have problems in the area of self-esteem and those known not to. Further, the *ISE* has very good construct validity, correlating well with a range of other measures with which it should correlate highly, e.g., depression, happiness, sense of identity, and scores on the *Generalized Contentment Scale* (depression).

PRIMARY REFERENCE: Hudson, W.W. (1982). *The clinical measurement package: A field manual.* Chicago: Dorsey.

Figure D₁ (Continued)

Basic Information about Hudson's *Index of Self-Esteem*

Appendix E
(Informed consent form, if applicable)

FIRST AND FOREMOST, reread the research ethics chapter in your research methods text before you write a consent form. As you know from Section 8a (on research design), Section 8b (on sampling), Section 8c (on instrumentation), Section 8d (on data collection), and Section 8e (on data analysis), ethical issues arise when you want to use research participants in your proposed study. You always need to address possible ethical issues in your proposal when you use humans as data sources.

You must plan to protect your participants' privacy. By collecting your research participants' anonymous responses to mailed questionnaires and surveys, for example, you provide them with this much-needed protection. If you will be providing anonymity, you should state that in your proposal. Remember that anonymity means you do not know who answered what on a particular measuring instrument.

You need to consider how to shield your research participants from psychological harm as you design your study (e.g., experimental or control groups), select your research participants and measuring instruments, and decide on your data collection and analysis plans. This all boils down to writing a consent form that your research participants need to sign.

A written consent form should be only part of the process of informing your research participants of their roles and rights as volunteers in your purposed study. It must give potential participants a basic description of the purpose of your study, the study's procedures, and their rights as voluntary participants. All information must be provided in plain and simple language:

- that participants are being asked to participate in a research study
- the names of the investigators and their affiliations
- the purposes of the research, simply explained

- the study's procedures
- the expected duration of participation
- any reasonably foreseeable risks or discomforts
- any safeguards to minimize the risks
- any benefits to the participant or to others that may reasonably be expected from the research study. (In most cases, the study is not being performed for the benefit of the participants but for the potential benefit of others. This broader social benefit to the public should be made explicit.)
- in cases where an incentive is offered, a description of the incentive and of how and under what conditions it is to be obtained
- appropriate alternative procedures or courses of treatment, if applicable
- the extent, if any, to which confidentiality of records identifying the participant will be maintained (not an issue unless participants can be identified)
- any restrictions on confidentiality. (For instance, if any of the information gained during the study might have to be disclosed as required by law, as in instances of child abuse, absolute confidentiality cannot be assured.)
- what monetary compensation or medical or psychological treatment will be provided for any research-related injury (if more than minimal risk)
- contact information for questions about the study (name, office address, and phone contacts for the researcher, faculty advisor, and IRB staff). Do not include home phone numbers.
- that participation is voluntary, and that the participant may discontinue participation at any time without penalty or loss of benefits to which he or she is otherwise entitled (e.g., in their standing as a patient, student, employee, and so forth)
- that the researcher will keep one copy of the signed consent form and give another signed copy to the participant

Most universities/colleges, and most large social service agencies for that matter, require that all research proposals be reviewed by their internal committees, which will consider all these issues. These committees are likely to pay special attention to what you will be measuring and how you will be measuring it, with an eye to whether participants are adequately protected. These committees will also be reviewing your informed-consent form, so you should obtain a copy of your institution's guidelines on preparing such a form early in the development of your proposal.

More than likely, your university/college will have examples of consent forms that can be found in their research offices or some other similar department. Many times universities/colleges have online templates you can use as guides.

In any event, if you are going to use human research participants in your study, you will probably have to submit your proposal to your university/college's institutional review board (IRB) for their approval before you start collecting data. You can easily get an expedited student review if your study is simple, straightforward, and doesn't involve assigning individuals to groups or collecting data through interviews. Your instructor would be the person in the know when it comes to helping you get your research proposal through the incredible maze of the university/college IRB.

Obviously, you do not have to submit your research proposal to your IRB if you do not plan on implementing your study.

BOX E	Example of a Consent Form from a Research Proposal

Chatham-Kent Children's Services (CKCS) Help-Seeking Project for Adolescents in Out-of-Home Placement: A Research Proposal[1]

You are invited to have your clients participate in Chatham-Kent Children's Services (CKCS) Help-Seeking Project for Adolescents in Out-of-Home Placement. The project is funded by the Provincial Centre of Excellence for Child and Youth Mental Health. The primary person in charge of the project is Mike Stephens, Chief Executive Officer of CKCS.

This handout describes our project and will help you decide if you want to have your clients participate. You are 100% free to choose whether or not you will have your clients take part in the study. Before you decide, however, you need to know what will be expected of them if you agree to have them participate and the risks and benefits of their participation. Please take time to read this handout.

There are no negative consequences for either you or your clients in reference to your decision as to their potential participation. Your clients can drop out of the study at any time. The services they receive from CKCS will not be affected by your decision to have them participate in this project.

If you agree to have your clients take part in the project they will be asked to sign a separate assent form. The assent form is a shorter version of this consent form and contains important information about the project. When they sign the assent form, they give their "consent," which means that they agree to participate in the project.

WHAT'S THE PROJECT ABOUT ANYWAY?

The main purpose of our project is to find out whether a workshop on help-seeking for youth living in out-of-home placement at CKCS will help them become more skilled at asking for help when personal or emotional problems arise. We don't yet know if our help-seeking workshop works. So we have designed a project that will involve about 120 youth, ages 12 years and older, who are living at CKCS.

Half of the youth who participate in the project will attend a special workshop, and the other half will not. The workshop will give them information and ideas about how to seek help when personal or emotional problems arise. We will then compare the help-seeking skills of those youth who attended the workshop with those who did not in order to learn whether the workshop was helpful. They will be assigned, by chance, to a group who attend the workshop, or to a group who do not attend. That is, they may or may not attend the workshop even though they agree to participate in the project (via an assent form).

If we learn that the workshop is helpful in the way we expect, then all youth who did not get to attend the workshop will be offered a chance to attend it at a later date, as long as they are still living at CKCS.

In total, about 120 youth will participate in the project. Everyone will be asked to complete a set of questionnaires at four different times: this week, 5 weeks from now, 10 weeks from now, and 5 months from now. Step by step, this is what will happen if you agree to have your clients participate in the project AND they have also agreed.

1 They will be contacted twice by telephone. Sometime this week, and then again 5 months from now, a CKCS staff member will call them by telephone and ask them questions. The phone interview takes about 30 minutes and includes questions about common emotional and behavioral problems experienced by teenagers. They do not have to answer any questions they don't want to.

2 They will be asked to come to CKCS four times over the next 5 months and to complete four other surveys. These surveys are completed at the CKCS computer lab using a special computer program. Sitting at their own computers and wearing headphones, they will see each question appear on the computer screen and hear the question being read through the headphones.

3 They will answer the questions by clicking the computer mouse. The computer surveys should take about 30 to 40 minutes to complete each time. As we said above, they do not have to answer any questions that they don't want to. They will be paid for their participation. They will receive $10 the first time they answer the survey questions, $15 the second time, $20 the third time, and $30 the fourth time.

4 Snacks also will be provided at each meeting, and bus fare to CKCS will be available if they need it. In addition to the above surveys, a project staff member will review their CKCS case files for information such as their placements, services they have received, and family contacts.

5 By chance, half of the youth participating in the project will be invited to attend a 2- to 3-hour workshop that will include six youths at a time. The workshop will take place at CKCS and be run by a CKCS staff member. The purpose of the workshop is to give them additional information about how they can best get help for their personal or emotional problems while living in a CKCS placement.

UNDER WHAT CIRCUMSTANCES WOULD CKCS END THEIR PARTICIPATION?

If they leave CKCS within 5 weeks of the start of the project, their participation in the project will automatically end.

HOW WILL THEIR PRIVACY BE PROTECTED?

Confidentiality describes what we do to keep information gathered about your clients completely private. In order to protect their privacy in this project:

1 We use numbers instead of names (or other identifiers) on all of the data we obtain so that no one can connect the data with you or them.

2 The data collected for this project will be sent to researchers at Western Michigan University. Once again, the data will not include anything that would individually identify you or them. The researchers and their staff have been trained in protecting everyone's confidentiality.

3 No CKCS staff member will have access to the data that your clients provide as part of this project. All data collected from your clients will not be shared with you (their Children's Service Worker and legal guardian), their foster parents or caregivers, or any other workers at CKCS. The data collected will only be used for this project.

4 All data will be stored in a safe, locked area. The computers for this project are protected by a firewall system, and all users are required to use passwords.

5 All of the adolescents' answers will be kept absolutely private unless a staff member thinks they might be in danger of hurting themselves. For example, if an adolescent tells us that he or she is using illegal drugs, or is thinking of harming him or herself or someone else, project staff are obligated to inform you since you are his or her legal guardian and CKCS Children's Service Worker.

6 The information from the project will be used to write papers, make presentations, and work with other education or research centers to improve out-of-home services for youth. Please remember that their names, or any information that could identify them, will never be used. We will evaluate the survey answers "as a group" and not for any one individual. They will not be identified (for example, by name or social security number) in any reports or publications of this project.

WILL WE SHARE INFORMATION WITH OTHERS?

Yes. As we have said before, if we know or think we know that one of your clients is being abused, under law we must take action to protect that person. We also must report if we hear that they intend to harm themselves or someone else. We will inform you immediately if this is the case.

WHAT ARE THEIR RIGHTS AS A PARTICIPANT IN OUR PROJECT?

As participants in our project, your clients have certain rights that protect them from potential harm. After you, as their legal guardian, have provided your consent to have them participate in the project (via signing this form), their specific rights are as follows:

1 It is up to them to decide if they want to be in our project. That means their participation is completely voluntary.

2 They have the right to change their minds at any time about being in the project. If they decide to leave the project, there will be no penalty of any kind.

3 They have the right to refuse to answer any question(s). Some questions might be personal or sensitive to them. These questions are important to our project and we would like them to answer the questions honestly. However, if there are questions they do not want to answer, they may skip them and move on to other questions.

4   They will be given copies of this Project Description (your consent form). If they want to participate in our project, they will also sign an Assent Form.

5   Their assent forms will also be explained verbally to them. If they have any difficulty in reading these forms, a staff person will read it to them.

6   At any time they can ask any staff member questions about our project. They may also call collect Mike Stephens (x-xxx-xxx-xxxx, extension xxx).

7   If they would like to contact someone outside the project staff with questions or concerns, they can Yvonne Unrau at xxx-xxx-xxxx or Rick Grinnell at xxx-xxx-xxxx, who are the two Western Michigan University researchers involved with the project. They may also contact the Chair, Human Subjects Institutional Review Board (xxx-xxx-xxxx) or the Vice President for Research (xxx-xxx-xxxx) at Western Michigan University if questions or problems arise during the course of the study. They may call collect.

RISKS ASSOCIATED WITH PARTICIPATING IN OUR PROJECT

There are very few risks in this project. The adolescents may, however, feel a little embarrassed or uncomfortable because of the personal nature of some questions on the surveys or due to certain project activities such as role plays in the workshop. Remember, they do not have to answer any questions or take part in any activities at any time.

WHAT ARE THE BENEFITS TO THEM?

Many people find it helpful to think and talk about personal information about themselves and their families. Being in the project gives them a chance to do this. The project may improve our knowledge about how youth in care can better seek help when they need it.

The information gained may help us understand more about how parents, foster parents, and CKCS can work together to help teenagers who are placed in foster or group care.

This information might be used to prevent problems for teenagers in the future and to help those that are having trouble.

As a participant, they will be part of a valuable project that might help other people in the future. Please sign below to show that you have reviewed this Project Description, you consent to have your clients participate, and that you have had all your questions answered.

_____

Social worker's signature (as legal guardian)

_____

Date

Names of your clients who you agree can participate in the project:

_____

_____

_____

[1]Unrau, Y., & Grinnell, R.M., Jr. (2005). *Chatham-Kent Children's Services (CKCS) Help-Seeking Project for Adolescents in Out-of-Home Placement: A Research Proposal.* Submitted to Provincial Centre of Excellence for Child and Youth Mental Health at CHEO. Ottawa, Ontario, Canada K1H 8L1.

Appendix F
(Informed assent form, if applicable)

FIRST AND FOREMOST, reread the research ethics chapter in your research methods text before you write an assent form. The procedures for obtaining informed assent are similar to those for obtaining informed consent. You should note, however, that an institutional review board (IRB) looks fastidiously at research proposals that require informed assent forms from prospective research participants.

When your proposed study involves populations where informed assent forms are required, plan on the IRB process taking a month or two. If your proposed study plans on using research settings such as schools, residential institutions, departments of human services, or nursing homes, then add another month onto the IRB process. Never underestimate the length of time it takes to get a research proposal through the IRB process when you plan to use vulnerable populations as research participants.

Box F contains an example of an assent form from a research proposal. This assent form was signed by the underage youths after their social workers (their legal guardians) gave their consent for them to participate. It should be noted that the youths could refuse to participate in the study regardless of their social workers' consent. So this study had to have the social workers' consent and their clients' assent.

BOX F	Example of an Assent Form from a Research Proposal

Chatham-Kent Children's Services (CKCS) Help-Seeking Project for Adolescents in Out-of-Home Placement: A Research Proposal[1]

I have been invited to be part of a study entitled "Chatham-Kent Children's Services (CKCS) Help-Seeking Project for Adolescents in Out-of-Home Placement."

The main purpose of the study is to see if a workshop and additional support given to youth living at CKCS will make youth more skilled at asking for help with personal or emotional problems. In this study:

1   I will be phoned by a CKCS staff member twice over 20 weeks and be asked to answer questions on the phone. This will take about 15 minutes each time.

2   I will be invited to come to CKCS four times over the next 20 weeks to answer questions from four other survey questionnaires about my help- seeking behaviors using a special computer program at CKCS.

3   After the first testing, CKCS will pay me $10 (or equivalent).

4   After the second testing point, CKCS will pay me $15 (or equivalent).

5   After the third testing point, CKCS will pay me $20 (or equivalent).

6   After the fourth (and final) time, CKCS will pay me $30 (or equivalent).

7   CKCS will provide food snacks at each testing time.

8   A project staff member will look at my case file to obtain basic information about me such as my age, sex, time in care, etc.

9   My name will not be recorded; instead of recording my name, a number code will be used.

10   I also may be invited to participate in a 2- to 3-hour workshop with a small group of about five other youth in care. The workshop will take place at CKCS and will be run by a CKCS mental health worker and possibly someone who formerly lived in an out-of-home placement.

11 At the workshop, I will get information and ideas about asking for help related to personal or emotional problems that are common with teenagers.

12 If I don't want to participate at this time, the service I receive from CKCS will not be affected.

13 Even if I agree today to participate by signing this form, I can change my mind at any time and withdraw from the study, and there will be no effect on the service I receive from CKCS.

14 If I choose to complete any or all of the questionnaires for the study, then my scores will be sent to researchers at Western Michigan University in Kalamazoo, Michigan.

15 As mentioned previously, my name will not be on any of the surveys that are sent to Michigan. The researchers will use a code number instead of my name. The researchers will keep a list of names and code numbers that will be destroyed once the researchers have looked at all of the questionnaires.

16 All of my answers will be kept private, which means even my Children's Service Worker or caregivers won't know what I say unless project staff members think I might be in danger of hurting myself or others. Then project staff will need to tell my Children's Service Worker.

17 Your signature below indicates that you agree to be interviewed by phone and surveyed on the computer.

YOUR SIGNATURE ALSO INDICATES THAT YOU AGREE:

1 To have your case file at CKCS reviewed for information it contains.

2 To be assigned to participate in a special help-seeking workshop for this project if selected.

3 To allow CKCS to give the researchers your survey results and case file information (your name will not be sent to the researchers).

4 That you have had a chance to ask any questions you may have.

_____

Print your name on above line.

_____ (Date: _____)

Sign your name on the above line and put in today's date.

Assent obtained by: _____

Thank you!

_____

[1]Unrau, Y., & Grinnell, R.M., Jr. (2005). *Chatham-Kent Children's Services (CKCS) Help-Seeking Project for Adolescents in Out-of-Home Placement: A Research Proposal.* Submitted to Provincial Centre of Excellence for Child and Youth Mental Health at CHEO. Ottawa, Ontario, Canada K1H 8L1

Appendix G
(Institutional Review Board approval, if required)

YOUR CONSENT FORMS (Appendix E) and your assent forms (Appendix F) were included in your research proposal that you sent to your college/university's institutional review board (IRB). Once your proposal is approved by the IRB, an official copy of their letter of approval is placed in Appendix G. Keep the original copy in a safe place. Read all the stipulations on the letter such as expiry dates and the like. Pay close attention to these dates.

Appendix G is left blank in the research proposal you send to your university/college's IRB because they have yet to approve your proposed study. In addition to the IRB's approval for your proposal, Appendix G should also contain additional IRB approvals from the agencies you will be using for your study.

Find out if your university/college's IRB requires any special forms or permissions that you will need to actually implement your proposed study. Box G provides a short example of how a Ph.D. student addressed the process of obtaining her university's IRB approval.

BOX G	Example of a Research Proposal That Addressed Institutional Review Board Issues

Students' Persistence in the University of Nebraska at Lincoln: A Mixed Methods Study[1]

RESEARCH PERMISSION AND ETHICAL CONSIDERATIONS

Ethical issues will be addressed at each phase in the study. In compliance with the regulations of the Institutional Review Board (IRB), the permission for conducting the research must be obtained (Institutional Review Board). The Request for Review Form will be filed, providing information about the principal investigator, the project title and type, source of funding, type of review requested, number and type of subjects.

Application for research permission will contain the description of the project and its significance, methods and procedures, participants, and research status. This project will be accorded an expedited-middle status, since the interviews with the participants will be audio taped, though the study will be conducted in a normal social setting, its topic does not fall in the sensitive category, and the subject population is over age nineteen.

An informed consent form will be developed. The form will state that the participants are guaranteed certain rights, agree to be involved in the study, and acknowledge their rights are protected. A statement relating to informed consent will be affixed to the web survey and reflect compliance by participation.

The anonymity of participants will be protected by numerically coding each returned questionnaire and keeping the responses confidential. While conducting the individual interviews with the selected respondents, they will be assigned fictitious names for use in their description and reporting the results.

All study data, including the survey electronic files, interview tapes, and transcripts, will be kept in locked metal file cabinets in the researcher's office and destroyed after a reasonable period of time. Participants will be told summary data will be disseminated to the professional community, but in no way it will be possible to trace responses to individuals.

[1]Ivankova, N.V. (2002). *Students' persistence in the University of Nebraska at Lincoln: A mixed methods study.* Doctoral dissertation proposal submitted for partial fulfillment of the requirements for the degree of Doctor of Philosophy. Graduate College at the University of Nebraska at Lincoln.

APPENDIX H IS WHERE YOU CLEARLY DELINEATE the instructions you will provide your research participants when it comes to filling out the measuring instruments. Sometimes the instructions for completing measuring instruments are contained within the measuring instruments themselves. Since copies of the measuring instruments are contained in Appendix D, you can simply refer the reader to that location for instructions on how to complete the measuring instruments in addition to copies of the measuring instruments themselves.

In the simplest of terms, Appendix H contains the verbal and written information given to research participants on how to fill out the measuring instruments that you did not describe in Section 8d, on data collection. You will need to include Appendix H in the research proposal you submit to your university/college's institutional review board (IRB) because they will be very concerned with how your research participants are going to be instructed on completing your measuring instruments. Sometimes this information is contained in the Informed Consent/Assent Form.

Obviously you will not need Appendix H if you do not use human research participants in your proposed study.

Appendix I
(Interview protocols, if needed)

APPENDIX I IS YOUR DESCRIPTION of how you plan to gather information from your interviewees, assuming you are going to use interviews as a data collection method. Appendix I is another place your university/college's institutional review board (IRB) is going to scrutinize very carefully. How you plan on conducting your interviews is a very important part of the research process. Your Data Collection section, Section 8d, doesn't go into specifics of how you will specifically conduct your interviews. It will only describe the general questions you will be asking, and a copy of your interview schedule will be included in Appendix D on measuring instruments.

So, for now, just remember that Appendix I is the place where you describe exactly how you are going to conduct the interviews contained in the Appendix D interview schedule.

You will refer to Appendixes D and I in your Data Collection section. Box I is a brief example of an actual interview protocol from a research proposal.

BOX I	Example of Interview Protocols from a Research Proposal

Students' Persistence in the University of Nebraska at Lincoln: A Mixed Methods Study[1]

INTERVIEW PROTOCOLS

The Interview Protocol will include ten to fifteen open-ended questions, and will be pilot tested. The content of the protocol questions will be grounded in the results of the statistical tests of the relationships between the participants' group membership and the predictor factors as related to students' persistence in the program, and will elaborate on them.

The questions will focus on the issue of persistence in the ELHE-DE program and about the details of the cases selected on maximal variation principle. The protocol will be pilot tested on three students selected from the same target population, but then excluded from the full study.

Debriefing with the participants will be conducted to obtain information on the clarity of the interview questions and their relevance to the study aim. The participants will receive the interview questions prior to the scheduled calling time, and will be informed the interview will be tape-recorded and transcribed verbatim.

Respondents will have an opportunity to review and, if necessary, correct the contents of the interview after it has been transcribed.

---

[1]Ivankova, N.V. (2002). *Students' persistence in the University of Nebraska at Lincoln: A mixed methods study.* Doctoral dissertation proposal submitted for partial fulfillment of the requirements for the degree of Doctor of Philosophy. Graduate College at the University of Nebraska at Lincoln.

Appendix J
(Data collection plan)

APPENDIX J IS NOT OPTIONAL; it's mandatory, as it contains your specific data collection plan (and its corresponding narrative) as described in Section 8d. The table shown here and the corresponding narrative is one of many ways you can convince your readers that your data-gathering activities are not haphazard, unsystematic enterprises but well-thought-out procedures.

Example of a Data-Collection Plan for Two Variables

a	b	c	d	e	f	g
Indicator	*How indicator is measured*	*Who provides the data*	*How data are gathered*	*When data are gathered*	*Where data are gathered*	*Who collects the data*
Increase the self-esteem of pregnant adolescents after they have their babies	*Rosenberg Self-Esteem Scale* (Appendix D$_1$)	Client	1. Self-administered 2. Self-administered 3. Self-administered	1. Intake 2. Exit interview 3. 3 months after intervention	1. Waiting room 2. Social worker's office 3. Client's home	1. Receptionist 2. Social Worker 3. Case-aid
Increase the social support systems of pregnant adolescents after they have their babies	*Scale of Perceived Social Support* (Appendix D$_2$)	Client	1. Self-administered 2. Self-administered in group setting 3. Self-administered in a group setting	1. Intake 2. Last day of intervention 3. 1 month after intervention	1. Waiting room 2. In last group session 3. Group interview in coffee shop	1. Receptionist 2. Group leader 3. Research assistant

209

a = This column is where you list specifically what indicator(s) you are going to use to measure each one of your variables. Theoretically, you can have multiple indicators to measure the same variable.

b = This column is where you list specifically how you are going to measure each indicator in column *a*. For example, the indicators for self-esteem and social support can be measured by many different means. In our example, we chose one standardized measuring instrument for each variable: the *Rosenberg Self-Esteem Scale* for our self-esteem variable and the *Scale of Perceived Social Support* for our social support variable.

c = This column is where you list specifically who is going to provide the data, via the use of your selected measuring instrument (*b*). In a nutshell, this person, called a data source, is the one who is going to provide the data for the measuring instrument. Once again, a measuring instrument can be completed by a variety of different data sources.

d = This column is where you list specifically how the measuring instrument is going to be administered. Not only can you use a variety of measuring instruments to measure an indicator (*b*), but you also have a variety of options for how to administer them. For example, you can read the items or questions on the measuring instrument to your clients, or you can have your clients fill out the instrument themselves. You can also have clients complete them individually with no one around or in group settings such as parks, waiting rooms, and coffee shops.

e = This column is where you state the exact time frame in which the measuring instrument is going to be completed. Once again, there are many options available. For example, clients could complete measuring instruments at home on Friday nights before bedtime or at the beginning of your interview.

f = This column, which is highly related to the previous column (*e*), is where you list the specific location where the measuring instrument will be completed. For example, you can have your clients complete the *Rosenberg Self-Esteem Scale* in your program's waiting room, at home, or in your office.

g = This column is where you list specifically who is going to collect the data via the measuring instrument when it is completed. After the data source (*c*) has provided the data for the measuring instrument (*b*), who's going to collect the completed instrument for analysis? And, more importantly, who is going to collate all the data into a databank for further analyses?

Appendix K
(Data analysis plan)

JUST AS YOU HAVE PUT TOGETHER a good data collection plan, as evidenced by Appendix J, you also need to do the same for your data analysis plan. You told your readers how you specifically were going to collect the data for your variables in Appendix J. Now the time has come for you to let them know how you are going to analyze the data that you have so meticulously collected. This is done with a data analysis plan, as shown here.

Example of a Data-Analysis Plan for One Variable Measured before and after Treatment

a	b	c	d	e
Name of variable	Name of measuring instrument	Measurement level	When data are going to be collected	How data are going to be analyzed
Self-Esteem	Index of Self-Esteem (Appendix D₃)	Ordinal (treated as interval)	Time 1: Intake interview Time 2: Exit interview	• Descriptive statistics • One group *t*-test between Time 1 and Time 2 self-esteem scores

Many times, you will describe how your data are going to be analyzed in the body of your proposal. It doesn't hurt to provide your readers with a simple graphic of the analysis process.

Appendix L
(Personnel, if applicable)

APPENDIX L IS THE PLACE where you let your reviewers know whom you plan on inviting to your party: here, you must list each and every person who will be involved in your proposed project. For each person, the following information should be included:

1 Name of person

2 Title of person, if person is based in a cooperating social work agency

3 Specific duties or roles within your project

4 Amount of involvement (e.g., part-time, hours per week)

5 Relevant experience

6 Résumé

If your proposed project involves collaboration with a social work agency, it's beneficial to present evidence of any past successful cooperation experiences you have had with the agency (see Box B in Appendix B for an example).

Writing a Personnel Appendix	QUICK TIPS

Check to see if you have read pages 6–7 on how to use our tips.				
#	**Answers**			**Tips**
319	NA	TA	Yes	No	Check to see that you have obtained written permission from all persons who will be involved in your proposed research study, stating that they have read your proposal and will contribute to your project as outlined within your proposal.
320	NA	TA	Yes	No	Check to see that you clarified how each person's role is essential to the success of your project and have delineated what each person will do.
321	NA	TA	Yes	No	Optional: Check to see if you have spelled out exactly what your Steering Committee (Advisory Committee, Governing Board, etc.) is supposed to do in your proposed project and describe how it will be organized and who will be included.

Appendix M
(Résumés)

APPENDIX M IS THE PLACE where your résumé goes. Each person who will be involved in your proposed project must include a résumé in this appendix. Unlike Appendix D where you have a separate appendix for each measuring instrument, you can group all the résumés together in Appendix M. Your readers have to know who you are, and this is where they will be able to see your research interests and qualifications.

214

Appendix N
(Dissemination plan, if applicable)

APPENDIX N IS THE LOCATION of your dissemination plan. A *dissemination plan* is simply a way to show how you will share with other audiences the information that was derived from your project. Most funding agencies are interested in seeing how their financial support of your project will extend to other audiences besides yourself. Dissemination could be done through newsletters, workshops, radio broadcasts, presentations, printed handouts, slide shows, training programs, or publications. If you have an advisory group involved with your project, they can be very helpful in disseminating your study's results to other audiences.

Appendix O
(Budget)

YOUR PROPOSAL'S BUDGET IS CONTAINED in the final appendix. None of your budget items should surprise your reviewers. Furthermore, all project financial needs must be itemized in detail as well as justified in the narrative component of your budget section.

Do not pad your budget! It should only be your best-guess estimate of what your project is going to cost if it is actually going to be implemented. Nevertheless, it has to be a fairly truthful estimate. A realistic estimate of your project's costs is a good indication of your managerial ability. It's also unlikely that a funding agency will, upon the award, increase your proposed budget. There is a general tendency for students to underestimate costs (and time), so be as realistic as you can. Unforeseen circumstances will inevitably increase your costs and take more of your time than you have budgeted for.

If you will be submitting your proposal to a funding agency such as those listed on www.grants.gov, you must include a budget for your proposed study. List what equipment you need (e.g., computer, software, interviewers, travel, tape or video recorder) as well as the kind of services you will have to pay for (e.g., transcription, photocopying, binding, postage, library loans). Different funding agencies each have their own interpretations of what they will permit and ultimately fund. Thus, you will obviously have to adapt your proposal accordingly.

Funding agencies customarily specify how budgets should be presented and what costs are allowable. Your budget must show the costs that you are asking the funding agency to fund, which will include personnel, nonpersonnel, administrative, and overhead expenses. Your budget should also contain items paid for by other funding agencies, if applicable.

At all costs (no pun intended), make your budget realistic. Sharpen your pencil, or the person who will be reading your proposal will sharpen it for you—probably too sharp! Carefully think through exactly what you will need to carry out your proposed project, and establish your budget around this amount. Have fellow students and your instructor review your budget to see how realistic you are. Incorporate their suggestions, if possible.

Here are a few general categories you may need address when preparing your budget.

A. Personnel

- Principal investigator, co-principal investigator
- Graduate students
- Undergraduate students
- Professional assistants (e.g., interviewers, coders)

B. Fringe Benefits

- Personnel retirement, worker's compensation, medical/dental/life insurances, Medicare, etc.
- Graduate student tuition

C. Consultant Fees

- Honorarium
- Transportation (air, ground)
- Per diem

D. Equipment

E. Materials and Supplies

F. Travel (e.g., local, out of state)

- Transportation (e.g., air, ground)
- Per diem

G. Other

- Communications (telephone, postage)
- Shipping, courier
- Printing and duplicating
- Equipment maintenance
- Other (with explanation)

Glossary

***A* phase:** In case-level evaluation designs, the phase (*A* phase) in which the baseline measurement of the target problem is established before the intervention (*B* phase) is implemented.

A priori: Latin for "from what comes before." Typically, conclusions drawn from self-evident or deductive propositions that a researcher decides to make before collecting the data or examining the results.

Abstract: A brief summary of the important parts of a research study.

Abstracting indexing services: Providers of specialized reference tools that make it possible to find information quickly and easily, usually through subject headings and/or author approaches.

Abstracts: Reference materials consisting of citations and brief descriptive summaries from positivist and interpretive research studies.

Accountability: A system of responsibility in which program administrators account for all program activities by answering to the demands of a program's stakeholders and by justifying the program's expenditures to the satisfaction of its stakeholders; taking personal responsibility for one's conduct.

Accounts: In an interview, an account is a representation of a situation. Successful analysis depends on treating what the participants say as subjective accounts that the researcher must interpret, rather than factual reports than can be simply accepted at face value.

Accreditation: A process in which an accrediting body determines whether an institution or organization meets certain standards developed by the body.

Acculturation difficulty: A problem stemming from an inability to appropriately adapt to a different culture or environment.

Achieved status: Social status and prestige of an individual acquired as a result of individual accomplishments.

Action research: Action research is a research approach that **occurs** when researchers design a field experiment, collect the data, and feed it back to the activists (i.e., participants) both as feedback and as a way of modeling the next stage of the experiment. "Action" refers to the process of identifying issues relevant to a teaching or social situation; "research" refers to the processes of systematically collecting, documenting, and analyzing data. Data can be numerical as well as textual. In the field of applied linguistics, action research is often used by teachers when they investigate their own classrooms.

Adverse event (AE): A medically undesirable event occurring in a research subject, such as an abnormal sign, symptom, or worsening of a disease or injury. A serious adverse event (SAE) results in death, hospitalization (or increased hospital stay), persistent disability, birth defect, or any other outcome that seriously jeopardizes the subject's health. AEs that are also unanticipated problems should be reported promptly to institutional review boards and other appropriate officials.

Aggregate: Any collection of individuals who do not interact with one another.

Aggregate-level data: Derived from micro-level data, aggregate-level data are grouped so that the characteristics of individual units of analysis are no longer identifiable; for example, the variable "gross national income" is an aggregation of data about individual incomes.

Aggregated case-level evaluation designs: The collection of a number of case-level evaluations to determine the degree to which a program objective has been met.

Aggregated statistics: Information, written as numbers, about whole groups, not individuals in the groups.

Alternate-forms method: A method for establishing reliability of a measuring instrument by administering, in succession, equivalent forms of the same instrument to the same group of research participants.

Alternative hypothesis: See Rival hypothesis.

Amendment: A change to a human subjects research protocol approved by an institutional review board or the board's chair (if the change is minor).

Analysis: The breakdown of something that is complex into smaller parts in such a way that leads to a better understanding of the whole.

Analysis of variance: A statistical technique for determining the statistical significance of differences among means; used with two or more groups.

Analytical memos: Notes made by the researcher in reference to interpretive data that raise questions or make comments about meaning units and categories identified in a transcript.

Analytic generalization: The type of generalizability associated with case studies and used as working hypotheses to test practice principles. The research findings of case studies are not assumed to fit another case, no matter how apparently similar; rather, research findings are tested to see if they do in fact fit.

Analytic induction: Use of constant comparison specifically in developing hypotheses, which are then tested in further data collection and analysis.

Analytic memos: Notes made by the researcher in reference to interpretive data that raise questions or make comments about meaning units and categories identified in a transcript.

Analytic strategies: The choices in statistical procedures made by the investigators based on their values or what they consider important in a study.

Analyzing: Evaluating data to reach a conclusion about a research study.

Anecdotal evidence: What people say about something, which is not provable.

Annotated bibliography: A list of sources that gives the publication information and a short description—or annotation—for each source. Each annotation is generally three to seven sentences long. In some bibliographies, the annotation merely describes the content and scope of the source; in others, the annotation also evaluates the source's reliability, currency, and relevance to a researcher's purpose.

Annual report: A detailed account or statement describing a program's processes and results over a given year, usually produced at the end of a fiscal year.

Anonymity: Research studies that are designed so that no one, not even the person doing the study, knows which research participant gave what response (not be confused with confidentiality).

ANOVA: See analysis of variance.

Antecedent variable: A variable that precedes the introduction of one or more dependent variables.

Antiquarianism: An interest in past events without reference to their importance or significance for the present; the reverse of presentism.

Applied research approach: A search for practical and applied research results that can be used in actual social work practice situations; complementary to the pure research approach.

Area probability sampling: A form of cluster sampling that uses a three-stage process to provide the means to carry out a research study when no comprehensive list of the population can be compiled.

Assent: A subject's affirmative agreement to participate in a research study. Assent may take place when the subject does not have the capacity to provide informed consent (e.g., the subject is a child or mentally disabled) but has the capacity to meaningfully assent.

Assessment: A test or other way of measuring something, such as a person's mental health or goals or needs; often the first test in a series of tests, or a test given before treatment starts.

Assessment rubric: A rubric for assessment, usually in the form of a matrix or grid; a tool used to interpret and grade a piece of work against criteria and standards. Rubrics are sometimes called "criteria sheets," "grading schemes," or "scoring guides."

Assessment-related case study: A type of case study that generates knowledge about specific clients and their situations; focuses on the perspectives of the study's participants.

Assimilation: A process of consistent integration whereby members of an ethnocultural group, typically immigrants or other minority groups, are "absorbed" into an established larger community.

Association (statistical): A measure of whether and how closely certain values (numbers, amounts) in a study go up or down at the same time.

Astrology: The study of the movements and relative positions of celestial objects as a means of divining information about human affairs and terrestrial events.

Attribute: A specific value (or label) for a variable.

Attrition: The dropout rate among people who are being studied. People may quit because they want to, or they may not be able to stay in the study group (because of illness, lack of time, moving to another city, etc.), or they may not fit into the study anymore (if they get a job or marry, for example, in a study about single people who are not working).

Audit: A formal review of research records, policies, activities, personnel, or facilities to ensure compliance with ethical or legal standards or institutional policies. Audits may be conducted regularly, at random, or for-cause (i.e., in response to a problem).

Audit trail: The documentation of critical steps in an interpretive research study that allows for an independent reviewer to examine and verify the steps in the research process and the conclusions of the research study.

Author: A person who makes a significant contribution to a creative work. Many journal guidelines define an author as someone who makes a significant contribution to (1) research conception and design, (2) data acquisition, or (3) data analysis or interpretation, and who drafts or critically reads the paper and approves the final manuscript.

Authority: The reliance on authority figures to tell us what is true; one of the five ways of knowing.

Authorship, ghost: Failing to list someone as an author on a work even though they have made a significant contribution to it.

Authorship, honorary: Receiving authorship credit when one has not made a significant contribution to the work.

Autonomy: The capacity for self-governance— the ability to make reasonable decisions; a moral principle barring interference with autonomous decision-making. See decision-making capacity.

Availability sampling: See convenience sampling.

Axes: Straight horizontal and vertical lines in a graph upon which values of a measurement or the corresponding frequencies are plotted.

***B* phase:** In case-level evaluation designs, the intervention phase, which may or may not include simultaneous measurements.

Back-translation: The process of translating an original document into a second language, then having an independent translator conduct a subsequent translation of the first translation back into the language of origin; the second translation is then compared with the original document for equivalency.

Bad apples theory: The idea that most research misconduct is committed by individuals who are morally corrupt or psychologically ill. This idea can be contrasted with the view that social, financial, institutional, and cultural factors play a major role in causing research misconduct.

Bar graph: A drawing that uses bars for various groupings. The height of the bar shows how many things or people are in that grouping.

Baseline: A period of time, usually three or four data collection periods, in which the level of the client's target problem is measured while no intervention is carried out; designated as the A phase in single-system designs (case-level designs).

Baseline analysis: An analysis of data collected before a treatment or intervention is applied.

Belief system: A way in which a culture collectively constructs a model or framework for how it thinks about something. A religion is a particular kind of belief system.

Beliefs and intuition: Two highly related ways of obtaining knowledge; together they form one of the five ways of knowing.

Bell curve: See normal frequency distribution curve.

Belmont Report: A report issued by the U.S. National Commission for the Protection of Human Subjects in Biomedical and Behavioral Research in 1979 that has had a significant influence over human subjects research ethics, regulation, and policy. The report provided a conceptual foundation for the Common Rule and articulated three principles of ethics: respect for persons, beneficence, and justice.

Benchmark: A standard, test, or point of reference (often a number).

Beneficence: Refraining from maltreatment and maximizing potential benefits to research participants while minimizing potential harm; the ethical obligation to do good and avoid causing harm; the ethical obligation to do good and avoid causing harm. See also Belmont Report.

Benefit: A desirable outcome or state of affairs, such as medical treatment, clinically useful information, or self-esteem. In the oversight of human subjects research, money is usually not treated as a benefit.

Between research methods approach: Triangulation by using different research methods available in both the interpretive and the positivist research approaches in a single research study.

Bias: Something that may lead a researcher to wrong conclusions, such as mistakes or problems in how the study is planned or how the information is gathered or looked at. If two different interviewers had different styles that caused people with the same thoughts to give different answers but the answers were all put together in one pool, there would be a bias. It is impossible to conduct completely bias-free research.

Biased sample: A sample unintentionally selected in such a way that some members of the population are more likely than others to be picked for sample membership.

Biculturalism: The simultaneous identification with two cultures when an individual feels equally at home in both cultures and feels emotional attachment with both cultures.

Bimodal distribution: A range of scores that has two most frequent scores instead of one.

Binomial effect size display (BESD): A technique for interpreting the r value in a meta-analysis by converting it into a 2×2 table displaying magnitude of effect.

Bioethics: The study of ethical, social, or legal issues arising in biomedicine and biomedical research.

Biography: Tells the story of one individual's life, often suggesting what the person's influence was on social, political, or intellectual developments of the times.

Bivariate analysis: The study of how two variables are related.

Boundedness: A term used in a case study to refer to the parameters of a case. These could include the individual or entity, such as a school, under investigation and the setting in which social action takes place.

Case: The basic unit of social work practice, whether it be an individual, a couple, a family, an agency, a community, a county, a state, or a country.

Case study: An in-depth study of a case or cases (a "case" can be a program, an event, an activity, an individual), studied over time, using multiple sources of information (e.g., observations, documents, archival data, interviews). Can be exploratory, explanatory, or descriptive, or a combination of these.

Case-level evaluation designs: Designs in which data are collected about a single-client system—an individual, group, or community—in order to evaluate the outcome of an intervention for the client system; a form of appraisal that monitors change for individual clients; also called single-system research designs.

Caste system: Hereditary system of stratification. Hierarchical social status is ascribed at birth and often dictated by religion or other social norms.

Categorical variable: A piece of information that can be put in a single category instead of being given a number: for example, the information about whether a person owns a car or about whether the person belongs to a certain race can be put in the category of "yes" or the category of "no."

Categories: Groupings of related meaning units that are given one name; used to organize, summarize, and interpret qualitative data. Categories in an interpretive study can change throughout the data-analysis process, and the number of categories in a given study depends upon the breadth and depth the researcher aims for in the analysis.

Category: In an interpretive data analysis, an aggregate of meaning units that share a common feature.

Category saturation: The point in a qualitative data analysis when all identified meaning units fit easily into the existing categorization scheme and no new categories emerge; the point at which first-level coding ends.

CATI: See computer-assisted telephone interviewing.

Causality: A relationship of cause and effect; the effect will invariably occur when the cause is present.

Causal relationship: A relationship between two variables for which we can state that the presence or absence of one variable determines the presence or absence of the other variable; a relationship of cause and effect; the effect will invariably occur when the cause is present.

CD-ROM sources: Computerized retrieval systems that allow searching for indexes and abstracts stored on compact computer discs (CDs).

Ceiling effects: A term used to describe what happens when a group of subjects in a study have scores that are close to or at the upper limit (ceiling) of a variable. For example, the majority of subjects score 100% correct because the task is too easy.

Censorship: Taking steps to prevent or deter the public communication of information or ideas. In science, censorship may involve prohibiting the publication of research or allowing publication only in redacted form (with some information removed).

Census data: Data from the survey of an entire population, in contrast to a survey of a sample.

Chi-square: A statistical significance test that is appropriate when the data are in the form of frequency counts.

Citation: A brief identification of a reference that includes name of author(s), title, source, page numbers, and year of publication.

Citation amnesia: Failing to cite important work in the field in a paper, book, or presentation.

Classic experimental design: An explanatory research design with randomly assigned experimental and control groups in which the dependent variable is measured before and after the treatment (the independent variable) for both groups, but only the experimental group receives the treatment (the dependent variable).

Classification: A way of putting facts, things, people, and so on into groups based on something they have in common.

Classifications of research questions: Questions that can be classified into seven categories: existence, composition, relationship, descriptive-comparative, causality, causality-comparative, and causality-comparative interaction.

Classified research: Research that the government keeps secret to protect national security. Access to classified research is granted to individuals with the appropriate security clearance on a need-to-know basis.

Client system: An individual client, a couple, a family, a group, an organization, or a community that can be studied with case- and program-level evaluation designs and with positivist and interpretive research approaches.

Clinical investigator: A researcher involved in conducting a clinical trial.

Clinical trial: An experiment designed to test the safety or efficacy of a type of therapy (such as a drug).

Clinical trial, active controlled: A clinical trial in which the control group receives a treatment known to be effective. The goal of the trial is to compare different treatments.

Clinical trial, placebo controlled: A clinical trial in which the control group receives a placebo. The goal of the trial is to compare a treatment to a placebo.

Clinical trial, registration: Providing information about a clinical trial in a public registry. Most journals and funding agencies require that clinical trials be registered. Registration information includes the name of the trial, the sponsor, study design and methods, population, inclusion/exclusion criteria, and outcome measures.

Clinical utility: The clinical usefulness of information, for example, for making decisions concerning diagnosis, prevention, or treatment.

Closed-ended questions: Items in a measuring instrument that require respondents to select one of several response categories provided; also known as fixed-alternative questions.

Cluster analysis: A study that puts people or things into a small number of separate groups, so that there will be as much likeness within each group and as much difference among the groups as possible.

Cluster diagram: An illustration of a conceptual classification scheme in which the researcher draws and labels circles for each theme that emerges from the data; the circles are organized in a way to depict the relationships between themes.

Cluster sampling: A multistage probability sampling procedure in which the population is divided into groups (or clusters); the groups, rather than the individuals, are selected for inclusion in the sample.

Code: The label assigned to a category or theme in a qualitative data analysis; shortened versions of the actual category or theme label; used as markers in a qualitative data analysis; usually no longer than eight characters in length and can use a combination of letters, symbols, and numbers.

Codebook: A device used to organize qualitative data by applying labels and descriptions that draw distinctions between different parts of the data that have been collected.

Coding: Coding is one aspect of data analysis. When researchers code, they are trying to make sense of the data by systematically looking through it, clustering or grouping together similar ideas, phenomena, people, or events, and labeling them. Coding helps researchers find similar patterns and connections across the data. It helps researchers get to know the data better and to organize their thinking, and it also makes storage and retrieval of data easier.

Coding frame: A specific framework that delineates what data are to be coded and how they are to be coded in order to prepare them for analyses.

Coding sheets: In a literature review, a sheet used to record for each research study the complete reference, research design, measuring instrument(s), population and sample, outcomes, and other significant features of the study.

Coercion: Using force, threats, or intimidation to make a person comply with a demand.

Cohort study: A longitudinal survey design that uses successive random samples to monitor how the characteristics of a specific group of people, who share certain characteristics or experiences (cohorts), change over time.

Collaboration agreement: An agreement between two or more collaborating research groups concerning the conduct of research. The agreement may address the roles and responsibilities of the scientists, access to data, authorship, and intellectual property.

Collaterals: Professionals or staff members who serve as indigenous observers in the data collection process.

Collective biographies: Studies of the characteristics of groups of people who lived during a past period and had some major factor in common.

Collectivist culture: Societies that stress interdependence and seek the welfare and survival of the group above that of the individual; collectivist cultures are characterized by a readiness to be influenced by others, preference for conformity, and cooperation in relationships.

Commercialization: The process of developing and marketing commercial products (e.g., drugs, medical devices, or other technologies) from research. See also copyright, intellectual property.

Common law: A body of law based on judicial decisions and rulings.

Common Rule: The U.S. Department of Health and Human Services regulations (45 CFR 46) for protecting human subjects, which has been adopted by 17 federal agencies. The Common Rule includes subparts with additional protections for children, neonates, pregnant women and fetuses, and prisoners.

Community review: A process for involving a community in the review of research conducted on members of the community. Some research studies include community advisory boards as a way of involving the community.

Comparability: A measure of whether things can really be compared in a way that is fair and helpful. For example, oranges and grapefruits, because they are both citrus fruits, would have comparability in a study of vitamin C content, but oranges and sausages would not.

Comparative rating scale: A rating scale in which respondents are asked to compare an individual person, concept, or situation with others.

Comparative research design: The study of more than one event, group, or society to isolate explanatory factors. There are two basic strategies in comparative research: (1) the study of elements that differ in many ways but that have some major factor in common, and (2) the study of elements that are highly similar but different in some important aspect, such as modern industrialized nations that have different health insurance systems.

Comparison group: A nonexperimental group to which research participants have not been randomly assigned for purposes of comparison with the experimental group. Not to be confused with control group.

Comparison group posttest-only design: A descriptive research design with two groups, experimental and comparison, in which the dependent variable is measured once for both groups, and only the experimental group receives the treatment (the independent variable).

Comparison group pretest-posttest design: A descriptive research design with two groups, experimental and comparison, in which the dependent variable is measured before and after the treatment for both groups, but only the experimental group receives the treatment.

Compensation: Attempts by researchers to compensate for the lack of treatment for control group members by administering it to them; a threat to internal validity.

Compensatory rivalry: Motivation of control group members to compete with experimental group members; a threat to internal validity.

Competence: The legal right to make decisions for one's self. Adults are considered to be legally competent until they are adjudicated incompetent by a court.

Completeness: One of the four criteria for evaluating research hypotheses.

Complete observer: A term describing one of four possible research roles on a continuum of participant observation research; the complete observer acts simply as an observer and does not participate in the events at hand.

Complete participant: The complete participant's research role, at the far end of the continuum from the complete observer in participant observation research, is characterized by total involvement.

Compliance: In research, complying with laws, institutional policies and ethical guidelines related to research.

Composite index: A combination of scores made of distinct factors or fundamental dimensions.

Comprehensive qualitative review: A nonstatistical synthesis of representative research studies relevant to a research problem, question, or hypothesis.

Computational formulas: A mathematical equation, of a fact or other logical relation, that helps to convey the conceptual basis of statistical tests.

Computer-assisted telephone interviewing (CATI): A method of interviewing people over the phone; CATI uses a computer to choose the interviewees and to ask questions and record answers as well as to keep track of information.

Computerized retrieval systems: Systems in which abstracts, indexes, and subject bibliographies are incorporated in computerized databases to facilitate information retrieval.

Concept mapping: Grouping ideas or results based on how alike they are and showing the groups in picture form.

Concept: An understanding, an idea, or a mental image; a way of viewing and categorizing objects, processes, relations, and events.

Conceptual classification system: The strategy for conceiving how units of qualitative data relate to each other; the method used to depict patterns that emerge from the various coding levels in qualitative data.

Conceptual framework: A frame of reference that serves to guide a research study and is developed from theories, findings from a variety of other research studies, and the author's personal experiences and values.

Conceptual validity: See construct validity.

Conceptualization: The process of selecting the specific concepts to include in positivist and interpretive research studies.

Conclusion: A summary of the key points and a statement of opinion or decisions reached about the research study.

Concurrent validity: A form of criterion validity that is concerned with the ability of a measuring instrument to predict accurately an individual's status by comparing concurrent ratings (or scores) on one or more measuring instruments.

Conduct: Action or behavior. For example, conducting research involves performing actions related to research, such as designing experiments, collecting data, analyzing data, and so on.

Confidence interval: Quantifies the uncertainty in measurement. It is usually reported as a 95% CI, which is the range of values within which it can be 95% certain that the true value for the whole population lies.

Confidentiality: The obligation to keep some types of information confidential or secret; the researcher knows how a particular participant responded and has agreed not to divulge the information to anyone else; not to be confused with anonymity.

Confirmability: A concept that researchers should fully explain or disclose the data that they are basing their interpretations on, or at least make those data available. Confirmability can be improved by maintaining precise data records and keeping all data for additional scrutiny.

Conflict of interest (COI): A situation in which a person has a financial, personal, political, or other interest that is likely to bias his or her judgment or decision making concerning the performance of his or her ethical or legal obligations or duties.

Conflict of interest, apparent or perceived: A situation in which a person has a financial, personal, political, or other interest that is not likely to bias his or her judgment or decision-making concerning the performance of his or her ethical or legal obligation or duties but which may appear to an outside observer to bias his or her judgement or decision-making.

Conflict of interest, institutional: A situation in which an institution (such as a university) has financial, political, or other interests that are likely to bias institutional decision-making concerning the performance of institutional ethical or legal duties.

Conflict of interest, management: Strategies for minimizing the adverse impacts of a conflict of interest, such as disclosure, oversight, or recusal/prohibition.

Confounding factors: The inability to tell between the separate impacts of two or more factors on a single outcome. For example, one may find it difficult to tell between the separate impacts of genetics and environmental factors on depression.

Confounding variable: A variable operating in a specific situation in such a way that its effects cannot be separated; the effects of an extraneous variable thus confound the interpretation of a research study's findings.

Consent: See informed consent.

Consequentialism: An approach to ethics, such as utilitarianism, that emphasizes maximizing good over bad consequences resulting from actions or policies.

Consistency: Holding steadfast to the same principles and procedures in the qualitative data-analysis process.

Constant: A concept that does not vary and does not change; a characteristic that has the same value for all research participants or events in a research study.

Constant comparative method: A method of data analysis from grounded theory in which the researcher constantly compares new data to data already placed in existing categories, to help develop and define that category and decide if a new category should be created.

Constant error: Systematic error in measurement; error due to factors that consistently or systematically affect the variable being measured and that are concerned with the relatively stable qualities of respondents to a measuring instrument.

Constant variable: A variable that is not changed during the research study.

Construct: A general idea that tries to explain something; for example, social status is a construct.

Constructivism: A belief that that there is no universally agreed upon reality or universal "truth." Rather, meaning is socially constructed by individuals interacting with their world. Through that interaction, each individual creates his or her own unique understandings of the world. As a result, there are multiple constructions and interpretations of reality, so multiple 'truths' exist. These interpretations change, depending upon time and circumstances, so reality is not universal but person, context, and time bound.

Construct validity: The degree to which a measuring instrument successfully measures a theoretical construct; the degree to which explanatory concepts account for variance in the scores of an instrument; also referred to as conceptual validity in meta-analyses.

Content analysis: A form of analysis that usually counts and reports the frequency of concepts/words/ behaviors held within the data. The researcher develops brief descriptions of the themes or meanings, called codes. Similar codes may at a later stage in the analysis be grouped together to form categories.

Content validity: The extent to which the content of a measuring instrument reflects the concept that is being measured and in fact measures that concept and not another.

Contextual detail: The particulars of the environment in which the case (or unit of analysis) is embedded; provides a basis for understanding and interpreting case study data and results.

Continuing review: In human subjects research, subsequent review of a study after it has been approved by an institutional review board. Continuing review usually happens on an annual basis.

Continuous variable: Something that has an unlimited number of possible values; for example, height, weight, and age are all continuous because a person's height, weight, or age could be measured in smaller and smaller fractions between the numbers of the whole inches, pounds, or years.

Contradictory evidence: Identifying themes and categories that raise questions about the conclusions reached at the end of qualitative data analysis; outliers or extreme cases that are inconsistent or contradict the conclusions drawn from qualitative data; also called negative evidence.

Contributing partner: A social work role in which the social worker joins forces with others who perform various roles in positivist and interpretive research studies.

Control group: A group of randomly assigned research participants in a research study who do not receive the experimental treatment and are used for comparison purposes; not to be confused with comparison group.

Control variable: A variable, other than the independent variable(s) of primary interest, whose effects we can determine; an intervening variable that has been controlled for in the study's research design.

Convenience sampling: A nonprobability sampling procedure that relies on the closest and most available research participants to constitute a sample.

Convergent validity: The degree to which different measures of a construct yield similar results, or converge.

Copyright: A right, granted by a government, that prohibits unauthorized copying, performance, or alteration of creative works. Copyright laws include a fair use exemption that allows limited, unauthorized uses for noncommercial purposes.

Correction (or errata): Fixing a minor problem with a published paper. A minor problem is one that does not impact the reliability or integrity of the data or results. Journals publish correction notices and identify corrected papers in electronic databases to alert the scientific community to problems with the paper. See also retraction.

Correlated variables: Variables whose values are associated; values of one variable tend to be associated in a systematic way with values in the others.

Correlation: A measure of how well two or more variables change together.

Correlation coefficient: A decimal number between 0.00 and ±1.00 that indicates the degree to which two variables are related.

Cost-benefit analysis: An analytical procedure that not only determines the costs of the program itself but also considers the monetary benefits of the program's effects.

Cost-effectiveness analysis: An analytical procedure that assesses the costs of the program itself; the monetary benefits of the program's effects are not assessed.

Council on Social Work Education (CSWE): The official educational organization that sets minimum curriculum standards for bachelor of social work (BSW) and master of social work (MSW) programs throughout the United States.

Covariance: When changes in one variable are accompanied by changes in another variable. For example, if a person takes a vocabulary test and a reading comprehension test, changes in scores on one test might be accompanied with changes in scores on the other test.

Covariate: A variable that may affect the relationship between two variables of interest, but is not of intrinsic interest itself. The researcher may choose to control for or statistically reduce the effect of a covariate.

Cover letter: A letter to respondents or research participants that is written under the official letterhead of the sponsoring organization and describes the research study and its purpose.

Credibility: A concept that researchers should maximize the accuracy of how they define concepts and how they characterize the people they are investigating—with a particular focus on how the various participants feel about the interpretations the researcher makes. Credibility can be enhanced by using prolonged engagement, careful observation, triangulation, peer debriefing, negative case analysis, and member checks.

Criterion validity: The degree to which the scores obtained on a measuring instrument are comparable with scores from an external criterion believed to measure the same concept.

Criterion variable: The variable whose values are predicted from measurements of the predictor variable.

Critical ethnography: A type of ethnography that examines cultural systems of power, prestige, privilege, and authority in society. Critical ethnographers study marginalized

groups from different classes, races, and genders to advocate the needs of these participants.

Critical thinking: Understanding the meaning of a statement, judging ambiguity, judging whether an inductive conclusion is warranted, and judging whether statements made by authorities are acceptable; sometimes called directional thinking.

Cronbach's alpha: A number showing whether all the items on a scale or test are related and pulling in the same direction.

Cross-comparability: The degree in which similarities and differences in the characteristics of research participants from different groups can be assessed.

Cross-cultural: An interaction between individuals from different cultures. The term cross-cultural is generally used to describe comparative studies of cultures. Intercultural is also used for the same meaning.

Cross-cultural awareness: Develops from cross-cultural knowledge as the learner understands and appreciates the deeper functioning of a culture.

Cross-cultural communication: A field of study that looks at how people from differing cultural backgrounds try to communicate; also referred to as intercultural communication.

Cross-cultural communication skills: Refers to the ability to recognize cultural differences and similarities when dealing with someone from another culture and also the ability to recognize features of one's own behavior that are affected by culture.

Cross-cultural comparisons: Research studies that include culture as a major variable; studies that compare two or more diverse cultural groups.

Cross-cultural competence: The final stage of cross-cultural learning that signals the individual's ability to work effectively across cultures.

Cross-cultural knowledge: Refers to a surface level familiarization with cultural characteristics, values, beliefs and behaviors. It is vital to basic cross-cultural understanding and without it cross-cultural competence cannot develop.

Cross-cultural method (comparative method): A way of studying different cultural groups to see how they are the same and how they are different.

Cross-cultural sensitivity: Refers to an individual's ability to read into situations, contexts, and behaviors that are culturally rooted; consequently the individual is able to react to them suitably.

Crossover participants: A type of intervention assignment in which participants may receive different interventions during the life of the study.

Crossover study design: The administration of two or more experimental therapies, one after the other, in a specified or random order to the same group of people.

Cross-sectional research design: A survey research design in which data are collected to indicate characteristics of a sample or population at a particular moment in time.

Cross-sectional study: Research studies that compare people at one time only. Cause and effect cannot be determined in this type of study.

Cross-tabulation table: A simple table showing the joint frequency distribution of two or more nominal-level variables.

Cross-validation: A method used to prove the validity of a test by administering it a second time on a new selected group from the same population.

Cultural alienation: The process of devaluing or abandoning one's own culture or cultural background in favor of another.

Cultural boundaries: Those invisible lines that divide territories, cultures, traditions, practices, and worldviews.

Cultural competency: The ability to respond respectfully and effectively to people of all cultures, classes, ethnic backgrounds, and religions in a manner that recognizes and values cultural differences and similarities.

Cultural components: Attributes that vary from culture to culture, including religion, language, architecture, cuisine, technology, music, dance, sports, medicine, dress, gender roles, laws, education, government, agriculture, economy, grooming, values, work ethic, etiquette, courtship, recreation, and gestures.

Cultural construct: The idea that the characteristics people attribute to social categories such as gender, illness, death, status of women, and status of men are culturally defined.

Cultural convergence: An idea that increased communication among the peoples of the world via the Internet will lead to the differences among national cultures becoming smaller over time, eventually resulting in the formation of a single global culture.

Cultural diversity: Differences (e.g., in race, language, or religion) in one community, organization, or nation.

Cultural encapsulation: The assumption that differences between groups represent some deficit or pathology.

Cultural identity: The identity of a group or culture, or of individuals as belonging to a group or culture that affects their view of themselves. People who feel they belong to the same culture share a common set of norms.

Culturally equivalent: Similarity in the meaning of a construct between two cultures.

Cultural relativity: The belief that human thought and action can be judged only from the perspective of the culture out of which they have grown.

Cultural sensitivity: A necessary component of cultural competence, meaning that we make an effort to be aware of the potential and actual cultural factors that affect our interactions with others.

Cultural traits: Distinguishing features of a culture such as language, dress, religion, values, and an emphasis on family; these traits are shared throughout that culture.

Cultural values: The individual's desirable or preferred way of acting or knowing.

Culture: The shared values, norms, traditions, customs, arts, history, folklore, and institutions of a group of people.

Culture of integrity: The idea that the institutional culture plays a key role in preventing research misconduct and promoting research integrity. Strategies to promote a culture of integrity include education and mentoring in the responsible conduct of research; research policy development; institutional support for research ethics oversight, consultation, and curriculum development; and ethical leadership.

Cumulative frequency distribution: A graphic depiction of how many times groups of scores appear in a sample.

Cut-and-paste method: A method of analyzing qualitative data whereby the researcher cuts segments of the transcript and sorts these cuttings into relevant groupings; it can be done manually or with computer assistance.

Data: Numbers, words, or scores, or other information generated by positivist and interpretive research studies. The word data is plural.

Data analysis: A systematic process of working with the data to provide an understanding of the research participant's experiences. While there are several methods of qualitative analysis that can be used, the aim is always to provide an understanding through the researcher's interpretation of the data.

Data and safety monitoring board (DSMB): A committee that monitors data from human subjects research to protect participants from harm and promote their welfare. DSMBs may recommend to an institutional review board that a study be stopped or altered.

Data archive: A place where many data sets are stored and from which data can be accessed.

Data auditing: See audit.

Database: A collection of information organized for retrieval. In libraries, databases usually contain references to sources retrievable by a variety of means. Databases may contain bibliographic citations, descriptive abstracts, full-text documents, or a combination.

Data coding: Translating data from one language or format into another, usually to make it readable for a computer.

Data collection: The gathering of information through surveys, tests, interviews, experiments, library records, and so on.

Data-collection method: Procedures specifying techniques to be employed, measuring instruments to be used, and activities to be conducted in implementing a positivist or interpretive research study.

Data imputation: The use of statistical methods to fill in or replace missing or lost data. Imputation is not considered to be fabrication if it is done honestly and appropriately.

Data management: Practices and policies related to recording, storing, auditing, archiving, analyzing, interpreting, sharing, and publishing data.

Data matrix: A table where the variable name is entered at the tops of the columns that will contain the data for that variable, and the case records are entered across the rows.

Data outlier: A data point that is more than two standards deviations from the mean. Removal of outliers without articulating a legitimate reason may constitute data, falsification.

Data processing: Recording, storing, calling up, and analyzing information with a computer program.

Data repository: A centralized data storage system containing the data collected from different research sites.

Data saturation: As researchers collect data and simultaneously create categories through data analysis, they will get to a point at which these categories are "saturated"—no new information adds to their understanding of the category.

Data set: A collection of related data items, such as the answers given by respondents to all the questions in a survey.

Data source: The provider of the data, whether it be primary (the original source) or secondary (an intermediary between the research participant and the researcher analyzing the data).

Data use agreement (DUA): An agreement between institutions for the sharing and use of research data.

Datum: Singular of data.

Debriefing: Involves explaining the true purpose of the research study to the participants after the study is completed, along with why the deception was necessary in the first place.

Deception: In human subjects research, using methods to deceive the participants about the goals and nature of a study or the methods, tests, interventions, or procedures used in the study; occurs as the result of researchers providing false or incomplete information to research participants for the purpose of misleading them. Should be used with extreme caution.

Deception and consent: Universal ethical concerns about the rights of participants to be informed honestly and openly, and not to be coerced into participating in a study.

Decision-making capacity (DMC): The ability to make sound decisions. DMC is often situational and comes in degrees; for example, a person may be able to order food from a menu but not be able to make a decision concerning complex medical treatment. Factors that can compromise DMC include mental illness or disability, extreme emotional stress, drugs, age, or serious physical illness. DMC is not the same as legal competence: a demented adult may be legally competent but lack DMC.

Deduction: A conclusion about a specific case(s) based on the assumption that it shares a characteristic with an entire class of similar cases.

Deductive thinking: A way of reasoning that works from the more general to the more specific. It begins with a general theory, which generates predictions about specific phenomena. These theories can be tested empirically by seeing if the predictions are true. The opposite is inductive thinking.

Degrees of freedom (df): The number of values/amounts that are free to vary in one calculation. Degrees of freedom are used in the formulas that test hypotheses statistically.

De-identified data or samples: Data or biological samples that have been stripped of information, such as name or medical record number, that personally identifies individuals.

Demand needs: When needs are defined by only those individuals who indicate that they feel or perceive the need themselves.

Demographic data: Vital and social facts that describe a sample or a population.

Demography: The study of a group of people, including its size, how old different members are, what sex and race different members belong to, how many people are married, how many years they went to school, and so on.

Demoralization: Feelings of deprivation among control group members that may cause them to drop out of a research study; a threat to internal validity.

Deontology: An approach to ethics, such as Kantianism, that emphasizes adherence to rules or principles of conduct.

Dependability: An emphasis on the need for researchers to account for the ever-changing context and shifting conditions within which research occurs; the soundness of both the steps taken in a qualitative data analysis and the conclusions reached. In their published accounts, the researcher should describe the changes that occur in the setting and how these changes affected the way the researcher approached the study.

Dependent events: Events that influence the probability of each other occurring.

Dependent *t*-test: A statistical test that assesses whether the means of two related groups are statistically different from each other.

Dependent variable: A variable dependent on, or caused by, another variable; an outcome variable that is not manipulated directly but is measured to determine whether the independent variable has had an effect.

Derived scores: Raw scores of research participants or groups converted in such a way that meaningful comparisons with other individuals or groups are possible.

Descriptive research: Research studies undertaken to increase precision in the definition of knowledge in a problem area where less is known than at the explanatory level; situated in the middle of the knowledge continuum.

Descriptive statistics: Methods used for summarizing and describing data in a clear and precise manner.

Design bias: Any effect that systematically distorts the outcome of a research study so that the study's results are not representative of the phenomenon under investigation.

Determinism: A contention in positivist research studies that only an event that is true over time and place and that will occur independent of beliefs about it (a predetermined event) permits the generalization of a study's findings; one of the four main limitations of the positivist research approach.

Deterministic causation: When a particular effect appears, the associated cause is always present; no other variables influence the relationship between cause and effect; the link between an independent variable that brings about the occurrence of the dependent variable every time.

Diary studies: First-person or third-person case studies in which individuals keep a reflective journal using introspection and/or retrospection.

Dichotomous variable: A variable that can take on only one of two values.

Differential scale: A questionnaire-type scale in which respondents are asked to consider questions representing different positions along a continuum and to select those with which they agree.

Differential selection: A potential lack of equivalency among preformed groups of research participants; a threat to internal validity.

Diffusion of treatments: Problems that may occur when experimental and control group members talk to each other about a research study; a threat to internal validity.

d index: A measure of effect size in a meta-analysis.

Direct observation: An obtrusive data-collection method in which the focus is entirely on the behaviors of a group, or persons, being observed.

Direct observation notes: The first level of field notes, usually chronologically organized, containing a detailed description of what was seen and heard and potentially also including summary notes made after an interview.

Directional hypothesis: See one-tailed hypotheses.

Directional test: See one-tailed hypotheses.

Direct relationship: A relationship between two variables such that high values of one variable are found with high values of the second variable.

Discourse analysis: The linguistic analysis of naturally occurring connected speech or written discourse. It is also concerned with language use in social contexts, and in particular with interaction or dialogue between speakers.

Discrete variables: Separate values or groupings, with no possible values (numbers, measurements) between them. The only choices are separate categories; for example, "male" and "female" are discrete variables.

Discriminant validity: The degree to which a construct can be empirically differentiated or discriminated from other constructs.

Discrimination: Treating people differently based on irrelevant characteristics, such as skin color, ethnicity, or gender.

Disinformation: False information that is intended to mislead, especially propaganda issued by a government organization to a rival power or the media.

Distractors: Any questions or events that divert attention from what is being tested. Usually, items in a questionnaire to keep subjects from understanding what's being tested.

Distribution: The measure of how often something is found in the group being studied; also the range of those measures.

Divergent validity: The extent to which a measuring instrument differs from other instruments that measure unrelated constructs.

Diversity: The understanding that each individual is unique, and the recognition of individual differences along the dimensions of race, ethnicity, gender, sexual orientation, socioeconomic status, age, physical abilities, religious beliefs, political beliefs, or other ideologies.

Domain: An area or topic or focus of a research study.

Dominant culture: Usually the one "dominant" culture in each area that forms the basis for defining that culture. This is determined by power and control in cultural institutions (church, government, education, mass media, and monetary systems.

Double-barreled question: A question in a measuring instrument that contains two questions in one, usually joined by an and or an or.

Double-blinding: Processes used to prevent human research subjects and researchers from discovering who is receiving an experimental treatment vs. a placebo. Double-blinding is used to control for the placebo effect.

Dropout: A person who was being studied but couldn't keep on with the study or didn't want to continue.

Dual use research: Research that can be readily used for beneficial or harmful purposes.

Dummy variable: A piece of information that has only one of only two possible values.

Duplicate publication: Republishing the same paper or data without proper acknowledgment.

Duration recording: A method of data collection that includes direct observation of the target problem and recording of the length of time each occurrence lasts within a specified observation period.

Ecological fallacy: A mistake based on believing that what is true for a group must also be true for each individual in the group.

Edge coding: Adding a series of blank lines on the right side of the response category in a measuring instrument to aid in processing the data.

Effectiveness: The measure of how well something does what it is supposed to do for a certain group of people under normal conditions.

Effect size: A measurement of the strength of a relationship between two variables. In meta-analysis, the most widely used measure of the dependent variable—the effect size statistic provides a measure of the magnitude of the relationship found between the variables of interest and allows for the computation of summary statistics that apply to the analysis of all the studies considered as a whole.

Efficacy study: A study comparing an experimental group (who receive the treatment) to a control group (who do not receive the treatment).

Egocentric thinking: Results from the unfortunate fact that humans do not naturally consider the rights and needs of others.

Elaboration: A way of studying or thinking about other causes that may also change an effect, instead of looking at only one cause.

Eligibility criteria: The detailed rules for what kind of people a researcher will let into a certain study. For example, being over age 60 and having a diagnosis of anxiety disorder could be the eligibility criteria for a study about how a new medication works for elderly, anxious people.

Embedded design: A mixed-methods design in which the researcher collects and analyzes quantitative and qualitative data within a traditional quantitative or qualitative design to enhance the overall design in some way.

Emergency research: In human subjects research, research that is conducted when a subject who cannot provide informed consent faces a life-threatening illness that requires immediate treatment and has no available legally authorized representative to provide consent. The Food and Drug Administration has developed special rules for emergency research involving products that it regulates.

Emergent mixed-methods designs: Designs where the use of mixed methods arises due to issues that develop while conducting the research.

Emerging themes: Concepts (explanatory ideas) that are identified from the data in the first stages of analysis and given a label or code that describes them. Concepts that are closely linked in meaning can be formed into categories, and categories that have similar meanings can be brought together into a theme. The term emerging themes refers to the development or "emergence" of themes from the data, and this overall method of analysis is referred to as thematic analysis.

Empirical: Knowledge derived from the five ways of knowing.

Empirical method: A kind of research that is based on believing that all real facts must come through the senses or a practical experiment, not just through reasoning. A conclusion must be proven by facts (results that can be measured, like blood pressure or body weight) rather than just "following" or "making sense."

Enculturation: A process whereby an established culture teaches an individual its accepted norms and values by establishing a context of boundaries and correctness that dictates what is and is not permissible within that society's framework.

Equipoise: Research studies that randomize their research participants to different treatment groups, which should be conducted only if there is a true uncertainty about which of the treatment alternatives is most likely to benefit them; also called the uncertainty principle.

Equivalency data: When there is more than one group (e.g., control and experimental) in a study, the researcher must ensure that both groups are equally represented by using equivalency data to avoid discrepancies (e.g., an equal number of females in both groups).

Error: An unintended adverse outcome; a mistake.

Error of central tendency: A measurement error due to the tendency of observers to rate respondents in the middle of a variable's value range, rather than consistently too high or too low.

Error of measurement: See measurement error.

Ethical dilemma: A situation in which two or more potential actions appear to be equally justifiable from an ethical point of view. That is, one must choose between the lesser of two evils or the greater of two goods.

Ethical reasoning: Making a decision in response to a moral dilemma based a careful and thorough assessment of the different options in light of the facts and circumstances and ethical considerations.

Ethical relativism: The view that ethical standards are relative to a particular culture, society, or historical period. (When in Rome, do as the Romans do.)

Ethical theory: A set of statements that attempts to unify, systematize, and explain our moral experience—our intuitions or judgments about right and wrong, good and bad, and so on.

Ethical universalism: The view that the same standards of ethics apply to all people at all times.

Ethics, applied: The study of ethics in specific situations, professions, or institutions; for example, medical ethics and research ethics.

Ethics in research: Positivist and interpretive data that are collected and analyzed with careful attention to their accuracy, fidelity to logic, and respect for the feelings and rights of the research participants; one of the four main criteria for evaluating research problem areas and formulating research questions out of the problem areas.

Ethics, meta: The study of the meaning, truth, and justification of ethical statements.

Ethics, normative versus descriptive: Normative ethics studies the standards of conduct and methods of reasoning that people ought to follow. Descriptive ethics studies the standards of conduct and reasoning processes that people in fact follow. Normative ethics seeks to prescribe and evaluate conduct, whereas descriptive ethics seeks to describe and explain conduct. Disciplines such as philosophy and religious studies take a normative approach to ethics, whereas sociology, anthropology, psychology, neuroscience, and evolutionary biology take a descriptive approach.

Ethnic group: A group characterized by cultural similarities (shared among members of that group) and differences (between that group and others).

Ethnicity: A term that implies a common ancestry and cultural heritage and encompasses customs, values, beliefs, and behaviors.

Ethnocentricity: Assumptions about normal behavior that are based on one's own cultural framework without taking cultural relativity into account; the failure to acknowledge alternative worldviews; a belief in the superiority of one's own

ethnic group; seeing the world through the lenses of one's own people or culture so that one's own culture always looks best and becomes the pattern everyone else should fit into.

Ethnograph: A computer program designed for qualitative data analyses.

Ethnographic: A form of content analysis used to document and explain the communication of meaning as well as to verify theoretical relationships; any of several methods of describing social or cultural life based on direct, systematic observation, such as becoming a participant in a social system.

Ethnography: A qualitative research methodology that enables a detailed description and interpretation of a cultural or social group to be generated. Data collection is primarily through participant observation or through one-to-one interviews. The importance of gathering data on context is stressed, as only in this way can an understanding of social processes and the behavior that comes from them be developed.

Ethnomethodology: A research method that focuses on the commonsense understanding of social life held by ordinary people (the ethos), usually as discovered through participant observation. Often the observer's own methods of making sense of the situation become the object of investigation.

Evaluation: A form of appraisal using valid and reliable research methods. There are numerous types of evaluations geared to produce data that in turn produce information that helps in the decision-making process. Data from evaluations are used to develop quality programs and services.

Evaluative research designs: Case- and program-level research designs that apply various research designs and data-collection methods to find out whether an intervention (or treatment) worked at the case level and whether a social work program worked at the program level.

Evidence-based guidelines: Sometimes referred to as practice guidelines, systematically compiled and organized statements of empirically tested knowledge and procedures that help social workers select and implement interventions that are most effective and appropriate for attaining the desired outcomes.

Evidence-based practice: A process in which practitioners integrate information about client needs and values with knowledge of research findings on effective interventions.

Evidence hierarchies: Hierarchies that are commonly used for ranking interventions or evidence-based practices.

Exclusion criteria: The basis for excluding subjects from the sample who do not meet the basic parameters for participation within the study because they do not have a certain characteristic or trait.

Exculpatory language: Language in an informed consent form, contract, or other document intended to excuse a party from legal liability.

Exempt research: Human subjects research that is exempted from review by an institutional review board. Some types of exempt research include research on existing human samples or data in which the researcher cannot readily identify individuals and anonymous surveys of individuals.

Existing documents: Physical records left over from the past.

Existing statistics: Previously calculated numerical summaries of data that exist in the public domain.

Expected outcome: The effects and unique contributions attributed to an intervention or specific treatment that the investigator expects to find.

Expedited review: In human subjects research, review of a study by the chair of an institutional review board (or designee) instead of by the full board. Expedited review may be conducted on new studies that pose minimal risks to subjects, for continuing review in which a study is no longer recruiting subjects, or on amendments to approved studies that make only minor changes.

Experience: Learning what is true through personal past experiences; one of the five ways of knowing.

Experiment: A research study in which we have control over the levels of the independent variable and over the assignment of research participants, or objects, to different experimental conditions; an organized process used to test hypotheses.

Experimental designs: (1) Explanatory research designs or "ideal experiments." (2) Case-level research designs that examine the question, "Did the client system improve because of social work intervention?"

Experimental group: In an experimental research design, the group of research participants exposed to the manipulation of the independent variable; also referred to as a treatment group.

Explanatory research: "Ideal" research studies undertaken to infer cause-and-effect and directional relationships in areas where a number of substantial research findings are already in place; situated at the top end of the knowledge continuum.

Explanatory research questions: Questions formulated to infer cause-and-effect and directional relationships in areas where a number of substantial research findings are already in place; situated at the top end of the knowledge continuum.

Exploitation: Taking unfair advantage of someone else.

Exploratory analysis: A type of analysis that is used to understand an observable fact or event when there are no assumptions or expectations about the outcomes.

Exploratory research: Research studies undertaken to gather data in areas of inquiry where very little is already known; situated at the lowest end of the knowledge continuum. See nonexperimental design.

Expression of concern: In a scholarly journal, a published statement that a paper has come under suspicion for wrongdoing or is being investigated for possible research misconduct.

External evaluation: An evaluation that is conducted by someone who does not have any connection with the program; usually an evaluation that is requested by the agency's funding sources. This type of evaluation complements an in-house evaluation.

External validity: The extent to which the findings of a research study can be generalized outside the specific research situation.

Extraneous data: Data that are not relevant to the specific question or area being analyzed.

Extraneous variables: See rival hypothesis.

Fabrication: Making up data or results.

Face-to-face interview: A meeting to ask and answer questions in person, not over the phone or by mail or e-mail.

Face validity: The degree to which a measurement has self-evident meaning and measures what it appears to measure.

Fact: A statement that can be proven true.

Factor analysis: A type of study used to find the underlying causes and characteristics of something. The general purpose of this test is to take the information in a large number of "variables" and to link it with a smaller number of "factors" or causes.

Fake news: A type of yellow journalism or propaganda that consists of deliberate disinformation or hoaxes spread via traditional print and broadcast news media or online social media; fabricated information that mimics news media content in form but not in organizational process or intent. The false information is often caused by reporters paying sources for stories, an unethical practice called checkbook journalism. The news then often reverberates as misinformation via social media and occasionally finds its way to the mainstream media as well.

Falsification: Changing, omitting, or manipulating data or results deceptively; or deceptive manipulation of research materials or experiments.

Feasibility: One of the four main criteria for evaluating research problem areas and formulating research questions out of the problem areas.

Feasibility study: A first, small study to see whether a larger study will be possible and to see what problems the larger study might have; also called a pilot study.

Feedback: When data and information are returned to the persons who originally provided or collected them; used for informed decision making at the case and program levels; a basic principle underlying the design of evaluations.

Fidelity: The observance of the actual treatment delivery to the set of rules originally developed. Fidelity assessment considers to what degree the program was implemented as planned. Alternatively referred to as "treatment integrity."

Field notes: Detailed notes written or recorded while observing in the research setting, or made during or after interviewing research participants. Some researchers also include their own personal ideas in their field notes, while others put them in analytic memos.

Field research: Research conducted in a real-life setting, not in a laboratory. The researcher neither creates nor manipulates anything within the study, only observes it.

Field-tested: The pilot of an instrument or research method in conditions equivalent to those that will be encountered in the research study.

Fieldwork: Refers to the research activity of collecting data through observation (and other means) in the "field," the designated research setting or settings.

File drawer problem: (1) In literature searches or reviews, the difficulty in locating studies that have not been published or are not easily retrievable. (2) In meta-analyses, errors in effect size due to reliance on published articles showing statistical significance.

First-hand data: Data obtained from people who directly experience the problem being studied.

First-level coding: A process of identifying meaning units in a transcript, organizing the meaning units into categories, and assigning names to the categories.

Flexibility: The degree to which the design and procedures of a research study can be changed to adapt to contextual demands of the research setting.

Floor effects: A term used to describe what happens when a group of subjects in a study have scores that are close to or at the lower limit (floor) of a variable. For example, the majority of subjects score very poorly because the task is too difficult.

Focus group interview: Used to elicit the views of a group (usually around 6 to 10 individuals) who have common experiences or interests. They are brought together with the purpose of discussing a particular subject, under the guidance of a facilitator.

Follow-up: Contact with a person being studied, made after the first stage of the study, to see if there have been changes since then, and to see how long changes last. The term can also mean the length of time a person is studied, or the length of time between stages in the study.

Formative evaluation: A type of evaluation that focuses on obtaining data that are helpful in planning the program and in improving its implementation and performance.

Framework: A method of qualitative data analysis involving five key stages: familiarization, identifying a thematic framework, indexing, charting, and mapping and interpretation.

Fraud: Knowingly misrepresenting the truth or concealing a material (or relevant) fact to induce someone to make a decision to his or her detriment. Some forms of research misconduct may also qualify as fraud. A person who commits fraud may face civil or criminal legal liability.

Freedom of Information Act (FOIA): A law enacted in the United States and other countries that allows the public to obtain access to government documents, including documents related to government-funded scientific research such as data, protocols, and e-mails. Several types of documents are exempt from FOIA requests, including classified research and confidential information pertaining to human subjects research.

Frequency distributions: A mathematical function showing the number of instances in which a variable takes each of its possible values.

Frequency polygons: Graphical devices for understanding the shapes of distributions.

Frequency recording: A method of data collection by direct observations in which each occurrence of the target problem is recorded during a specified observation period.

F-test: A statistical test (also known as analysis of variance) used to compare two or more groups for statistically significant differences between/among them.

Fugitive data: Informal information found outside regular publishing channels.

Gaining access: A term used in interpretive research studies to describe the process of engagement and relationship development between the researcher and the research participants.

Gatekeeper: A person whose permission or approval is necessary for a researcher to gain access to a research site or setting.

Generalizable explanation evaluation model: An evaluation model whose proponents believe that many solutions are possible for any one social problem and that the effects of programs will differ under different conditions.

Generalizing results: Extending or applying the findings of a research study to individuals or situations not directly involved in the original research study; the ability to extend or apply the findings of a research study to subjects or situations that were not directly investigated.

Goal Attainment Scale (GAS): A modified measurement scale used to evaluate case or program outcomes.

Good clinical practices (GCPs): Rules and procedures for conducting clinical trials safely and rigorously.

Good record-keeping practices (GRKPs): Rules and procedures for keeping research records. Records should be thorough, accurate, complete, organized, signed and dated, and backed up.

Government documents: Documents issued by local, state, and federal governments; they include reports of legislative committee hearings and investigations, studies commissioned by legislative commissions and executive agencies, statistical compilations such as the census, the regular and special reports of executive agencies, and much more.

Grand tour questions: Queries in which research participants are asked to provide wide-ranging background information; mainly used in interpretive research studies.

Graph: A diagram that shows the relationship between two variables.

Graphic rating scale: A rating scale that describes an attribute on a continuum from one extreme to the other, with points of the continuum ordered in equal intervals and then assigned values.

Grounded theory: A qualitative research methodology with systematic guides for the collection and analysis of data that aims to generate a theory that is "grounded in" or formed from the data and is based on inductive reasoning. This contrasts with other approaches that stop at the point of describing the participants' experiences. The researcher uses qualitative data collection methods like interviews to collect information until data saturation is reached, then groups ideas together into categories using the constant comparison method to develop a context-specific or "substantive" theory.

Group evaluation designs: Evaluation designs that are conducted with groups of cases for the purpose of assessing to what degree program objectives have been achieved.

Group research designs: Research designs conducted with two or more groups of cases, or research participants, for the purpose of answering research questions or testing hypotheses.

Guideline: A nonbinding recommendation for conduct.

Halo effect: A measurement error due to the tendency of an observer to be influenced by a favorable trait of a research participant.

Harassment: Repeatedly annoying, bothering, or intimidating research participants.

Hawthorne effect: Effects on research participants' behaviors or attitudes attributable to their knowledge that they are taking part in a research study; a reactive effect; a threat to external validity.

Helsinki Declaration: Ethical guidelines for conducting medical research involving human subjects research adopted by the World Medical Association.

Heterogeneity of respondents: The extent to which a research participant differs from other research participants.

Heuristic: A theory used to stimulate creative thought and scientific activity.

Historical data: Collected in an effort to study the past.

Historical research: The process by which we study the past; a method of inquiry that attempts to explain past events based on surviving artifacts.

History in research design: The possibility that events not accounted for in a research design may alter the second and subsequent measurements of the dependent variable; a threat to internal validity.

Homogeneity of respondents: The extent to which a research participant is similar to other research participants.

Honesty: The ethical obligation to tell the truth and avoid deceiving others. In science, some types of dishonesty include data fabrication or falsification, and plagiarism; a key ingredient of a social work researcher and practitioner.

Human subjects protections: Rules and laws to make sure the people being studied in a research project are treated fairly.

Human subjects research: Research involving the collection, storage, or use of private data or biological samples from living individuals by means of interactions, interventions, surveys, or other research methods or procedures.

Hypothesis: A prediction of whether the independent variable will have an effect on the dependent variable or a prediction of the nature of the effect; an educated guess that explains why or how something occurs; a theory-based prediction of the expected results of a research study; a tentative explanation that a relationship between or among variables exists.

Hypothetico-deductive method: A hypothesis-testing approach that a hypothesis is derived on the deductions based from a theory.

Ideographic research: Research studies that focus on unique individuals or situations.

Incidental finding: Information inadvertently discovered during medical treatment or research that was not intentionally sought. For example, if a research subject receives an MRI as part of a brain-imaging study and the researcher notices an area in the fontal cortex that appears to be a tumor, this information would be an incidental finding.

Independence or independently: When one factor does not exert influence on another. For example, what one study participant does should not influence what another participant does. They make decisions independently. Independence is critical for a meaningful statistical analysis.

Independent *t*-test: A statistical test used to determine whether there is a statistically significant difference between the means of two independent samples.

Independent variable: A variable that is not dependent on another variable but is believed to cause or determine changes in the dependent variable; an antecedent variable that is directly manipulated to assess its effect on the dependent variable.

Index: A group of individual measures that, when combined, are meant to indicate some more general characteristic.

Indigenous observers: People who are naturally a part of the research participants' environment and who perform the data-collection function; includes relevant others (e.g., family members, peers) and collaterals (e.g., social workers, staff members).

Indirect measures: A substitute variable, or a collection of representative variables, used when there is no direct measurement of the variable of interest; also called a proxy variable.

Individualism: In individualistic cultures, such as the mainstream North American culture, people work toward individual goals and achievement.

Individualized research results: In human subjects research, results pertaining to a specific individual in a study, such as the subject's pulse, blood pressure, or the results of laboratory tests (e.g., blood sugar levels, blood cell counts, genetic or genomic variants). Individualized results may include intended findings or incidental findings. There is an ongoing ethical controversy concerning whether, when, and how individualized research results should be shared with human subjects. Some argue that individualized results should be returned if they are based on accurate and reliable tests and have clinical utility because inaccurate, unreliable, or uncertain results may be harmful. Others claim that the principle of autonomy implies that subjects should be able to decide whether to receive their results.

Induction (an inductive process): Logical thought process in which generalizations are developed from specific observations: reasoning moves from the particular to the general.

Inductive reasoning: A method of reasoning whereby a conclusion is reached by building on specific observations of events, things, or processes to make inferences or more general statements; applied to data collection and research results to make generalizations to see if they fit a theory.

Inductive thinking: Working from the specific to the more general; taking specific observations or instances, noting patterns, then extrapolating from them to create general conclusions or a general theory. The opposite is deductive thinking.

Infer: To predict something based on what is true about a smaller group of people or about parts of the larger whole; building a larger idea or conclusion from blocks of smaller examples.

Inference: A logical explanation or conclusion based on observations and/or facts.

Inferential statistics: Using a random sample of data taken from a population to describe and make inferences about the population from which the sample was drawn.

Inferring: The process of making an inference, an interpretation based on observations and prior knowledge.

Informant: A person from within the cultural group being studied who provides the researcher with "insider" information.

Information: Something you hope to get from the data once you have analyzed them.

Information anxiety: A feeling attributable to a lack of understanding of information, being overwhelmed by the amount of information to be accessed and understood, or not knowing whether certain information exists.

Informed consent: Based on the principles of beneficence and respect for persons, the process of ensuring that participants understand their role in a study, agree to participate voluntarily, and can withdraw from the study at any time without prejudice.

Informed consent, blanket (general): A provision in an informed consent document that gives general permission to researchers to use the subject's data or samples for various purposes and share them with other researchers.

Informed consent, documentation: A record (such as a form) used to document the process of consent. Research regulations require that consent be documented; however, an institutional review board may decide to waive documentation of consent if the research is minimal risk and (1) the principle risk of the study is breach of confidentiality and the only record linking the subject to the study is the consent form or (2) the research involves procedures that normally do not require written consent outside of the research context.

Informed consent, specific: A provision in an informed consent document that requires researchers to obtain specific permission from the subject before using samples or data for purposes other than those that are part of the study or sharing them with other researchers.

Informed consent, tiered: Provisions in an informed consent document that give the subject various options concerning the use and sharing of samples or data. Options may include blanket consent, specific consent, and other choices.

Informed consent, waiver: In human subjects research, the decision by an institutional review board to waive (or set aside) some or all of the informed consent requirements. Waivers are not usually granted unless they are necessary to conduct the research and pose minimal risks to the subjects.

In-house evaluation: An evaluation that is conducted by someone who works within a program; usually an evaluation for the purpose of promoting better client services; also known as an internal evaluation. This type of evaluation complements an external evaluation.

Institutional review board (IRB): A committee responsible for reviewing and overseeing human subjects research; boards set up by institutions to protect research participants and to ensure that ethical issues are recognized and responded to in a study's research design. An IRB may also be called a research ethics committee (REC) or research ethics board (REB). IRBs usually include members from different backgrounds and disciplines.

Instrumentation: Weaknesses of a measuring instrument, such as invalidity, unreliability, improper administration, or mechanical breakdowns; a threat to internal validity.

Intellectual property: Legally recognized property pertaining to the products of intellectual activity, such as creative works or inventions. Forms of intellectual property include copyrights on creative works and patents on inventions.

Interaction effects: Effects produced by the combination of two or more threats to internal validity.

Internal consistency: The extent to which the scores on two comparable halves of the same measuring instrument are similar; inter-item consistency.

Internal validity: The extent to which it can be demonstrated that the independent variable within a research study is the only cause of change in the dependent variable; overall soundness of the experimental procedures and measuring instruments.

Internet: A global system of interconnected computer networks that use the Internet protocol suite (TCP/IP) to link devices worldwide.

Internet café approach: An approach to assessing research findings in an effort to help one become a better critical thinker.

Interobserver reliability: The stability or consistency of observations made by two or more observers at one point in time.

Interpretation: The researcher's explanation of why participants behave or think in the way that they do. In qualitative research, this is usually based on the data, and is developed through inductive thinking.

Interpretative: Exploration of the human experiential interpretation of any observed phenomena, enabling researchers to gain a better understanding of the underlying processes that may influence behavior.

Interpretive analysis: Analysis emphasizing the role of the researcher as an interpreter of the data, and the self-reflective nature of qualitative research.

Interpretive notes: Notes on the researcher's interpretations of events that are kept separate from the record of the facts noted as direct observations.

Interpretive research approach: Research studies that focus on the facts of nature as they occur under natural conditions and emphasize qualitative description and generalization; a process of discovery sensitive to holistic and ecological issues; a research approach that is complementary to the positivist research approach.

Interquartile range: A measure of statistical dispersion being equal to the difference between the third and first quartiles.

Interrater reliability: The degree to which two or more independent observers, coders, or judges produce consistent results.

Interrupted time-series design: An explanatory research design in which there is only one group of research participants and the dependent variable is measured repeatedly before and after treatment; used in case and program evaluation designs.

Interval level of measurement: The level of measurement with an arbitrarily chosen zero point that classifies its values on an equally spaced continuum.

Interval recording: A method of data collection that involves a continuous direct observation of an individual during specified observation periods divided into equal time intervals.

Intervening variable: See Rival hypothesis.

Intervention: A planned change, such as a new therapy or a new medication; or the act of making this change.

Interview data: Isolated facts that are gathered when research participants respond to carefully constructed research questions; data in the form of words, recorded by transcription.

Interview guide: Also known as an interview schedule, a list of topics and questions that the researcher writes before an interview. It helps the researcher prepare for the interview, ensuring that all the important areas of interest are being considered, and it can also guide the interview itself.

Interviewing: A conversation with a purpose.

Interview protocol: A form used in qualitative research to collect qualitative data. On the form are questions to be asked during an interview and space for recording data gathered during the interview. This protocol also provides space to record essential data such as the time, day, and place of the interview.

Interview schedule: A measuring instrument used to collect data in face-to-face and telephone interviews.

Intraobserver reliability: The stability of observations made by a single observer at several points in time.

Intrusion into lives of research participants: The understanding that specific data-collection methods can have negative consequences for research participants; a criterion for selecting a data-collection method.

Inview: Involves a detailed and careful reading of the subject matter, ensuring that one understands the concepts and follows the author's argument.

Itemized rating scales: A measuring instrument that presents a series of statements that respondents or observers rank in different positions on a specific attribute.

Iteration (an iterative process): Relates to the process of repeatedly returning to the source of the data to ensure that the understandings are truly coming from the data. In practice this means a constant process of collecting data, carrying out a preliminary analysis, and using that to guide the next piece of data collection then continuing this pattern until the data collection is complete.

Journal: A type of periodical usually sold by subscription and containing articles written for specialized or scholarly audiences. Alternatively, a written record of the process of an interpretive research study. Journal entries are made on an ongoing basis throughout the study and include study procedures as well as the researcher's reactions to emerging issues and concerns during the data-analysis process.

Justice: (1) Fair treatment of people. (2) An ethical principle that obligates one to treat people fairly. Distributive justice refers to allocating benefits and harms fairly; procedural justice refers to using fair processes to make decisions that affect people; formal justice refers to treating similar cases in the same way. In human subjects research, the principle of justice implies that subjects should be selected equitably. See also Belmont Report.

Key informants: A subpopulation of research participants who seem to know much more about "the situation" than other research participants.

Knowledge base: A body of knowledge and skills specific to a certain discipline.

Knowledge creator and disseminator: A social work role in which the social worker actually carries out and disseminates the results of a positivist and/or interpretive research study to generate knowledge for our profession.

Knowledge-level continuum: The range of knowledge levels, from exploratory to descriptive to explanatory, at which all research questions can be answered.

Law: A rule enforced by the coercive power of the government. Laws may include statutes drafted by legislative bodies (such as Congress), regulations developed and implemented by government agencies, and legal precedents established by courts (i.e., common law).

Legal authorized representative (LAR): A person, such as a guardian, parent of a minor child, health care agent, or close relative, who is legally authorized to make decisions for another person when they cannot make decisions for themselves. LARs may also be called surrogate decision-makers. See competence, decision-making capacity.

Latent content: In a content analysis, the true meaning, depth, or intensity of a variable or concept under study.

Levels of measurement: The degree to which characteristics of a data set can be modeled mathematically; the higher the level of measurement, the more statistical methods that are applicable.

Lifelong learning: A process where we continue to learn new and exciting stuff throughout our entire life span.

Likert Scale: A scale to show how a person feels about something. It usually includes a range of possible answers, from "strongly agree" to "strongly disagree," which each have a number. The total score is found by adding all these numbers.

Limited review: An existing literature synthesis that summarizes in narrative form the findings and implications of a few research studies.

Linear relationship: A relationship between two variables that are directly related.

Literature review: An article or paper describing published research on a particular topic. The purpose of a literature review (sometimes called a review article) is to select the most important publications on the topic, sort them into categories, and comment on them to provide a quick overview of leading scholarship in that area. Published articles often include a literature review section to place their research in the context of other work in the field.

Literature search: Scanning books and journals for basic, up-to-date research articles on studies relevant to a research question or hypothesis; should be sufficiently thorough to maximize the chance of including all relevant sources.

Logical consistency: The requirement that all the steps within a positivist research study must be logically related to one another.

Logical positivism: A philosophy of science holding that the scientific method of

inquiry is the only source of certain knowledge; in research, focuses on testing hypotheses deduced from theory.

Logistics: In evaluation, refers to getting research participants to do what they are supposed to do, getting research instruments distributed and returned; in general, activities that ensure that the procedural tasks of a research or evaluation study are carried out.

Longitudinal case study: An exploratory research design in which there is only one group of research participants and the dependent variable is measured more than once.

Longitudinal data: Data collected over time from a variable or group of subjects.

Longitudinal research design: A survey research design in which a measuring instrument is administered to a sample of research participants repeatedly over time; used to detect dynamic processes such as opinion change.

Magnitude recording: A direct-observation method of soliciting and recording data on the amount, level, or degree of the target problem during each occurrence.

Mail survey: A questionnaire mailed to people or groups who fill out the form and mail it back to the researcher.

Management Information System (MIS): A way of storing, accessing, and managing data in electronic form.

Manifest content: Content of a communication that is obvious and clearly evident.

Matching: A random assignment technique that assigns research participants to two or more groups so that the experimental and control groups are approximately equivalent in terms of pretest scores or other characteristics, or so that all differences except the experimental condition are eliminated.

Matrix of categories: A method of displaying relationships among themes in analyzing case study data that shows whether changes in categories or degrees along one dimension are associated with changes in the categories of another dimension.

Maturation: Unplanned change in research participants due to mental, physical, or other processes operating over time; a threat to internal validity.

Mean: The sum of the scores in a distribution divided by the number of scores in the distribution.

Meaning units: In a qualitative data analysis, a discrete segment of a transcript that can stand alone as a single idea; can consist of a single word, a partial or complete sentence, a paragraph, or more; used as the basic building blocks for developing categories.

Measurement: The assignment of labels or numerals to the properties or attributes of observations, events, or objects according to specific rules.

Measurement error: Any variation in measurement that cannot be attributed to the variable being measured; variability in responses produced by individual differences and other extraneous variables.

Measures of central tendency: A central or typical value for a probability distribution; the most common measures of central tendency are the mean, median, and mode.

Measuring instrument: Any instrument used to measure a variable.

Media embargo: A policy, adopted by some journals, that allows journalists to have access to a scientific paper before publication provided they agree not to publicly disclose the contents of the paper until it is published. Some journals will refuse to publish papers that have already appeared in the media.

Media myths: The content of television shows, movies, and newspaper and magazine articles.

Median: The midpoint or number in a distribution having 50% of the scores above it and 50% of the scores below it.

Member checking: A process of obtaining feedback and comments from research participants on interpretations and conclusions made from the qualitative data they provided; asking research participants to confirm or refute the conclusions made.

Mentor: Someone who provides education, training, guidance, critical feedback, or emotional support to a student. In science, a mentor may be the student's advisor but need not be.

Merging: A mixing strategy in which quantitative and qualitative results are brought together through a combined analysis.

Meta-analysis: A statistical technique that integrates the results of several independent randomized controlled trials that are similar enough statistically that the results can be combined and analyzed as if they were one study.

Methodology: The procedures and rules that detail how a single research study is conducted.

Micro-level data: Data derived from individual units of analysis, whether these data sources are individuals, families, or corporations; for example, age and years of formal schooling are two variables requiring micro-level data.

Minimal risk: A risk that is not greater than the risk of routine medical or psychological tests or exams or the risk ordinarily encountered in daily life activities.

Minority group: A group that occupies a subordinate position in a society. Minorities may be separated by physical or cultural traits disapproved of by the dominant group and as a result often experience discrimination.

Misconduct: See research misconduct.

Misinformation: False or inaccurate information, especially that which is deliberately intended to deceive.

Mismanagement of funds: Spending research funds wastefully or illegally; for example, using grant funds allocated for equipment to pay for travel to a conference. Some types of mismanagement may also constitute fraud or embezzlement.

Missing data: Data not available for a research participant about whom other data are available, such as when a respondent fails to answer one of the questions in a survey.

Missing links: When two categories or themes seem to be related but not directly so, it may be that a third variable connects the two.

Mixed-methods case study: Variant of the embedded design in which the researcher collects both qualitative and quantitative data within a case study.

Mixed-methods research questions: Questions in a mixed-methods study that address the mixing or integration of quantitative and qualitative data.

Mixed research model: A model combining aspects of interpretive and positivist research approaches within all (or many) of the methodological steps contained within a single research study.

Mode: Most frequent score in a distribution.

Monitoring approach to evaluation: Evaluation that aims to provide ongoing feedback so that a program can be improved while it is still under way; it contributes to the continuous development and improvement of a human service program; this approach complements the project approach to evaluation.

Monochronic: In monochronic cultures people try to sequence actions on the "one thing at a time" principle. Interpersonal relations are subordinate to time schedules and deadlines.

Morality: See ethics.

Mortality: Loss of research participants through normal attrition over time in an experimental design that requires retesting; a threat to internal validity.

Multiculturalism: A belief or policy that endorses the principle of cultural diversity of different cultural and ethnic groups so that they retain distinctive cultural identities.

Multicultural research: Representation of diverse cultural factors in the subjects of study; such diversity variables may include religion, race, ethnicity, language preference, and gender.

Multigroup posttest-only design: An exploratory research design in which there is more than one group of research participants and the dependent variable is measured only once for each group.

Multiple-baseline design: A case-level evaluation design with more than one baseline period and intervention phase, which allows causal inferences to be made regarding the relationship between a treatment intervention and its effect on clients' target problems and which helps control for extraneous variables. See interrupted time-series design.

Multiple-group design: An experimental research design with one control group and several experimental groups.

Multiple-treatment interference: Effects of the results of a first treatment on the results of second and subsequent treatments; a threat to external validity.

Multistage probability sampling: Probability sampling procedures used when a comprehensive list of the population does not exist and it is not possible to construct one.

Multivariate: (1) A relationship involving two or more variables. (2) A hypothesis stating an assertion about two or more variables and how they relate to one another.

Multivariate analysis: A statistical analysis of the relationship among three or more variables.

N: A measure of how many people or things in a group were studied by the researcher; followed by an equal sign and a number, such as $N = 45$.

Narrative inquiry: A qualitative research approach that employs a variety of data collection methods, particularly interviews, to elicit, document, and analyze life experiences as they are recounted by the individuals who live them.

Narrative interviewing: Research participants tell stories in their own words.

Narrowband measuring instrument: Measuring instruments that focus on a single variable or a few variables.

National Association of Social Workers (NASW): A professional organization of social workers in the United States; provides guidance, research, up-to-date information, advocacy, and other resources for its members and for social workers in general.

Nationality: Refers to country of origin.

Naturalist: A person who studies the facts of nature as they occur under natural conditions.

Natural settings: Refers to the ordinary, everyday worlds of participants—where they live, work, and study. These natural settings include such places as homes and workplaces, staffrooms, classrooms and self-access centers, and online chat rooms. These settings are complex, dynamic, and multifaceted.

Nazi research on human subjects: Heinous experiments conducted on concentration camp prisoners, without their consent, during World War II. Many of the subjects died or received painful and disabling injuries. Experiments included wounding prisoners to study healing, infecting prisoners with diseases to test vaccines, and subjecting prisoners to electrical currents, radiation, and extremes of temperature or pressure.

Needs assessment: Program-level evaluation activities that aim to assess the feasibility for establishing or continuing a particular social service program; an evaluation that aims to assess the need for a human service by verifying that a social problem exists within a specific client population to an extent that warrants services.

Negative case sampling: Purposefully selecting research participants based on the fact that they have different characteristics than previous cases.

Negligence: A failure to follow the standard of care that results in harm to a person or organization. In science, research that is sloppy, careless, or poorly planned or executed may be considered negligent.

Nominal level of measurement: The level of measurement that classifies variables by assigning names or categories that are mutually exclusive and exhaustive.

Noncompliance: The failure to comply with research regulations, institutional policies, or ethical standards. Serious or continuing noncompliance in human subjects research should be promptly reported to the institutional review board and other authorities. See compliance.

Nondirectional test: See two-tailed hypotheses.

Nonexperimental design: A research design at the exploratory, or lowest, level of the knowledge continuum; also called pre-experimental.

Nonlinear relationship: A relationship between two variables that are not directly related to each other.

Nonoccurrence data: In the structured-observation method of data collection, a recording of only those time intervals in which the target problem did not occur.

Nonparametric tests: Refers to statistical tests of hypotheses about population probability distributions, but not about specific parameters of the distributions.

Nonprobability sampling: Sampling procedures in which all of the persons, events, or objects in the sampling frame have an unknown, and usually different, probability of being included in a sample.

Nonreactive: Methods of research that do not allow the research participants to know that they are being studied; thus, they do not alter their responses for the benefit of the researcher.

Nonresponse: The rate of nonresponse in survey research is calculated by dividing the total number of respondents by the total number in the sample, minus any units verified as ineligible.

Nonresponse bias: A research fault based on the people who didn't agree to be studied, although they were chosen. People who didn't agree may have been different in other important ways from people who did, so the study's results might be true for only part of the chosen group.

Nonsampling errors: Errors in a research study's results that are not due to the sampling procedures.

Norm: In measurement, an average or set group standard of achievement that can be used to interpret individual scores; normative data describing statistical properties of a measuring instrument such as mean and standard deviation.

Normal distribution: An arrangement of a data set in which most values cluster in the middle of the range and the rest taper off symmetrically toward either extreme.

Normal frequency distribution curve: A bell-shaped curve of values (amounts, numbers, scores) in which the average, the midpoint, and the most frequent score are all the same.

Normalization group: The population sample to which a measuring instrument under development is administered to establish norms; also called the norm group.

Normative needs: When needs are defined by comparing the objective living conditions of a target population with what society— or, at least, that segment of society concerned with helping the target population—deems acceptable or desirable from a humanitarian standpoint.

Null hypothesis: A statement concerning one or more parameters that is subjected to a statistical test; a statement that there is no relationship between the two variables of interest.

Numbers: The basic data unit of analysis used in positivist research studies.

Nuremberg Code: The first international ethics code for human subjects research, adopted by the Nuremberg Council during the war crimes tribunals in 1947. The code was used as a basis for convicting Nazi physicians and scientists for war crimes related to their experiments on concentration camp prisoners.

Objective inclusion scales: A set of items in a questionnaire designed to measure objective and impartial information about the participant (e.g., "How often do you feel sad?").

Objective measures: Any measure that is based on fact rather than opinion.

Objectivity: (1) The tendency for the results of scientific research to be free from bias. (2) An ethical and epistemological principle instructing one to take steps to minimize or control for bias.

Objectivity: A research stance in which a study is carried out and its data are examined and interpreted without distortion by personal feelings or biases.

Observation: A strategy for data collection, involving the process of watching participants directly in the natural setting. Observation can be participative (i.e., taking part in the activity) or nonparticipative (the researcher watches from the outside)

Observational research: A type of research design in which there's no interaction between the researcher and the research participants.

Observer: One of four roles on a continuum of participation in participant observation research; the level of involvement of the observer participant is lower than of the complete participant and higher than of the participant observer.

Observer (or Hawthorne) effect: The tendency for individuals to change their behavior when they know they are being observed. Some social science experiments use deception to control for the observer effect.

Obtrusive data-collection methods: Direct data-collection methods that can influence the variables under study or the responses of research participants; data-collection methods that produce reactive effects.

Occurrence data: In the structured-observation method of data collection, a recording of the first occurrence of the target problem during each time interval.

Office of Human Research Protections (OHRP): A federal agency that oversees human subjects research funded by the Department of Health and Human Services, including research funded by the National Institutes of Health. OHRP publishes guidance documents for interpreting the Common Rule, sponsors educational activities, and takes steps to ensure compliance with federal regulations, including auditing research and issuing letters to institutions concerning noncompliance.

Office of Research Integrity (ORI): A U.S. federal agency that oversees the integrity of research funded by the Public Health Service, including research funded by the National Institutes of Health. ORI sponsors research and education on research integrity and reviews reports of research misconduct inquiries and investigations from institutions.

One-group posttest-only design: An exploratory research design in which the dependent variable is measured only once.

One-group pretest-posttest design: A descriptive research design in which the dependent variable is measured twice—before and after treatment.

One-stage probability sampling: Probability sampling procedures in which the selection of a sample that is drawn from a specific population is completed in a single process.

One-tailed hypotheses: Statements that predict specific relationships between independent and dependent variables.

One-way analysis of variance: An extension of the independent group t-test when there are more than two groups.

Online sources: Computerized literary retrieval systems that provide printouts of indexes and abstracts.

Open-ended questions: Questions that let people answer in their own words instead of having to choose from set answers like "a" or "b" or "true" or "false"; questions in which the response categories are not specified or detailed.

Open interviews: Interviews that develop naturally, rather than being guided by a preprepared interview guide or list of questions. They are also known as "open-ended," "in-depth," or "unstructured" interviews.

Openness: The ethical obligation to share the results of scientific research, including data and methods.

Operational definition: Explicit specification of a variable in such a way that its measurement is possible.

Operationalization: The process of developing operational definitions of the variables that are contained within the concepts of a positivist and/or interpretive research study.

Opinion: Expresses someone's belief, feeling, view, idea, or judgment about something or someone; statements that cannot be validated.

Ordinal level of measurement: The level of measurement that classifies variables by rank-ordering them from high to low or from most to least.

Ordinal scale: A ranking of values (amounts, numbers, scores) from greatest to least, lowest to highest, first to last, but by a category instead of a number.

Outcome: The effect of the manipulation of the independent variable on the dependent variable; the end product of a treatment intervention; the way something, often a treatment or a program or a study, turns out; the effect it has on people; or the record or measure of the effects.

Outcome-oriented case study: A type of case study that investigates whether client outcomes were in fact achieved.

Outcome variables: Variables that are used to measure the overall impact of the study.

Outliers: Abnormal values in the data that are unusually large or unusually small compared to the others.

Outside observers: Trained observers who are not a part of the research participants' environment and who are brought in to record data.

Overview: One slightly engages with the literature.

Paired observations: An observation involving two variables, where the intent is to examine the relationship between them.

Panel research study: A longitudinal survey design in which the same group of research participants (the panel) is followed over time by surveying them on successive occasions.

Parametric tests: Statistical methods for estimating parameters or testing hypotheses about population parameters.

Participant observation: An obtrusive data-collection method in which the researcher, or the observer, participates in the life of those being observed; both an obtrusive data-collection method and a research approach, this method is characterized by the one doing the study undertaking roles that involve establishing and maintaining ongoing relationships with research participants who are often in the field settings, and observing and participating with the research participants over time.

Participant observer: One of four roles on a continuum of participation in participant observation research; the level of involvement of the participant observer is higher than of the complete observer and lower than of the observer participant.

Participants: People in a research study. They are also called respondents (particularly when data are collected using interviews or questionnaires); in the quantitative research approach, they are often referred to as "subjects."

Participatory action research (PAR): A type of study in which a researcher becomes a member of the group being studied and finds out information by doing what the group is doing.

Paternalism: Restricting a person's decision-making for their own good. In soft paternalism, one restricts the choices made by someone who has a compromised ability to make decisions (see decision-making capacity). In hard paternalism, one restricts the choices made by someone who is fully autonomous (see autonomy).

Peer review: Part of the publication process for scholarly publications in which a group of experts examines a document to determine whether it is worthy of publication. Journals and other publications use a peer review process—usually arranged so that reviewers do not know who the author of the document is—to assess articles for quality and relevance. See also refereed publication.

Peer review, double-blind: A peer review process in which neither the authors nor the reviewers are told each other's identities.

Peer review, open: A peer review process in which the authors and reviewers are told each other's identities.

Peer review, single-blind: A peer review process, used by most scientific journals, in which the reviewers are told the identities of the authors but not vice versa.

Percentage: A part of a whole, when the whole is divided in hundredths.

Percentile: A number showing how many cases, out of every hundred, fall below the point (score, amount) in question.

Periodical: A publication issued at regular intervals. Periodicals may be magazines, journals, newspapers, or newsletters. See also serial.

Periodical index: A list of all the articles that have been published in a magazine, journal, newspaper, newsletter, or a set of periodicals. Many periodical indexes have been converted to online databases, though many online versions are limited to recent decades.

Permanent product recording: A method of data collection in which the occurrence of the target problem is determined by observing the permanent product or record of the target problem.

Phenomenology: An approach that allows the meaning of having experienced the phenomenon under investigation to be described, as opposed to a description of what the experience was. This approach allows the reader to have a better understanding of what it was like to have experienced a particular phenomenon.

Phenomenon: Any observable fact or event that occurs.

Pie chart: A drawing of a circle that is divided into pieces like a pie. Each piece shows how much of the whole is taken up by that group, thing, or process.

Pilot study: Administration of a measuring instrument to a group of people who will not be included in the study to determine any difficulties the research participants may have in answering questions and the general impression given by the instrument; sometimes called a pretest.

Placebo: A biologically or chemically inactive substance or intervention given to a research subject that is used to control for the placebo effect.

Placebo effect: A person's psychosomatic response to the belief that they are receiving an effective treatment. Researchers may also be susceptible to the placebo effect if they treat subjects differently who they believe are receiving effective treatment. See also double-blinding.

Placebo treatment: A fake treatment that should have no effect, outside of the power of suggestion.

Plagiarism: The unattributed use of a source of information that is not considered common knowledge. In general, the following acts are considered plagiarism: (1) failing to cite quotations or borrowed ideas, (2) failing to enclose borrowed language in quotation marks, (3) failing to put summaries or paraphrases in your own words, and (4) submitting someone else's work as your own.

Plot: A way of summarizing data and to illustrate the major characteristics of the distribution of the data in a convenient form.

Plural society: A society that combines ethnic contrasts and economic interdependence of the ethnic groups.

Poll: A survey that asks people questions about certain issues, topics, or candidates, either face to face, by mail, by phone, or by computer.

Pooling: Term used to describe the act of combining data from more than one group of subjects or combining scores from different variables to produce a single score.

Population: An entire set, or universe, of people, objects, or events of concern to a research study, from which a sample is drawn.

Positivism: See positivist research approach.

Positivist research approach: A research approach to discover relationships and facts that are generalizable; research that is "independent" of subjective beliefs, feelings, wishes, and values; a research approach that is complementary to the interpretive research approach.

Posttest: Measurement of the dependent variable after the introduction of the independent variable.

Potential for testing: One of the four criteria for evaluating research hypotheses.

Power: The odds that you will observe a treatment effect when it occurs.

Practitioner/researcher: A social worker who guides practice through the use of research findings; collects data throughout an intervention using research methods, skills, and tools; and disseminates practice findings.

Pragmatists: Researchers who believe that both interpretive and positivist research approaches can be integrated in a single research study.

Precautionary principle (PP): An approach to decision-making that holds we should take reasonable measures to prevent, minimize, or mitigate harms that are plausible and serious. Some countries have used the PP to make decisions concerning environmental protection or technology development. See also risk/benefit analysis, risk management.

Predicting: The process of forecasting what will happen in the future based on past experience or evidence.

Predictive validity: A form of criterion validity that is concerned with the ability of a measuring instrument to predict future performance or status on the basis of present performance or status.

Predictor variable: The variable that, it is believed, allows us to improve our ability to predict values of the criterion variable.

Preexposure: Tasks to be carried out in advance of a research study to sensitize the researcher to the culture of interest; these tasks may include participation in cultural experiences, intercultural sharing, case studies, ethnic literature reviews, value statement exercises, and so on.

Preliminary plan for data analysis: A strategy for analyzing qualitative data that is outlined in the beginning stages of an interpretive research study. The plan has two general steps: (1) previewing the data and (2) outlining what to record in the researcher's journal.

Preponderance of evidence: In the law, a standard of proof in which a claim is proven if the evidence shows that it is more likely true than false (i.e., probability >50%). Preponderance of evidence is the legal standard generally used in research misconduct cases. This standard is much lower than the standard used in criminal cases (i.e., proof beyond reasonable doubt).

Pre-post testing: Giving the same test before treatment and just after treatment.

Presentism: Applying current thinking and concepts to interpretations of past events or intentions; the reverse of antiquarianism.

Pretest: (1) Measurement of the dependent variable before the introduction of the independent variable. (2) Administration of a measuring instrument to a group of people who will not be included in the study to determine difficulties the research participants may have in answering questions and the general impression given by the instrument; also called a pilot study.

Pretest-treatment interaction: Effects that a pretest has on the responses of research participants to the introduction of the independent variable or the experimental treatment; a threat to external validity.

Preview: One does a broad and superficial sweep of the literature.

Previous research: Research studies that have already been completed and published and that provide information about data-collection methods used to investigate research questions that are similar to our own; a criterion for selecting a data-collection method.

Primary data: Data in their original form, as collected from the research participants. A primary data source is one that puts as few intermediaries as possible between the production and the study of the data.

Primary language: The preferred language of the research participants.

Primary reference source: A report of a research study by the person who conducted the study, usually an article in a professional journal.

Primary source: An original source, such as a speech, a diary, a novel, a legislative bill, a laboratory study, a field research report, or an eyewitness account. While not necessarily more reliable than a secondary source, a primary source has the advantage of being closely related to the information it conveys and as such is often considered essential for research, particularly in history. In the sciences, reports of new research written by the scientists who conducted it are considered primary sources.

Principal investigator (PI): The main person running a research study.

Privacy: A state of being free from unwanted intrusion into one's personal space, private information, or personal affairs. See also confidentiality.

Probability sampling: Sampling procedures in which every member of the designated population has a known probability of being selected for the sample.

Problem area: In social work research, a general expressed difficulty about which something researchable is unknown; not to be confused with research question.

Problem-solving process: A generic method with specified phases for solving problems; sometimes called the scientific method.

Procedure: A list that describes all the steps taken during a research study. The list should provide enough detail for any person to be able to repeat the study exactly the same way, like a recipe in a cookbook.

Process measure: A measure of things that matter during actual treatment. These might include whether the client had easy access to services or whether the client was involved in treatment planning.

Process-oriented case study: A type of case study that illuminates the micro-steps of intervention that lead to client outcomes; describes how programs and interventions work and gives insight into the "black box" of intervention.

Professional journal: A journal containing scholarly articles addressed to a particular professional audience such as doctors, lawyers, teachers, engineers, or accountants. Professional journals differ from trade publications, which usually do not include in-depth research articles.

Professional judgments: A conscious process whereby facts, as far as they are known, are supplemented with the knowledge derived from all five ways of knowing to form the basis for rational decisions.

Professional standards: Rules for making judgments about evaluation activity that are established by a group of persons who have advanced education and usually have the same occupation.

Program: An organized set of political, administrative, and clinical activities that function to fulfill some social purpose.

Program development: The constant effort to improve program services to better achieve outcomes; a basic principle underlying the design of evaluations.

Program efficiency: Assessment of a program's outcome in relation to the costs of obtaining the outcome.

Program evaluation: A form of appraisal, using valid and reliable research methods, that examines the processes or outcomes of an organization that exists to fulfill some social purpose.

Program goal: A statement defining the intent of a program that cannot be directly evaluated; it can, however, be evaluated indirectly by the program's objectives, which are derived from the program goal; not to be confused with program objectives.

Program-level evaluation: A form of appraisal that monitors change for groups of clients and organizational performance.

Program objectives: A statement that clearly and exactly specifies the expected change, or intended result, for individuals receiving program services; qualities of well-chosen objectives are meaningfulness, specificity, measurability, and directionality; not to be confused with program goal.

Program participation: The philosophy and structure of a program that will support or supplant the successful implementation of a research study within an existing social service program; a criterion for selecting a data-collection method.

Program process: The coordination of administrative and clinical activities that are designed to achieve a program's goal.

Program results: A report on how effective a program is at meeting its stated objectives.

Project approach to evaluation: Evaluation that aims to assess a completed or finished program. This approach complements the monitoring approach.

Propensity scores: Measure of an individual's predicted probability of being a program participant given his/her observed characteristics.

Proprietary research: Research that a private company owns and keeps secret.

Protocol: A set of steps, methods, or procedures for performing an activity, such as a scientific experiment.

Protocol, deviation: A departure from a protocol. In human subjects research, serious or continuing deviations from approved protocols should be promptly reported to the institutional review board.

Proxy: An indirect measure of a variable that a researcher wants to study; often used when the variable of inquiry is difficult to measure or observe directly.

Psychometrics: Psychological tests that are standardized (formal, set); for example, an IQ test.

Publication: The public dissemination of information. In science, publication may occur in journals or books, in print or electronically. Abstracts presented at scientific meetings are generally considered to be a form of publication.

Publication bias: Bias related to the tendency publish or not publish certain types of research. For example, some studies have documented a bias toward publishing positive results.

Pure research approach: A search for theoretical results that can be used to develop theory and expand our profession's knowledge bases; complementary to the applied research approach.

Purists: Researchers who believe that interpretive and positivist research approaches should never be mixed.

Purpose statement: A declaration of words that clearly describes a research study's intent.

Purposive sampling: A nonprobability sampling procedure in which research participants with particular characteristics are purposely selected for inclusion in a research sample; also known as judgmental or theoretical sampling.

p-value: The way in which statistical significance is reported (i.e., $p < .05$ means that there is a less than 5% chance that the results of a study are due to random chance).

Qualitative data: Data that measure a quality or kind. When referring to variables, qualitative is another term for categorical or nominal variable values; when speaking of kinds of research, qualitative refers to studies of subjects that are hard to quantify.

Qualitative data analysis: Process that involves coding the data set, dividing the text into small units (phrases, sentences, or paragraphs), assigning a label to each unit, and then grouping the codes into themes.

Qualitative methods: Methods used in research studies involving detailed, verbal descriptions of characteristics, cases, and settings. Qualitative research typically uses observation, interviewing, and document review to examine the quality, meaning, and context of people's answers.

Qualitative observation: An observation using descriptive words.

Qualitative research: In qualitative research, researchers try to understand participants' experiences with the central phenomenon (the focus of the study) in a natural setting, using research approaches such as ethnography or case study. Instead of numbers, researchers collect words (text, such as interviews or observation notes), and images (pictures or audiovisual footage) about the phenomenon of the study. As much as possible without preconceived hypotheses or ideas, they analyze the data for common patterns (themes) in order to allow multiple interpretations of participants' individual experiences.

Qualitative research questions: Research questions that can be answered by gathering and analyzing data in forms such as words or diagrams.

Qualitative validity: Assessing whether the information obtained through qualitative data collection is accurate through such strategies as member checking, triangulation of evidence, searching for disconfirming evidence, and asking others to examine the data.

Quality control/quality assurance: Processes for planning, conducting, monitoring, overseeing, and auditing an activity (such as research) to ensure that it meets appropriate standards of quality.

Quantification: In measurement, the reduction of data to numerical form in order to analyze them by way of mathematical or statistical techniques.

Quantitative data: Data that measure a quantity or amount.

Quantitative data analysis: Process that involves analyzing the data based on the type of questions or hypotheses and using the appropriate statistical test to address the questions or hypotheses.

Quantitative observation: An observation that deals with a number or amount.

Quantitative research: A research approach in which numeric data are collected and statistically analyzed in an objective and unbiased manner.

Quantitative research questions: Research questions that can be answered by gathering and analyzing numerical data.

Quasi-experiment: A research design at the descriptive level of the knowledge continuum that resembles an "ideal" experiment but does not allow for random selection or assignment of research participants to groups and often does not control for rival hypotheses.

Questionable research practices (QRPs): Research practices that are regarded by many as unethical but are not considered to be research misconduct. Duplicate publication and honorary authorship are considered by many to be QRPs.

Questionnaire-type scale: A type of measuring instrument in which multiple responses are usually combined to form a single overall score for a respondent.

Quota sampling: A nonprobability sampling procedure in which the relevant characteristics of the sample are identified, the proportion of these characteristics in the population is determined, and research participants are selected from each category until the predetermined proportion (quota) has been achieved.

Race: A variable based on physical attributes that can be subdivided into the Caucasoid, Negroid, and Mongoloid races.

Racism: Theories, attitudes, and practices that display dislike or antagonism toward people seen as belonging to particular ethnic groups. Social or political significance is attached to culturally constructed ideas of difference.

Random assignment: The process of assigning individuals to experimental or control groups so that the groups are equivalent; also referred to as randomization.

Random error: Variable error in measurement; error due to unknown or uncontrolled factors that affect the variable being measured and the process of measurement in an inconsistent fashion.

Randomization: A process for randomly assigning subjects to different treatment groups in a clinical trial or other biomedical experiment.

Randomized controlled trial (RCT): An experiment, such as a clinical trial, in which subjects are randomly assigned to receive an experimental intervention or a control; considered the gold standard for evaluating the effectiveness of different treatments or interventions.

Randomized cross-sectional survey design: A descriptive research design in which there is only one group, the dependent variable is measured only once, the research participants are randomly selected from the population, and there is no independent variable.

Randomized longitudinal survey design: A descriptive research design in which there is only one group, the dependent variable is measured more than once, and research participants are randomly selected from the population before each treatment.

Randomized one-group posttest-only design: A descriptive research design in which there is only one group, the dependent variable is measured only once, and the research participants are randomly selected from the population.

Randomized posttest-only control group design: An explanatory research design in which there are two or more randomly assigned groups, the control group does not receive treatment, and the experimental groups receive different treatments.

Random numbers table: A computer-generated or published table of numbers in which each number has an equal chance of appearing in each position in the table.

Random sampling: An unbiased selection process conducted so that all members of a population have an equal chance of being selected to participate in a research study.

Range: The distance between the minimum and the maximum score in any given data set.

Rank-order scale: A comparative rating scale in which the rater is asked to rank specific individuals in relation to one another on some characteristic.

Rating scale: A type of measuring instrument in which responses are rated on a continuum or in an ordered set of categories, with numerical values assigned to each point or category.

Ratio level of measurement: The level of measurement that has a nonarbitrary, fixed zero point and classifies the values of a variable on an equally spaced continuum.

Raw scores: Scores derived from administration of a measuring instrument to research participants or groups.

Reactive effect: (1) An effect on outcome measures due to the research participants' awareness that they are being observed or interviewed; a threat to external and internal validity. (2) Alteration of the variables being measured or the respondents' performance on the measuring instrument due to administration of the instrument.

Reactivity: The belief that things being observed or measured are affected by the fact that they are being observed or measured; one of the four main limitations of the positivist research approach.

Reassessment: A step in a qualitative data analysis in which the researcher interrupts the data-analysis process to reaffirm the rules used to decide which meaning units are placed within different categories.

Recoding: Developing and applying new variable value labels to a variable that has previously been coded. Usually, recoding is done to make variables from one or more data sets comparable.

Reductionism: In the positivist research approach, the operationalization of concepts by reducing them to common measurable variables; one of the four main limitations of the positivist research approach.

Refereed publication: A publication for which every submission is screened through a peer review process. Refereed publications are considered authoritative because experts have reviewed the material in advance of publication to determine its quality. See also peer review.

Reference: (1) A source used in research and mentioned by a researcher in a paper or article. (2) In libraries, a part of the library's collection that includes encyclopedias, handbooks, directories, and other publications that provide useful overviews, common practices, and facts. (Note: Reference may also indicate a desk or counter where librarians provide assistance to researchers.)

Reflexive: Being "reflexive" means critically thinking about the research process and your role in it.

Reflexivity: The open acknowledgement by the researcher of the central role they play in the research process. A reflexive approach considers and makes explicit the effect the researcher may have had on the research findings.

Relevancy: One of the four main criteria for evaluating research problem areas and formulating research questions out of the problem areas.

Reliability: (1) The degree of accuracy, precision, or consistency in results of a measuring instrument, including the ability to produce the same results when the same variable is measured more than once or repeated applications of the same test on the same individual produce the same measurement. (2) The degree to which individual differences on scores or in data are due either to true differences or to errors in measurement.

Reliance agreement: An agreement between two institutions in which one institution agrees to oversee human subjects research for the other institution for a particular study or group of studies.

Remuneration: In human subjects research, providing financial compensation to subjects.

Replication: Repetition of the same research procedures by a second researcher for the purpose of determining whether earlier results can be confirmed.

Reproducibility: The ability for an independent researcher to achieve the same results of an experiment, test, or study under the same conditions. A research paper should include information necessary for other scientists to reproduce the results. Reproducibility is not the same as repeatability, in which researchers repeat their own experiments to verify the results. Reproducibility is one of the hallmarks of good science.

Request for proposals (RFP): An announcement that a grant or other funding is available.

Research: A systematic attempt to develop new knowledge.

Researchability: The extent to which a research problem is in fact researchable and the problem can be resolved through the consideration of data derived from a research study; one of the four main criteria for evaluating research problem areas and formulating research questions out of the problem areas.

Research approach: A tradition such as narrative inquiry, case study, ethnography, phenomenology, grounded theory, or action research that employs generally accepted research methods.

Research attitude: A way that we view the world; an attitude that highly values craftsmanship, with pride in creativity, high-quality standards, and hard work.

Research compliance: See compliance.

Research consumer: A social work role reflecting the ethical obligation to base interventions on the most up-to-date research knowledge available.

Research design: The entire plan of a positivist and/or interpretive research study from problem conceptualization to the dissemination of findings.

Researcher bias: The tendency of researchers to find the results they expect to find; a threat to external validity.

Research findings: Findings derived from research studies that used the scientific method of inquiry; the most objective way of knowing; one of the five ways of knowing.

Research hypothesis: A statement about a study's research question that predicts the existence of a particular relationship between the independent and dependent variables; can be used in both the positivist and interpretive approaches to research.

Research institution: An institution, such as a university or government or private laboratory, that is involved in conducting research.

Research integrity: Following ethical standards in the conduct of research.

Research integrity official (RIO): An administrator at a research institution who is responsible for responding to reports of suspected research misconduct.

Research misconduct: Intentional, knowing, or reckless behavior in research that is widely viewed as highly unethical and often illegal. Most definitions define research misconduct as fabrication or falsification of data or plagiarism; some include other behaviors in the definition such as interfering with a misconduct investigation, significant violations of human research regulations, or serious deviations from commonly accepted practices. Honest errors and scientific disputes are not regarded as misconduct.

Research misconduct, inquiry versus investigation: If suspected research misconduct is reported at an institution, the research integrity official may appoint an inquiry committee to determine whether there is sufficient evidence to conduct an investigation. If the committee determines that there is sufficient evidence, an investigative committee will be appointed to gather evidence and interview witnesses. The investigative committee will determine whether there is sufficient evidence to prove misconduct and make a recommendation concerning adjudication of the case to the research integrity official.

Research participants: Those participating in research studies; sometimes called research subjects.

Research question: A clear statement in the form of a question of the specific issue that a researcher wishes to answer in order to address a research problem. A specific research question that is formulated directly out of the general research problem area; answered by the interpretive and/or positivist research approach; not to be confused with problem area.

Research sponsor: An organization, such as a government agency or private company, that funds research.

Research subject (also called research participant): A living individual who is the subject of an experiment or study involving the collection of the individual's private data or biological samples. See also human subjects research.

Resources: The costs associated with collecting data in any given research study; includes materials and supplies, equipment rental, transportation, training staff, and staff time; a criterion for selecting a data-collection method.

Respect for persons: A moral principle, with roots in Kantian philosophy, that holds that we should respect the choices of autonomous decision-makers (see autonomy, decision-making capacity) and that we should protect the interests of those who have diminished autonomy (see vulnerable subject). See also Belmont Report.

Respondent validation: Refers to seeking the participants' views of the initial interpretations of the data. The aim is not to ensure that the researcher agrees about the meaning of the data but that the researcher has the opportunity to incorporate the participants' responses into the analysis.

Response categories: Possible responses assigned to each question in a standardized measuring instrument, with a lower value generally indicating a low level of the variable being measured and a larger value indicating a higher level.

Response rate: The total number of responses obtained from potential research participants to a measuring instrument divided by the total number of responses requested, usually expressed in the form of a percentage.

Response set: Personal style; the tendency of research participants to respond to a measuring instrument in a particular way, regardless of the questions asked, or the tendency of observers or interviewers to react in certain ways; a source of constant error.

Responsible conduct of research (RCR): Following ethical and scientific standards and legal and institutional rules in the conduct of research. See also ethics, research integrity.

Retraction: Withdrawing or removing a published paper from the research record because the data or results have subsequently been found to be unreliable or because the paper involves research misconduct. Journals publish retraction notices and identify retracted papers in electronic databases to alert the scientific community to problems with the paper. See correction.

Review of the literature: (1) A search of the professional literature to provide background knowledge of what has already been examined or tested in a specific problem area. (2) Use of any information source, such as a computerized database, to locate existing data or information on a research problem, question, or hypothesis.

Right: A legal or moral entitlement. Rights generally imply duties or obligations. For example, if A has a right not be killed, then B has a duty not to kill A.

Risk: The product of the probability and magnitude (or severity) of a potential harm.

Risk/benefit analysis: A process for determining an acceptable level of risk, given the potential benefits of an activity or technology. See also risk minimization, precautionary principle.

Risk minimization: In human subjects research, the ethical and legal principle that the risks to the research participants should be minimized using appropriate methods, procedures, or other safety measures.

Risks, reasonable: In human subjects research, the ethical and legal principle that the risks to the subjects should be reasonable in relation to the benefits to the subjects or society. See risk/benefit analysis, social value.

Rival hypothesis: A hypothesis that is a plausible alternative to the research hypothesis and might explain the results as well or better; a hypothesis involving extraneous or intervening variables other than the independent variable in the research hypothesis; also referred to as an alternative hypothesis.

Rules of correspondence: A characteristic of measurement stipulating that numerals or symbols are assigned to properties of individuals, objects, or events according to specified rules.

Salami science: Dividing a scientific project into the smallest papers that can be published (least publishable unit) to maximize the total publications from the project. See questionable research practices.

Sample: A subset of a population of individuals, objects, or events chosen to participate in or to be considered in a research study.

Sampling error: (1) The degree of difference that can be expected between the sample and the population from which it was drawn. (2) A mistake in a research study's results that is due to sampling procedures.

Sampling frame: A listing of units (people, objects, or events) in a population from which a sample is drawn.

Sampling plan: A method of selecting members of a population for inclusion in a research study, using procedures that make it possible to draw inferences about the population from the sample statistics.

Sampling theory: The logic of using methods to ensure that a sample and a population are similar in all relevant characteristics.

Saturation: The point at which no further themes are generated when data from more participants are included in the analysis. The sampling process can be considered to be complete at this point.

Scale: A measuring instrument composed of several items that are logically or empirically structured to measure a construct.

Scattergram: A graphic representation of the relationship between two interval- or ratio-level variables.

Science: Knowledge that has been obtained and tested through use of positivist and interpretive research studies.

Scientific community: A group that shares the same general norms for both research activity and acceptance of scientific findings and explanations.

Scientific determinism: See determinism.

Scientific method: A generic method with specified steps for solving problems; the principles and procedures used in the systematic pursuit of knowledge.

Scientific (or academic) freedom: The institutional and government obligation to refrain from interfering in the conduct or publication of research, or the teaching and discussion of scientific ideas. See censorship.

Scientific validity (or rigor): Processes, procedures, and methods used to ensure that a study is well designed to test a hypothesis or theory.

Scope of a study: The extent to which a problem area is covered in a single research study; a criterion for selecting a data-collection method.

Score: A numerical value assigned to an observation; also called data.

Search statement: A statement developed by the researcher before a literature search that contains terms that can be combined to elicit specific data.

Secondary analysis: An unobtrusive data-collection method in which available data that predate the formulation of a research study are used to answer the research question or test the hypothesis.

Secondary content data: Existing text data.

Secondary data: The term refers to data that were collected for other studies. For the first researcher they are primary data, but for the second researcher they are secondary data.

Secondary data sources: A data source that provides nonoriginal, secondhand data.

Secondary source: A source that comments on, analyzes, or otherwise relies on primary sources. An article in a newspaper that reports on a scientific discovery or a book that analyzes a writer's work is a secondary source. See also primary source.

Secondhand data: Data obtained from people who are indirectly connected to the problem being studied.

Selection-treatment interaction: The relationship between the manner of selecting research participants and their response to the independent variable; a threat to external validity.

Self-administered questionnaire (self-report): A set of written questions that the person being studied fills out and returns to the researcher.

Self-anchored scales: A rating scale in which research participants rate themselves on a continuum of values, according to their own referents for each point.

Self-awareness: A psychological state in which individuals focus their attention on and evaluate different aspects of their self-concepts.

Self-deception: In science, deceiving one's self in the conduct of research. Self-deception is a form of bias that may be intentional or unintentional (subconscious).

Self-disclosure: Shared communication about oneself, including one's behaviors, beliefs, and attitudes.

Self-regulation: Regulation of an activity by individuals involved in that activity as opposed to regulation by the government. See also law.

Self-selection: A way of choosing the people for a study by letting them set themselves apart from a larger group in some way; for example, by responding to a questionnaire or by going to a program.

Semantic differential scale: A modified measurement scale in which research participants rate their perceptions of the variable under study along three dimensions—evaluation, potency, and activity.

Sequential triangulation: When two distinct and separate phases of a research study are conducted and the results of the first phase are considered essential for planning the second phase; research questions in phase 1 are answered before research questions in phase 2 are formulated.

Service recipients: People who use human services—individuals, couples, families, groups, organizations, and communities; also known as clients or consumers; a stakeholder group in evaluation.

Setting: A place where the research study is carried out. "Place" here refers to more than just the physical location—it also includes the people, artifacts, language used, and intangible aspects (like beliefs) of that location.

Sharing: A key ingredient of a social work researcher and practitioner.

Significance: A mathematical test of whether a study's results could be caused by chance or whether they really show what they seem to show.

Simple random sampling: A one-stage probability sampling procedure in which members of a population are selected one at a time, without a chance of being selected again, until the desired sample size is obtained.

Simultaneous triangulation: When the results of a positivist and interpretive research question are answered at the same time; results to the interpretive research questions, for example, are reported separately and do not necessarily relate to, or confirm, the results from the positivist phase.

Situationalists: Researchers who assert that certain research approaches (interpretive or positivist) are appropriate for specific situations.

Situation-specific variable: A variable that may be observable only in certain environments and under certain circumstances, or with particular people.

Size of a study: The number of people, places, or systems that are included in a single research study; a criterion for selecting a data-collection method.

Skeptic: A key ingredient of a social work researcher and practitioner.

Snowball sampling: A nonprobability sampling procedure in which individuals selected for inclusion in a sample are asked to identify other individuals from the population who might be included; useful to locate people with divergent points of view.

Social desirability: (1) A response set in which research participants tend to answer questions in a way that they perceive as giving favorable impressions of themselves. (2) The inclination of data providers to report data that present a socially desirable impression of themselves or their reference groups; also referred to as "impression management."

Socially acceptable response: Bias in an answer that comes from research participants trying to answer questions as they think a "good" person should, rather than in a way that reveals what they actually believe or feel.

Social problems: Problems social work researchers wish to solve. The problems must be changeable.

Social responsibility: In science, the obligation to avoid harmful societal consequences from one's research and to promote good ones.

Social value: (1) The social benefits expected to be gained from a scientific study, such as new knowledge or the development of a medical treatment or other technology. (2) The ethical principle that human subjects research should be expected to yield valuable results for society.

Social work research: A systematic and objective inquiry that utilizes the scientific method of inquiry to solve human problems and creates new knowledge that is generally applicable to the social work profession.

Sociocentric thinking: Results when people do not understand the degree to which they have uncritically internalized the dominant prejudices of their society or culture.

Socioeconomic variables: Any one of several measures of social rank, usually including income, education, and occupational prestige; the combined measure indicates socioeconomic status (SES).

Solomon four-group design: An explanatory research design with four randomly assigned groups, two experimental and two control; the dependent variable is measured before and after treatment for one experimental and one control group, but only after treatment for the other two groups, and only experimental groups receive the treatment.

Special populations: Groups of people who cannot be studied in the same way and by the same rules as other groups for some reason.

Specificity: One of the four criteria for evaluating research hypotheses.

Split-half method: A method for establishing the reliability of a measuring instrument by dividing it into comparable halves and comparing the scores between the two halves.

Split-half reliability: A measure of how well the different parts of a measuring instrument are working together; found by comparing half the items with the other half (for example, the odd-numbered items with the even-numbered items).

Spot-check recording: A method of data collection that involves direct observation of the target problem at specified intervals rather than on a continuous basis.

Stakeholder: A person or group of people having a direct or indirect interest in the results of an evaluation.

Stakeholder service evaluation model: According to proponents of this evaluation model, program evaluations will be more likely to be used—and thus have a greater impact on social problems—when they are tailored to the needs of stakeholders. In this model, the purpose of program evaluation is not to generalize findings to other sites but rather to restrict the evaluation effort to a particular program.

Standard deviation: Provides a picture of how the scores distribute themselves around the mean.

Standardized measuring instrument: A professionally developed measuring instrument that provides for uniform administration and scoring and generates normative data against which later results can be evaluated.

Standard operating procedures (SOPs): Rules and procedures for performing an activity, such as conducting or reviewing research.

Statistical significance: A measure of the degree that an observed result (such as relationship between two variables) is due to chance. Statistical significance is usually expressed as a p value. A p value of 0.05, for example, means that the observed result will probably occur as a result of chance only 5% of the time.

Statistics: The branch of mathematics concerned with the collection and analysis of data using statistical techniques.

Stereotypes: Generalizations or assumptions that people make about the characteristics of all members of a group based on an inaccurate image about what people in that group are like.

Stratification: A way of ordering individual people within a social system. The different rungs of the ladder depend on, for example, income, education, work, or power. The term can also mean ranking anything on different levels, by group or category.

Stratified random sampling: A one-stage probability sampling procedure in which a population is divided into two or more strata to be sampled separately, using simple random or systematic random sampling techniques.

Structured interview schedule: A complete list of questions to be asked and spaces for recording the answers. The interview schedule is used by interviewers when questioning respondents.

Structured observation: A data-collection method in which people are observed in their natural environments using specified methods and measurement procedures. See direct observation.

Study blind policy: Guidelines designed to limit or prohibit access of data by unauthorized users in a study.

Subject selection: Rules for including/excluding human subjects in research. Subject selection should be equitable; that is, subjects should be included or excluded for legitimate scientific or ethical reasons. For example, a clinical trial might exclude subjects who do not have the disease under investigation or are too sick to take part in the study safely. See risk minimization, justice.

Subjective inclusion scales: A set of items in a questionnaire designed to measure personal impressions or feeling about a subject. An example of a question might be, "How do you feel about other people?"

Subjective measures: Any measure that is based on the researcher's feelings or intuitions about the topic being studied.

Subscale: A component of a scale that measures some part or aspect of a major construct; also composed of several items that are logically or empirically structured.

Summated scale: A questionnaire-type scale in which research participants are asked to indicate the degree of their agreement or disagreement with a series of questions.

Summative evaluation: A type of evaluation that examines the ultimate success of a program and assists with decisions about whether a program should be continued or chosen in the first place among program options.

Summative measuring instrument: A type of measuring instrument in which multiple responses are usually combined to form a single overall score for a respondent; also called a questionnaire-type scale.

Surrogate decision-maker: See legal authorized representative.

Survey research: A data-collection method that uses survey-type instruments to obtain opinions or answers from a population or sample of research participants in order to describe or study them as a group.

Synthesis: Undertaking the search for meaning in our sources of information at every step of the research process; combining parts such as data, concepts, and theories to arrive at a higher level of understanding.

Systematic error: Measurement error that is consistent, not random.

Systematic random sampling: A one-stage probability sampling procedure in which every person at a designated interval in a specific population is selected to be included in a research study's sample.

Systematic: Methodical; used to refer to how the steps of a research study are arranged.

Systematic review: A comprehensive review of a body of data, or a series of studies, that uses explicit methods to locate primary studies representing the gold standard of evidence (i.e., randomized controlled trials), appraise them, and then summarize them according to a standard methodology.

Target population: The group about whom a researcher wants to draw conclusions; another term for a population about whom one aims to make inferences.

Target problem: (1) In case-level evaluation designs, the problem social workers seek to solve for their clients. (2) A measurable behavior, feeling, or cognition that is either a problem in itself or symptomatic of some other problem.

Temporal research design: A research study that includes time as a major variable. The purpose of this design is to investigate change in the distribution of a variable or in relationships among variables over time. There are three types of temporal research designs: cohort, panel, and trend.

Temporal stability: Consistency of responses to a measuring instrument over time; reliability of an instrument across forms and across administrations.

Testability: The ability to test a hypothesis or theory. Scientific hypotheses and theories should be testable.

Testing effect: The effect that taking a pretest might have on posttest scores; a threat to internal validity.

Test-retest reliability: Reliability of a measuring instrument established through repeated administration to the same group of individuals.

Thematic notes: In observational research, a record of emerging ideas, hypotheses, theories, and conjectures. They provide a place for the researcher to speculate and identify themes, link ideas and events, and articulate thoughts as they emerge in the field setting.

Theme: In a qualitative data analysis, a concept or idea that describes a single category or a grouping of categories; an abstract interpretation of qualitative data.

Theoretical framework: A frame of reference that serves to guide a research study and is developed from theories, findings from a variety of other studies, and the researcher's personal experiences.

Theoretical sampling: A procedure in grounded theory for selecting participants on the basis of whether or not they will contribute to the development of the theory.

Theory: A reasoned set of propositions, derived from and supported by established data, that serves to explain a group of phenomena; a conjectural explanation that may or may not be supported by data generated from interpretive and positivist research studies.

Therapeutic misconception: The tendency for human subjects in clinical research to believe that the study is designed to benefit them personally; the tendency for the subjects of clinical research to overestimate the benefits of research and underestimate the risks.

Thick description: Refers to the rich, vivid descriptions and interpretations that researchers create as they collect data. It encompasses the circumstances, meanings, intentions, strategies, and motivations that characterize the participants, research setting, and events. Thick description helps researchers paint a meticulous picture for the reader.

Thought units: In discourse analysis, thought units are segments of the transcribed text that reflect a particular thought or idea.

Three Rs: Ethical guidelines for protecting animal welfare in research, including reduction (reducing the number of animals used in research), replacement (replacing higher species with lower ones, or replacing animals with cells or computer models), and refinement (refining research methods to minimize pain and suffering).

Time orientation: An important cultural factor that considers whether one is more focused on the future, the present, or the past. For instance, individuals who are "present oriented" would not be as preoccupied with advance planning as those who are "future oriented."

Time-series design: See interrupted time-series design.

Tools: Ways of testing or measuring, such as questionnaires or rating scales.

Tradition: Traditional cultural beliefs that we accept without question as true; one of the five ways of knowing.

Transcribing data: A process of converting verbal data to written data for analysis.

Transcript: An electronic, written, printed, or typed copy of interview data or any other written material that have been gathered for an interpretive research study.

Transferability: Refers to the degree to which the results of qualitative research can be generalized or transferred to other contexts or settings. That decision is made by the reader; the qualitative researcher can enhance transferability by thoroughly describing the research setting using thick description, and clearly stating the assumptions that were central to the research study.

Transition statements: Sentences used to indicate a change in direction or focus of questions in a measuring instrument.

Transparency: In science, openly disclosing information that concerned parties would want to know, such as financial interests or methodological assumptions. See also conflict of interest, management.

Treatment group: See experimental group.

Trend study: A longitudinal study design in which data from surveys carried out at periodic intervals on samples drawn from a particular population are used to reveal trends over time.

Trials: Repetition of a research study, or parts of it. Increasing the number of times a research study is repeated allows for averaging of data and "better" analysis.

Triangulation: The idea of combining different research methods in all steps associated with a single research study; assumes that any bias inherent in one particular method will be neutralized when used in conjunction with other research methods; seeks convergence of a study's results, often using more than one research method and source of data to study the same phenomenon and to enhance validity. There are several types of triangulation, but the essence of the term is that multiple perspectives are compared. It can involve multiple data sources or multiple data analyzers; the hope is that the different perspectives will confirm each other, adding weight to the credibility and dependability of qualitative data analysis.

Triangulation design: A mixed methods design in which quantitative and qualitative data are collected and analyzed concurrently and then compared to understand the research problem more completely.

Triangulation of analysts: Using multiple data analysts to code a single segment of a transcript and comparing the amount of agreement between them; a method used to verify coding of qualitative data.

Trustworthiness: Refers to standards for judging the quality and usefulness of qualitative research studies, which are composed of criteria for methodologically.

t-**test:** A statistical test of the difference between two group "means."

Tuskegee Syphilis Study: A study, sponsored by the U.S. Department of Health, Education, and Welfare, conducted in Tuskegee, Alabama, from 1932 to 1972, which involved observing the progression of untreated syphilis in African American men. The men were not told they were in a research study; they thought they were

getting treatment for "bad blood." Researchers also steered them away from clinics where they could receive penicillin when it became available as a treatment for syphilis in the 1940s.

Two-phase research model: A model combining interpretive and positivist research approaches in a single study where each approach is conducted as a separate and distinct phase of the study.

Two-tailed hypotheses: Statements that do not predict specific relationships between independent and dependent variables.

Type I error: A mistake based on saying there is a difference when there is not.

Type II error: A mistake based on saying there isn't a difference when there is.

Typology: A system that groups information into different types.

Unanticipated problem (UP): An unexpected problem that occurs in human subjects research. Serious UPs that are related to research and suggest a greater risk of harm to subjects or others should be promptly reported to institutional review boards and other authorities.

Undue influence: Taking advantage of someone's vulnerability to convince them to make a decision.

Unit of analysis: A specific research participant (person, object, or event) or the sample or population relevant to the research question; the persons or things being studied; what size or number is being counted as separate within a larger group in a study. Units of analysis in research are often persons but may be groups, political parties, newspaper editorials, unions, hospitals, or schools. A particular unit of analysis from which data are gathered is called a case.

Univariate: A hypothesis or research design involving a single variable.

Universe: See population.

Unobtrusive methods: Data-collection methods that do not influence the variable under study or the responses of research participants; methods that avoid reactive effects.

Unstructured interviews: A series of questions that allow flexibility for both the research participant and the interviewer to make changes during the process.

Utilitarianism: An ethical theory that holds that the right thing to do is to produce the greatest balance of good/bad consequences for the greatest number of people. Act utilitarians focus on good resulting from particular actions; rule utilitarians focus on happiness resulting from following rules. Utilitarians may equate the good with happiness, satisfaction of preferences, or some other desirable outcomes. See also consequentialism, ethical theory.

Validity: (1) The extent to which a measuring instrument measures the variable it is supposed to measure and measures it accurately. (2) The degree to which an instrument is able to do what it is intended to do, in terms of both experimental procedures and measuring instruments (internal validity) and generalizability of results (external validity). (3) The degree to which scores on a measuring instrument correlate with measures of performance on some other criterion.

Value: Something that is worth having or desiring, such as happiness, knowledge, justice, or virtue.

Value awareness: A key ingredient of a social work researcher and practitioner.

Value, instrumental: Something that is valuable for the sake of achieving something else; for example, a visit to the dentist is valuable for dental health.

Value, intrinsic: Something that is valuable for its own sake, such as happiness, human life.

Value, scale of: The idea that some things can be ranked on a scale of moral value. For example, one might hold that human beings are more valuable than other sentient animals, sentient animals are more valuable than nonsentient animals, and so on. Some defenders of animal experimentation argue that harming animals in research to benefit human beings can be justified because human beings are more valuable than animals.

Value (statistical): An amount written in numbers, not in words or pictures.

Variable: A concept with characteristics that can take on different values.

Verbatim recording: Recording interview data word for word and including significant gestures, pauses, and expressions of persons in the interview.

Virtue: A morally good or desirable character trait, such as honesty, courage, compassion, modesty, and fairness.

Virtue ethics: An ethical theory that emphasizes developing virtue as opposed to following rules or maximizing good/bad consequences.

Visual diagram: A graphical representation of the research procedures used in a mixed methods study.

Voluntariness: The ability to make a free (uncoerced) choice.

Vulnerable subject: A research subject who has an increased susceptibility to harm or exploitation due to his or her compromised ability to make decisions or advocate for his/her interests or dependency. Vulnerability may be based on age, mental disability, institutionalization, language barriers, socioeconomic deprivation, or other factors. See decision-making capacity, informed consent.

Whistleblower: A person who reports suspected illegal or unethical activity, such as research misconduct or noncompliance with human subjects or animal regulations. Various laws and institutional policies protect whistleblowers from retaliation.

Wideband measuring instrument: An instrument that measures more than one variable.

Within-methods research approach: Triangulation by using different research methods available in either the interpretive or the positivist research approaches in a single research study.

Words: The basic data unit of analysis used in interpretive research studies.

Worker cooperation: The actions and attitudes of program personnel when carrying out a research study within an existing social service program; a criterion for selecting a data-collection method.

Working hypothesis: An assertion about a relationship between two or more variables that may not be true but is plausible and worth examining.

Credits

Tips were adapted and modified from: Black, T. R. (2001). *Understanding social science research: An introduction* (2nd ed.). Thousand Oaks, CA: Sage; Bonaccorsi, A. (2018). *The evaluation of research in social sciences and humanities: Lessons from the Italian experience.* New York: Springer; Carr, S., & Bostock, L. (2015). Appraising the quality of evidence. In M. Webber (Ed.). *Applying research evidence in social work practice* (pp. 44–58). London: Palgrave Macmillan; Evans, T. (2015). Using evidence to inform decision-making. In M. Webber (Ed.). *Applying research evidence in social work practice* (pp. 77–90). London: Palgrave Macmillan; Fischer, J. (1981). A framework for evaluating empirical research reports. In R. M. Grinnell, Jr. (Ed.). *Social work research and evaluation* (pp. 569–589). Itasca, IL: F. E. Peacock; Hart, V. (2015). Using research evidence in practice: A view from the ground. In M. Webber (Ed.). *Applying research evidence in social work practice* (pp. 91–107). London: Palgrave Macmillan; Grinnell, R. M., Jr., & Unrau, Y. A. (2013). *Social work research proposals: A workbook.* Kalamazoo, MI: Pair Bond Publications; Harris, S. R. (2014). *How to critique journal articles in the social sciences.* Thousand Oaks, CA: Sage; Holosko, M. J. (2005). *A primer for critiquing social research: A student guide.* Belmont, CA: Thomson Nelson, Brooks/Cole; Holosko, M. J. (2006). A suggested authors' checklist for submitting manuscripts to *Research on Social Work Practice. Research on Social Work Practice, 16,* 449–454; Holosko, M. J. (2018). Evaluating quantitative studies. In R. M. Grinnell, Jr., & Y. A. Unrau. (Eds.). *Social work research and evaluation: Foundations of evidence-based practice* (11th ed., pp. 573–596). New York: Oxford University Press; Litz, C. A., & Zayas, L. E. (2018). Evaluating qualitative studies. In R. M. Grinnell, Jr., & Y. A. Unrau. (Eds.). *Social work research and evaluation: Foundations of evidence-based practice* (11th ed., pp. 597–611). New York: Oxford University Press; Lomand, T. C. (2012). *Social science research: A cross section of journal articles for discussion & evaluation* (7th ed.). New York: Routledge; National Association of Social Workers. (2005). *Perspectives: Peer review & publication standards in social work journals:* The Miami statement. *Social Work Research, 29,* 119–121; Pyrczak, F. (2016). *Evaluating research in academic journals: A practical guide to realistic education* (6th ed.). Los Angeles, CA: Pyrczak Publications; Ross, P. D. S. (2015). Locating evidence for practice. In M. Webber (Ed.). *Applying research evidence in social work practice* (pp. 22–43). London: Palgrave Macmillan; Stern, P. C. (1979). *Evaluating social science research.* New York: Oxford University Press; Thyer, B. A. (1991). Guidelines for evaluating outcome studies on social work practice. *Research on Social Work Practice, 1,* 76–91; Thyer, B. A. (1994). *Successful publishing in scholarly journals.* Thousand Oaks, CA: Sage; Webber, M., & Carr, S. (2015). Applying research evidence in social work practice: Seeing beyond paradigms. In M. Webber (Ed.). *Applying research evidence in social work practice* (pp. 3–21). London: Palgrave Macmillan; and The Writing Center. (2018). *Checklist for analyzing research material.* Chapel Hill, NC: University of North Carolina.